Günther Blaschek   Gustav Pomberger

Introduction to Programming with Modula-2

With 26 Figures

Springer-Verlag

Berlin Heidelberg New York London
Paris Tokyo Hong Kong Barcelona

Authors

Günther Blaschek
Gustav Pomberger

Institut für Wirtschaftsinformatik
und Organisationsforschung
Johannes-Kepler-Universität Linz
Altenbergstraße 69, A-4040 Linz-Auhof, Austria

Translator

Robert Bach
180 Seyler Drive
Petersburg, VA 28305, USA

CR Subject Classification (1987): D.3, D.2.1–2, D.2.5

ISBN 3-540-52038-4 Springer-Verlag Berlin Heidelberg New York
ISBN 0-387-52038-4 Springer-Verlag New York Berlin Heidelberg

Library of Congress Cataloging-in-Publication Data
Blaschek, Günther, 1957–
[Einführung in die Programmierung mit Modula-2. English] Indroduction to programming
with Modula-2 / Günther Blaschek, Gustav Pomberger; [translator, Robert Bach].   p.   cm.
Translation of: Einführung in die Programmierung mit Modula-2.
Includes bibliographical references (p.) and index.
ISBN 0-387-52038-4 (U.S.)
1. Modula-2 (Computer program language) I. Pomberger, Gustav, 1949–   . II. Title
QA76.73.M63B5813 1990   005.13'3–dc20 90-10220   CIP

© Springer-Verlag Berlin Heidelberg 1990
Printed in the United States of America

2145/3140-543210 – Printed on acid-free paper

Preface

This book is intended for the novice as well as for the experienced programmer who wants to learn Modula-2. We do not limit ourselves to just a description of Modula-2. Instead, we seek to familiarize the reader with the concept of algorithms and to show him/her how to implement algorithms in Modula-2.

The programming language Modula-2 was developed by Niklaus Wirth (also the father of world-famous Pascal) and made public in 1978. Compared to other programming languages such as Ada, COBOL or PL/I, Modula-2 is a compact language, which makes it easy to learn. Nevertheless, Modula-2 contains all important language elements necessary for formulating complicated algorithms and for implementing the modern concepts of software engineering. Modula-2 is distinguished by a systematic structure that makes it possible to write easily readable programs. The language supports many of the principles of modern software engineering. All this makes Modula-2 a useful instrument for an introduction to the basics of programming.

This textbook strives to establish a solid foundation in the techniques of programming with up-to-date methods of program development. Use of the programming language Modula-2 is reinforced with numerous hands-on exercises. This book does not presuppose any knowledge of programming, but it does require a certain ability in the realm of abstract thinking, some pleasure in problem solving, and a desire to come to terms with complex interrelationships.

The book consists of two parts, each divided into three chapters. One part treats the basic concepts of programming (Chapters 1, 2 and 5); the other deals with programming in Modula-2 (Chapters 3, 4 and 6).

Chapter 1 introduces the term "algorithm" and attempts to broaden the reader's understanding of various types of problems and their algorithmic solutions. This chapter is intended primarily for novices.

The basic concepts of program development are treated in *Chapter 2*. We show how difficult and intractable problems can be solved by systematic reduction to constituent subproblems. We further present the criteria by which the resulting subtasks can be combined as modules to solve the original task. This chapter likewise addresses the novice. The program development strategies discussed here are, however, by no means trivial and are foreign to many experienced programmers, who might also profit from this section.

Chapter 3 describes the programming language Modula-2 progressively from simple to complex elements. It is organized in such a way that it serves as a reference for the programmer, i.e., the chapter contains all details relevant to the Modula-2 programmer.

With the basics covered in the first three chapters, specialized problems in the application of Modula-2 can now be discussed in *Chapter 4*.

The problem of program testing and a discussion of what comprises good programming style are the subjects of *Chapter 5*. Even experienced programmers should take this chapter to heart, although they could argue that it still treats basics. Good programming style can by no means be taken for granted out in the field.

The area of hardware has produced breathtaking advances in recent years. The development of the principles of software engineering was somewhat less rapid but no less important. *Chapter 6* discusses how Modula-2 supports the concepts of software engineering.

Most of the chapters and their sections contain exercises intended to help the reader to enrich his/her knowledge and to help monitor progress.

Above all, the collective experience of the authors in teaching such courses as Introduction to Programming, Algorithms and Data Structures, Compilers, Software Engineering, and various programming projects was channelled into this book. Most of the examples and exercises were taken from preparations for these courses.

Acknowledgements

It is impossible to list all the people who influenced the publication of this book. We are particularly indebted to *Prof. N. Wirth* of Zurich; his work in the area of programming languages—above all the definitions of Pascal, Modula-2 and Oberon—have had an immense impact on computer science and have greatly influenced our work. We owe special thanks to *Prof. P. Rechenberg* for valuable suggestions and discussion as well as for reading the manuscript. We are also indebted to our colleagues *P. Mössenböck* and *P. Schnorf*, who meticulously studied the manuscript and suggested valuable improvements. We also want to thank our publisher for the fine cooperation. Finally, we wish to express special thanks to *R. Bach* for his diligent English translation that included updating our German version.

Linz, Austria
March 1990

G. Blaschek
G. Pomberger

Table of Contents

1 Algorithms

The goal of this book is to convey the knowledge needed to make effective use of the programming language Modula-2. Before learning how to use a programming language, a student first needs to know what a program is and how programs are designed. Therefore, this chapter introduces some of the most important basics of programming. Since these are fundamentals, we cannot simply define them with the help of other concepts. Instead, we will describe them on the basis of examples.

Algorithms and *programs* are closely related. Computer science has no monopoly on algorithms. We encounter algorithms in everyday life without recognizing them as such. In computer science, however, they play a very central role. That is why we need to come to terms with what is meant by the term "algorithm," what attributes algorithms possess, and what meaning they have for programming. We will first present several examples of algorithms, then point out the properties of algorithms in general, and then arrive at a definition of the term algorithm. After describing various methods of representing algorithms, we give typical examples of simple algorithms and, in conclusion, discuss the connection between algorithms and programs.

1.1 Examples of Algorithms

In order to solve a problem, we need an unambiguous set of instructions that determines exactly which actions are to be executed and in which order. The formal description of such an approach to a solution is known as an algorithm.

Here is a simple example:

    (1) Add two natural numbers, a and b.

    (2) Assign the sum to the variable s.

An algorithm consists of a sequence of more or less complicated *actions*. Each action requires the presence of *objects* upon which it is to act and whose change in state represents the result of the action. The objects in the above algorithm, for example, are a, b and s.

Each object is associated with a *range*. In our example, all three objects have the same range: the natural numbers.

Examples of algorithms are by no means restricted to mathematics; rather, everyday proceedings can be described algorithmically. In order to show this clearly, let's take an example that has nothing to do with computational steps or with a computer program.

Assume someone is given the task of arranging an appointment with Mr. Smith. The statement

> "Arrange an appointment with Mr. Smith."

is already an algorithm, although it can only be executed by a *processor* which understands what actions are included in arranging an appointment. By processor we mean the driving force that executes the actions of an algorithm (compare Wirth 1978). Whether this force is a person or a machine is irrelevant to the definition. The important thing is agreement regarding the meaning of the description of actions. If such consensus does not exist (that is, if the formulation is not yet precise enough), then the instruction needs to be further refined. The set of instructions needs to be stepwise refined to a sequential list of actions until the meaning of each action is unambiguous to the processor.

We have developed a sequence of actions for the instruction "Arrange an appointment with Mr. Smith." The sequence is precise enough for a human processor to carry out.

The nomenclature used in the description is of particular importance. We have chosen to formulate the individual actions in stylized English and terminate each action with a period. If a complex action consists of simpler actions, we write the simpler actions indented. For example:

```
As long as Smith's number is busy, repeat:
  Replace receiver.
  Pick up receiver again.
  Redial Mr. Smith's number.
```

The instruction "Arrange an appointment with Mr. Smith" can then be written as follows:

```
Find Mr. Smith's number in the New York City telephone book.
If Mr. Smith's number is not found
  then:
    Write a letter.
    End.
  else:
    While Mr. Smith has not yet been reached, repeat:
      Pick up receiver.
      Dial Mr. Smith's number.
      While Mr. Smith's number is busy, repeat:
        Replace receiver.
        Pick up receiver again.
        Redial Mr. Smith's number.
```

```
                If someone answers
                  then:
                     Ask if it is Mr. Smith.
                     If it is Mr. Smith
                        then:
                           Make appointment.
                        else:
                           Apologize for error.
                  Replace receiver.
        End.
```

This example shows an important property of algorithms, the sequential execution of actions. As with our first example, this algorithm also consists of a set of actions and a set of objects (e.g., Mr. Smith, telephone book, receiver) which are to be manipulated.

Furthermore, we see that complex algorithms can be subdivided into subsets of actions. We also note that certain situations require sequences of actions that vary depending on certain conditions. We call these *conditional actions* or *selections* and use the following notation:

```
        If condition X is satisfied
          then:
             action sequence 1.
          else:
             action sequence 2.
        action sequence 3.
```

This means that if X is true, then *action sequence 1* is to be executed, followed by *action sequence 3*. Otherwise (if X is false) *action sequence 2* is to be executed, with *action sequence 3* following.

Often we find it necessary to execute a sequence of actions repeatedly as determined by some criterion. Such repeated action is called a *loop* and is represented by the following notation:

```
        While condition Y is true, repeat:
             action sequence 1.
        action sequence 2.
```

The first step is to check whether condition Y is true. If this is not the case, then *action sequence 2* is executed immediately. Otherwise (if Y is true) *action sequence 1* is executed. Then condition Y has to be tested again to determine if it is still true. If this is the case, then *action sequence 1* is executed and the cycle is repeated as long as Y remains true. The loop is ended and execution continued with *action sequence 2* when testing Y returns false.

In the development of an algorithm, care must be taken that the included actions can be carried out in an unambiguous fashion. In our example, if we happen to find multiple Mr. Smiths in the New York telephone directory, then the action "dial Mr. Smith's number" cannot be performed without further knowledge.

An algorithm is a set of instructions which does not permit interpretive freedom. This is particularly important when the processor is a computer. Thus, in the formulation of algorithms, all special cases need to be considered in advance. If the case arises that Mr.

Smith is out of town for some duration, then the condition "someone answers" could require a long wait, while the dutiful processor continues to dial the same number again and again. In order to show how much care must be taken in the formulation of an algorithm, we will develop an algorithm for finding the roots of a quadratic equation.

Before we can even begin with the task, we must determine what is given and what is expected of the algorithm. This is what is called the *specification of the algorithm*. Clearly this specification must be described so that it is both *complete* and *unambiguous*.

The statement

"Formulate an algorithm that solves the equation $a_2x^2+a_1x+a_0=0$"

proves inadequate for solving our problem. We do not know what is given and cannot determine exactly what we expect of the algorithm, and we have no information about restrictions or special cases that might arise.

We can make our specification more precise as follows:

"The values of the coefficients a_0, a_1, and a_2 are given. They can assume any real values.

Formulate an algorithm that computes all (real and complex) values of x for which the equation $a_2x^2+a_1x+a_0=0$ is satisfied."

We now have a specification that is precise and unambiguous, and we can begin the development of our algorithm with an idea for a solution.

We know from mathematics that our quadratic equation can be transformed to $x^2+b_1x+b_2=0$ and yield the general solution:

$$x_{1,2} = \frac{-b_1}{2} \pm \sqrt{\left(\frac{-b_1}{2}\right)^2 - b_2}$$

Armed with this knowledge, we now need to begin our algorithm with the computation of the discriminant, $(b_1/2)^2-b_2$, so that we can determine the real or complex roots based on the value of the discriminant. However, we also need to take special cases into consideration (for example, if one or more coefficients equal zero). This could lead to finding the root of a linear instead of a quadratic equation if $a_2=0$, or to no solution in case $a_2=0$, $a_1=0$, $a_0\neq0$. The algorithm can now be described as follows:

```
If a₂=0
   then:
      If a₁=0          (i.e., a₂=a₁=0)
         then:
            If a₀≠0
               then:   (a₀=0 and a₀≠0 are contradictory ⇒ error)
               End.    (with no solution)
               else:   (a₀=a₁=a₂=0 ⇒ 0x²+0x+0=0, satisfied for all x)
            End.
         else:  (i.e., a₂=0, a₁≠0)
            x=-a₀/a₁  (the special case of a linear equation).
         End.
```

```
else:    (a₂≠0)
   b₁=a₁/a₂.
   b₂=a₀/a₂.
   d=(b₁/2)²-b₂.
   If d<0
      then:
         x₁=-b₁/2+i√|d|.
         x₂=-b₁/2-i√|d|.
         End.
      else:
         x₁=-b₁/2+√|d|.
         x₂=-b₁/2-√|d|.
         End.
```

This example shows how meticulous we must be in both the specification and the design of an algorithm. One of the most common errors in algorithm specification is that the human processor subconsciously considers most of the special cases, but does not treat them in the description of the algorithm. When a machine is then used as the processor, undefined conditions or erroneous solutions readily result.

1.2 Definition of the Term "Algorithm"

Many specialists (mathematicians and computer scienctists) have defined the term algorithm in different ways. After reviewing some of these definitions, we will compare them with the characteristics of algorithms as we observed them in our examples. Then we will derive a definition that serves our purposes.

Knuth (1973) requires the following features of an algorithm:

1) Finiteness. An algorithm must always terminate after a finite number of steps.

2) Definiteness. Each step of an algorithm must be precisely defined; the actions to be carried out must be rigorously and unambiguously specified for each case.

3) Input. An algorithm has zero or more inputs, i.e., quantities which are given to it initially before the algorithm begins. These inputs are taken from specified sets of objects.

4) Output. An algorithm has one or more outputs, i.e., quantities which have a specified relation to the inputs.

5) Effectiveness. An algorithm is also generally expected to be effective. This means that all of the operations to be performed in the algorithm must be sufficiently basic that they can in principle be done exactly in a finite length of time by a man using pencil and paper.

Aho, Hopcroft and Ullman (1975) contribute the following definition:

> An algorithm is a finite sequence of instructions, each of which has a clear meaning and can be performed with a finite amount of effort in a finite length of time. In an algorithm instructions can be executed any number of times, provided the instructions themselves indicate the repetition. However, we require that, no matter what the input values may be, an algorithm terminate after executing a finite number of instructions. Thus, a program is an algorithm as long as it never enters an infinite loop on any input.

In Kronsjö (1979) we find:

> A procedure consisting of a finite set of unambiguous rules which specify a finite sequence of operations that provides the solution to a problem, or to a specific class of problems, is called an algorithm.

Bauer and Goos (1982) write:

> An algorithm is a precise (i.e., formulated in an established language) finite description of a general procedure using executable elementary (processing) steps.

Rechenberg (1974) defines the algorithm as follows:

> An algorithm is a stepwise finite process for the computation of desired quantities from given quantities; every step consists of a number of executable unambiguous operations and the determination of the next step.

Although these definitions are all similar, there are significant differences in their precision and their content.

All the definitions agree that algorithms are descriptions of a problem solving procedure with texts of finite length. They unanimously require that the actions in the procedure must be unambiguous and executable. Although Bauer and Goos do not make any statements concerning the duration of an algorithm, the other authors explicitly restrict their definitions of algorithms to only those procedures that terminate in finite time. Knuth and Rechenberg further expressly demand that an algorithm return at least one resulting quantity, while the other definitions do not handle this aspect.

Analysis of the examples that we have already discussed yields the following characteristics of algorithms:

1. Algorithms are problem solving procedures that consist of individual steps.

2. Every action has an effect that can (but need not) change values of objects and (whether implicitly or explicitly) determines which action is to be carried out next.

   Examples

   (1) The action "assign the sum of a and b to the variable s" changes the state of object s and determines implicitly that the next action in the text of the algorithm is to be carried out.

(2) The action "branch to action 3" only determines which action is to be carried out next (assuming that they are numbered), but does not change any objects in the algorithm.

3. Every action must be unambiguously interpretable. This precision of meaning applies to the algorithm's executing processor, for which no interpretive freedom can be permitted.

Examples

(1) The action "turn at the next intersection" becomes ambiguous as soon as more than one possibility for turning exists (e.g., left or right).

(2) The action "add 1 to the result of the operation $\sqrt{a}$ " fails in its precision of meaning because the result of the operation $\sqrt{a}$ can be interpreted as positive or negative.

4. Every action must be executable, i.e., each action must be of such a nature that the processor which is to execute it is able to do so. An example of a non-executable action is:

```
If 2 is the largest integer for which the equation
   xⁿ + yⁿ = zⁿ has integral solutions,
      then:
         set x = 2.
      else:
         set x = 0.
```

because there is no processor that can answer the given question (Fermat's problem).

5. Every algorithm must be statically finite, i.e., its formulation must be possible in a finite number of characters. The dynamic finiteness of an algorithm is a separate question. Although most algorithms (as we use the term) do end in finite time, there are processes which can be construed as infinite. Examples of such dynamically infinite algorithms are the regulation of a traffic light and the control of the dialog between a computer and its user. If we accept these processes as algorithms, then algorithms do not necessarily have to end. Thus dynamic finiteness need not serve as a criterion for *our* concept of algorithms.

6. Algorithms usually have objects whose values are established before execution of the algorithm—the *input objects*—and objects which are assigned values in the course of execution. Some of these latter objects' values represent the result of the algorithm— the *output objects*. All other objects are termed local *auxiliary objects*.

Example

The algorithm in Section 1.1 for solving quadratic equations uses the input objects a_0, a_1 and a_2, the output objects x, x_1 and x_2, and the auxiliary objects b_1, b_2 and d.

There are, however, algorithms without input objects. One example is an algorithm for generating the first 1000 prime numbers. This algorithm does not need any input.

Likewise, there are algorithms that have no output objects. An example in this category is an algorithm that handles the task of waiting until a key is pressed. This algorithm can be formulated without an output object, and we cannot even predict when or if the algorithm will end.

The question of whether an algorithm possesses input or output objects depends upon its specification. The presence of input and/or output objects proves not to be a characteristic of algorithms as we understand them.

On the basis of the above explanations, our definition of an algorithm is:

An *algorithm* is a stepwise problem solving procedure which is formulated in a text of finite length and in which each step (action) is unambiguous and executable for a particular class of processors. The execution of a step can (although need not) cause a change in state of objects and includes the determination of the next step to be executed.

This definition is adequately clear and precise for our purposes. It is not, however, precise in the mathematical sense and differs from other definitions in that it does not handle the dynamic finiteness or the number of input/output objects.

1.3 Objects and Actions

If we intend to formulate algorithms in preparation for writing computer programs, we need to know what actions and objects are permitted. It makes sense to allow only actions that a computer can execute and to define objects that a computer can manipulate. This section determines what objects and actions will be permitted (for the time being) for the formulation of algorithms.

Valid Objects

Two types of objects need to be differentiated: those whose value can be changed during execution of the algorithm—called *variables* —and those whose value cannot be changed— called *constants*.

Each object has a *range of values*. Computer science refers to this as the object's *data type*. The data type defines the set of values which a variable can assume or from which a constant comes, as well as the operations which are permitted on this set of values.

The most important data types that we will be using in the formulation of algorithms are:

> integers
> real numbers
> characters (e.g., letters, digits, special symbols)
> sequences of characters (character strings)
> boolean values (TRUE or FALSE)

It is often useful to combine several objects into a larger unit and refer to this unit (e.g., a vector or matrix) by a name. In mathematics, the designation $v_1, v_2, \ldots v_n$ represents the components of the vector v and $m_{11}, m_{12}, \ldots$ represents the elements of the two-dimensional matrix m.

We want to permit the use of such objects and shall call them *arrays*. All elements of an array are of the same data type. The customary mathematical notation will be used. Arrays can, among other things, be used to represent character strings. z_5 designates the fifth character in the string z.

We also want to include objects that combine objects of different data types into a larger unit. Such structured objects consist of an hierarchic set of objects, e.g.:

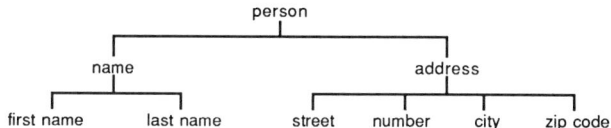

Fig. 1.1 Address book entry as structured object

The lowest level of this hierarchy contains the individual data objects that can be ordinary objects or arrays. The two higher levels constitute structures and represent combinations of individual objects. The object "name" is written as "person.name"; the object "first name" as "person.name.firstname".

The kinds of objects introduced thus far suffice for the formulation of algorithms for a large class of tasks.

Valid Actions

As the examples in Section 1.1 show, the formulation of algorithms requires above all two types of actions:

(1) the assignment of a value to an object, and

(2) the determination of the action to be executed next (flow control structures)

1. Assignment

A special *assignment operator*, whose symbol is ":=", is used to describe the assignment of a value to an object. The action *m:=n* is to be read as follows: "Assign to the object m the value of the object n." The value of the object to the left of the operator is changed; the value of the object to the right of the operator:assignment remains unchanged.

The major application of assignments is not, however, simply to assign the current value of one object to another. Instead, the values of several objects can be combined by operations and the result thereof assigned to a certain object. Therefore, *expressions* are permitted on the right side of assignment statements.

Expressions represent values and consist of *operands* (the objects) and *operators*. The value of an expression results from the values of its operands, the effect of its individual operators, and an explanation of the sequence in which the operators are to be applied.

For the present, we will include the following kinds of expressions on the right side of an assignment statement:

- *arithmetic expressions*, consisting of constants, variables and mathematical functions, and the comon arithmetic operators (+, -, *, /, modulo, etc.; * is the multiplication operator, and x modulo y yields the remainder in the division x/y).

  Examples

  ```
  a+b+c        √a        10*(a+SIN(b))        a        100
  ```

  The result of an arithmetic expression is always an arithmetic value.

- *boolean expressions*, consisting of boolean operands (expressions which are to be evaluated as either TRUE or FALSE) and the usual boolean operators from mathematics (AND, OR, NOT).

  Examples

  ```
  TRUE      FALSE      p AND q      NOT p      (p OR q) AND r
  ```

- *relational expressions*, consisting of boolean and/or arithmetic expressions connected by relational operators (< for less than, ≤ for less than or equal, = for equal, > for greater than, ≥ for greater than or equal, ≠ for not equal).

  Examples

  ```
  x≤y        b>10        (p AND q) = r        x≠y+z
  ```

  The result of a relational expression is always a boolean value (TRUE or FALSE).

- *character and character string constants,* which are placed in quotation marks in order to distinguish them from object names.

  Examples

  ```
  "A"      "y"      " "      "Modula-2"
  ```

Two special cases of assignments are:

(1) `count:=count+1`.

  This is a very common special case of an assignment that causes problems for beginners. The action means: "Add one to the current value of the variable `count` and assign this new value to the variable `count` itself." This action increments the value of `count` by one.

(2) `correct:=count≤100`.

  This action assumes that `correct` is an object whose range (data type) encompasses the values TRUE and FALSE. The object `correct` is assigned the value TRUE if the value of the (integer) object `count` has a value less than or equal to the integer constant 100; otherwise, `correct` receives the value FALSE.

Operations which are used with objects must also correspond to the data types of the objects. If we were to write the following in an algorithm:

```
x:="John".
```

```
y:=x+10.
```

then the sequence of assignments would be nonsensical because the range of x first covers all possible character strings, then the same x is used in an arithmetic expression. If we assume that x is a character string, then the expression x+10 is not valid.

2. Control Structures

The following actions serve to deviate from the simplest control structure, sequential control, in which actions are executed in linear form, one after the other. These actions control the execution sequence of actions in an algorithm. We define two such actions:

(1) selection

(2) repetition

Selection

The examples in Section 1.1 showed that we often need to execute different series of actions depending on the result of a boolean expression, e.g.:

```
If Mr. Smith's number is found in the directory
   then:  telephone him.
   else:  write a letter.
```

There is a choice between two possibilities. Contrary to sequential control, the processor selects *one* of the two *branches*, depending on the result of the evaluation of the condition (number found?). Regardless of what the result of the evaluation is, *one and only one* of the actions is executed.

We can generalize the above example by permitting a series of from zero to several actions instead of single actions in each of the branches.

Still, two possibilities might not suffice in all cases. We want the number of alternatives to be unlimited. If, for example, we want to base our actions on whether the value of an object is less than, equal to, or greater than some given bound, then we need an action that permits a choice among several alternatives.

For the formulation of algorithms, we shall therefore define two kinds of actions for selection: one that makes its decision based on the result of a single *boolean* expression (i.e., two alternatives), and one that permits any number of alternative branches (*multiway selection*).

We will use plain English words (written in all capital letters) to describe these actions because the transition from algorithm to program is thereby made easier.

We will use the following notation to describe simple selection structures:

```
IF boolean expression                    IF boolean expression THEN
   THEN                                      action sequence 1
       action sequence 1        or        END
   ELSE
       action sequence 2
END
```

Boolean expression stands for an expression of any complexity, so long as its result is a boolean value (TRUE or FALSE). The *action sequences* *1* and *2* can represent a series of actions of any length and, in particular, actions that can themselves be selection statements (i.e., selection statements can be nested).

The action as a whole is to be read as follows:

The value of the *boolean expression* is computed. If this value is TRUE, then *action sequence 1* is executed (THEN branch). Control is then be passed to the statement after the END. If the evaluation of the *boolean expression* yields FALSE, then *action sequence 2* in the ELSE branch is executed (if present). Control is then likewise passed to the statement following the END. If the ELSE branch is not present and the value of the *boolean expression* is FALSE, then the action following the END is executed immediately.

Examples

```
1.   i := 0
     IF   x < 0   THEN i := 1 END
     j := 0
```

If "x<0" is TRUE, then, after execution of the IF action, "i:=1" applies and execution continues with the assignment "j:=0". Otherwise, "i:=0" is performed and execution likewise continues with the assignment "j:=0."

```
2.   IF x < 0
        THEN
           ok := TRUE
           i := 1
        ELSE
           ok := FALSE
           i := 2
     END
     j := 0
```

If x<0, the following actions will be executed: ok:=TRUE, i:=1, j:=0. Otherwise (if x≥0) the sequence looks like this: ok:=FALSE, i:=2, j:=0.

To make the algorithm more readable, the action sequences in the THEN and ELSE branches are indented.

Multiway selections employ the following notation:

```
CASE expression
   case 1: action sequence 1
   case 2: action sequence 2
        .   .   .
```

```
    case n: action sequence n
    ELSE action sequence m
END
```

whereby *expression* symbolically stands for any valid expression and *case 1, case 2, ...
case n* stand for any values or subranges within the range of *expression. action sequence
1, ... action sequence m* stand for action sequences of any length, including action
sequences that themselves contain multiway selections (i.e., multiway selections can be
nested).

Subranges employ the notation `lo..hi`, whereby `lo` stands for the lower bound and
`hi` for the upper bound. `-3..2` designates the values `-3, -2, -1, 0, 1, 2`.

The entire action is to be read as follows:

The value of *expression* is computed. If the value matches the value designated by
case 1, then *action sequence 1* is executed; then control is passed to the statement
appearing after END. The situation is analogous if the computed value is equal to
case 2 (or *case 3,* or *... case n*). Each time the respective action sequence is executed
and control passes to the statement following END. If the computed value does not
match any of the listed cases, then *action sequence m* (the ELSE branch) is executed
with control again passing to the statement after END.

Example

```
CASE dayNumber
    1..5:  day := "weekday"
    6..7:  day := "weekend"
    ELSE errorMessage := "incorrect dayNumber"
END
```

If the object `dayNumber` has the value 1 at execution time, then the object `day` is
assigned the value "weekday"; for 6, `day` would be assigned "weekend", etc.

Repetition (Loops)

The examples in Section 1.1 also showed that it is often necessary to describe the repetition
of an action sequence. For example, if we were to describe an algorithm for procuring a
number of books from a library, we could formulate it like this:

```
While at least one book title is still on the list, repeat:
Get book.
Strike book title from list.
```

A repetition, as its name suggests, contains an action sequence that is to be carried out as
long as a certain condition (the loop continuation condition) is satisfied. In this example,
the loop condition is "at least one book title is still on the list."

If the loop continuation condition is not satisfied initially, i.e., if the list contains no
books to start with, then the actions contained in the loop are *never executed.*

We discover a second variety of repetition when we begin to refine the action "get
book." We can describe this loop in the following action sequence:

```
Repeat:
    Read the title of the next book on the shelf.
until the desired book title is found.
Remove book from shelf.
```

As we compare the first example to this repetition, we determine that in the former, the actions are carried out *while* the continuation condition is satisfied. In the latter, the action is executed *until* a certain condition (the loop termination condition) is satisfied.

Contrary to the *while loop*, the *repeat/until loop* is always executed *at least once*.

For the formulation of algorithms, we will define two kinds of loops and use the following notation:

```
1.   WHILE loop (continuation) condition
        action sequence                        "while loop"
     END

2.   REPEAT
        action sequence                        "repeat/until loop"
     UNTIL loop (termination) condition
```

Both *continuation condition* and *termination condition* can be boolean expressions of any complexity, their result being TRUE or FALSE. *action sequence* stands for any series of actions, even those including loops (i.e., loops can be nested).

The *while loop* is to be read as follows:

> The expression which serves as the *loop (continuation) condition* is evaluated. If the result is TRUE, the *action sequence* is carried out and the *loop condition* is evaluated again (it could have changed in the meantime). The *action sequence* is executed and the *loop condition* evaluated as long as the evaluation yields TRUE, or until the evaluation yields FALSE. Control is then passed to the statement following the END.

> The action sequence can be entirely bypassed or it can be executed repeatedly.

The *repeat/until* loop is to be read as follows:

> The *action sequence* is executed, then the expression serving as *loop (termination) condition* is tested. If the result is FALSE, then the entire process is repeated, and it is repeated over again until the loop condition yields TRUE. Then control is passed to the statement following the loop (i.e., following the loop condition).

> The action sequence is thus always executed *at least once*.

Examples

```
.  .  .
angle := 0
WHILE angle ≤ 2*π                        prints a table of sines
    sinevalue := SIN(angle)              for angles 0 to 2π
    print angle, sinevalue               in steps of π/8
    advance to next line
    angle := angle+π/8
END
```

```
. . .
y₂ := x
scount := 0
REPEAT
    y₁ := y₂
    y₂ := (2*y₁+x/(y₁*y₁))/3
    scount := scount+1
UNTIL (|y₁-y₂| < ε) OR (scount = 30)
y := y₂
. . .
```

computes the cube root
using Newton's approximation
formula (max 30 steps)
within a given tolerance ε

The actions discussed so far will suffice for the time being in order to be able to formulate algorithms. We still need to regularly give every algorithm a descriptive name that reflects the task it is to solve.

Furthermore, we will abide by the practice of following the name of the algorithm with parentheses that enclose the algorithm's *input* and *output objects* (see Section 1.2). These objects are collectively known as *parameters*. To distinguish the two types of objects, we will mark input objects with the symbol ↓, output objects with the symbol ↑ and input/output objects with ↕. All together, this is known as the *interface description* of the algorithm since it depicts the algorithm's interaction with its environment.

Examples

```
algorithm QuadEquat(↓a₀ ↓a₁ ↓a₂ ↑x₁ ↑x₂):
algorithm TeleAppt:    (no input/output objects)
algorithm DayOfYear(↓year ↓month ↓day ↑daynumber):
```

1.4 Means of Representing Algorithms

We formulated the algorithms in Section 1.1 in a combination of natural language and mathematical symbols. In Section 1.3 we established (for the time) permissible actions and used a semi-formal means of representation for the description of actions. There are also other methods for expressing algorithms. Some common representation techniques for algorithms are presented in this section along with a discussion of their advantages and disadvantages (compare Pomberger 1986).

For clarity, we shall use the example of the greatest common divisor (gcd) of two given positive integers ($m,\ n > 0$). Our solution is based on the Euclidean algorithm.

Natural Language. Algorithms can be formulated in everyday language. A description of this form has the advantage that any amount of text can be included and the possibilities for expression are practically unlimited. However, everyday language as a rule is not precise in meaning (i.e., it is ambiguous) and therefore not suitable for describing complex algorithms. Natural language does serve the purpose of recording initial ideas about the structure of algorithms. The Euclidean algorithm in everyday language looks like this:

Algorithm GCD: (* greatest common divisor *)

The positive integers m and n are given.

If m is smaller than n, swap the values of the two.

Divide m by n and call the remainder r.

If r is zero, then n is the greatest common divisor (gcd) and the algorithm ends.

If r is not equal to zero, then set m equal to n and n equal to r and again divide m by n and name the rest r. Repeat this until r is equal to zero. Then n is the greatest common divisor (gcd) and the algorithm ends.

Let's follow the flow of the algorithm in a concrete example in order to see how the Euclidean algorithm works and how we can simplify the understanding of a given algorithm. We will use the input values m=9 and n=12:

Since m is less than n, swap their values	$\Rightarrow$ m=12, n=9
Dividing m/n produces a remainder of 3	$\Rightarrow$ m=12, n=9, r=3
r is not equal 0; m is assigned the value of n, n is assigned the value of r	$\Rightarrow$ m=9, n=3, r=3
Dividing m/n produces a remainder of 0	$\Rightarrow$ m=9, n=3, r=0
r is 0, so the repetition ends, and n (3) is the greatest common divisor	$\Rightarrow$ gcd=3

Stylized Prose. Here we proceed with the algorithm as a sequence of individual actions. Each action is numbered and begins with a key word that summarizes the action. The action itself is described in prose. At the end of the action, the action which is to be executed next is given, if necessary.

This representation technique is used especially by Knuth (compare Knuth 1973). It has the advantage that any amount of text can be included in the description of any action. The major disadvantages are the length, the ambiguity and the lack of clarity of this method of formulation. Comparing expression in everyday language to stylized prose, the individual actions are more distinct in the latter, but the interrelationships within the algorithm remain clouded.

The Euclidean algorithm for determining the greatest common divisor looks like this in stylized prose:

Algorithm GCD($\downarrow$m $\downarrow$n $\uparrow$gcd):

Action 1 [swap].

If m < n then exchange the values of m and n.

Action 2 [modular division].

Divide m by n and name the remainder r.

Action 3 [end ?].

If r=0 then the value of the object n is the greatest comon divisor of m and n; assign this value to the object gcd and terminate the algorithm.
If r≠0 then proceed with Action 4.

Action 4 [replacement].

Assign the value of n to the object m.
Assign the value of r to the object n.
Return to Action 2.

Pseudocode is a semiformal method of formulation. It permits the description of algorithms without the precision that is required in programming languages. In pseudocode, flow control actions are expressed in a well-defined notation, while everything else can be freely formulated. Such languages are often based on some common programming language, but this is not required. The advantage is that the structure of the algorithm can be clearly represented without requiring too much preciseness from the formulator. The transition from algorithm to a programming language is also simplified. Furthermore, pseudocode facilitates the description of (data) objects, and commentary can easily be added and visually discerned (see the following example). This representation technique is being applied more and more in computer science literature. Section 1.3 employs such a pseudocode in establishing permissible actions. The Euclidean Algorithm in this representation looks like this:

```
Algorithm GCD(↓m ↓n ↑gcd):
objects m, n, gcd, r: integer, ≥0
   IF m < n THEN swap m and n END
   r := m modulo n     (* r is the remainder when m is divided by n *)
   WHILE r≠0
     m := n
     n := r
     r := m modulo n
   END
   gcd := n
END GCD.
```

Flow Charts are graphic representations of algorithms. A flow chart consists of various graphic symbols (which stand for individual actions) and arrows to depict flow control in an algorithm. Figure 1.2 shows the symbols that we will be using to represent the actions that were defined in Section 1.3. No further explanation is required for the reader to understand their meaning. There are various standards for flow chart symbols (ANSI X3.5, ISO R1028). We will, however, use the simplified form from Rechenberg 1974 because it usually achieves clarity equal to the standards, yet with a smaller set of symbols.

Flow charts show the structural properties of an algorithm better than nongraphic means—a picture is worth a thousand words. Comments can easily be added and emphasized. The disadvantages are that object descriptions are not explicitly representable in flow charts (they can only be added as commentary) and that control structures can be formulated with any level of complexity since the use of arrows has no limits. This freedom can encourage programmers who use flow charts to formulate algorithms with incomprehensible structures. Flow charts serve as a suitable means for representing algorithms if the discipline and judiciousness of the programmer counterbalance this freedom.

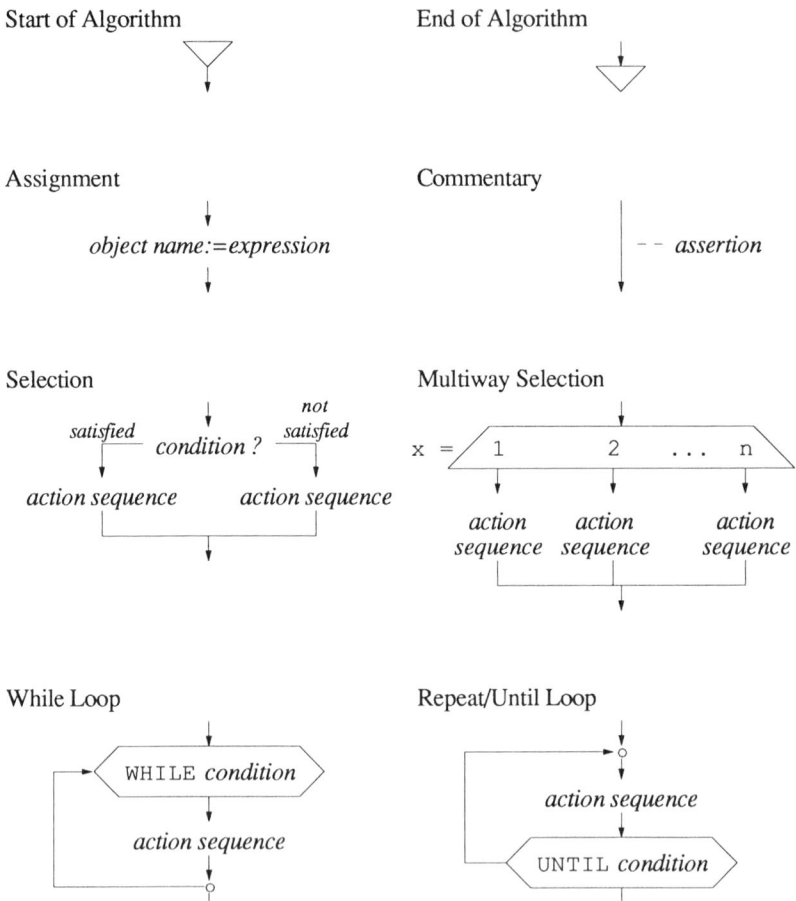

Fig. 1.2 Symbols for flow charts

Figure 1.3 shows the Euclidean Algorithm in flow chart form.

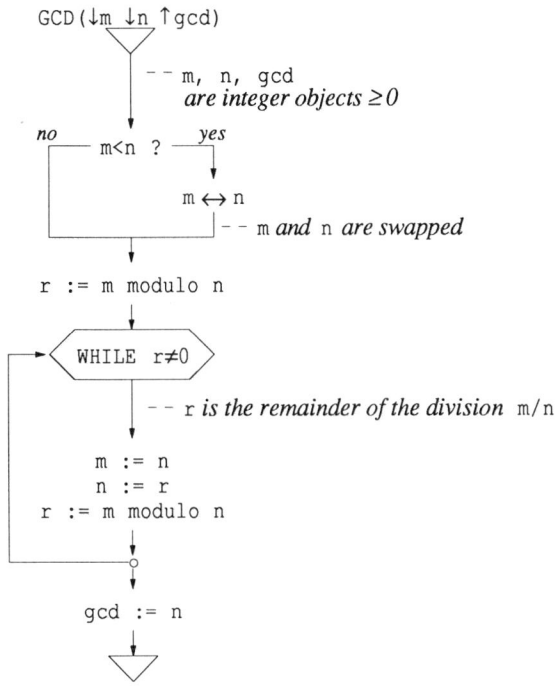

Fig. 1.3 The Euclidean algorithm in flow chart representation

Nassi-Shneiderman diagrams, named after their founders (Nassi and Shneiderman 1973), are graphic tools for the development and documentation of algorithms. In many ways they replace the older flow charts, and they force their users to create more structured algorithms by encouraging them to use less (albeit reliable) control structures. Nassi-Shneiderman diagrams employ graphic symbols for exactly the types of actions that we introduced in Section 1.3 (assignment, branching, multiway selections, and loops). The respective symbols are shown in Figure 1.4. Although several systems of notation are used with Nassi-Shneiderman diagrams, they are very similar and the differences do not create difficulty in interpretation. As flow charts, Nassi-Shneiderman diagrams do not permit the explicit representation of (data) objects. Comments are not as readily included as with flow charts. One serious disadvantage is that Nassi-Shneiderman diagrams are difficult to produce and more difficult to change without machine support.

Assignment

Selection

Multiway Selection

While Loop

Repeat/Until Loop

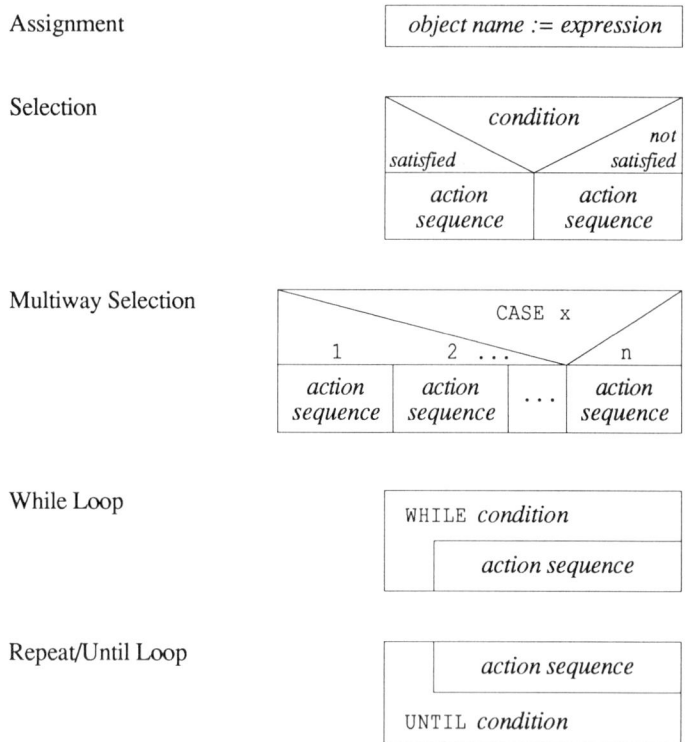

Fig. 1.4 Symbols for Nassi-Shneiderman diagrams

The Nassi-Shneiderman diagram for the Euclidean Algorithm is shown in Figure 1.5:

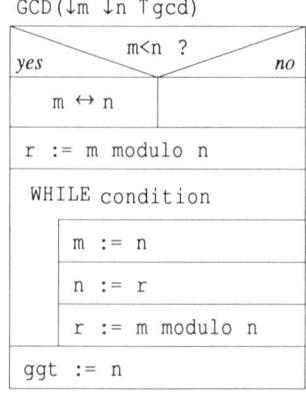

Fig. 1.5 The Euclidean algorithm as Nassi-Shneiderman diagram

Programming Languages. One thing that all the representation techniques discussed so far have in common is that they are not suitable for implementation and execution on a computer. In order to achieve that goal, formalisms were developed that are suitable for writing algorithms, yet so simple that a computer can "understand" them. Such a formalism must contain all the elements necessary for the complete description of algorithms (i.e., their objects and actions), and it must guarantee that everything which it expresses can be precisely and unambiguously interpreted. Furthermore, these formalisms must be easy to learn for humans and easy to read.

On the other hand, a disadvantage of programming languages for expression of algorithms is their preciseness itself, since their strict rules make every symbol and its position crucial. This means of representation is therefore more difficult to use and to read than others (e.g., graphic representation). However, with rational methodology (programming style) and thanks to the high degree of documentation inherent in the symbols of modern programming languages (as exemplified by Modula-2), algorithms can be written as clear and easily readable programs.

The Euclidean algorithm depicted in Modula-2 is shown below. This example is intended to give the reader a first impression of what algorithms look like in Modula-2. The characteristics of Modula-2 and the formulation of algorithms therein is handled in detail in Chapter 3.

```
PROCEDURE GCD(m,n: CARDINAL; VAR gcd: CARDINAL);
(*   m, n are input objects (value parameters). CARDINAL describes
     the data type for positive integers. gcd is an output object
     (variable parameter). *)

(* description of local objects *)
  VAR r,h:CARDINAL;  (* declaration of local auxiliary
                          objects r and h *)

BEGIN                    (* description of the actions *)
  IF m<n THEN            (* swap m and n *)
    h := m;
    m := n;
    n := h
  END;
  r := m MOD n; (* divide m by n and assign the remainder to r *)
  WHILE r <> 0 DO
    m := n ;
    n:= r ;
    r := m MOD n
  END;
  gcd := n
END GCD;
```

All text inserted between "(*" and "*)" serves as commentary and makes the algorithmic description more understandable.

We have now mastered the prerequisites for formulating and understanding algorithms. The next section will present some specific algorithms for simple tasks.

1.5 Some Simple Algorithms

This section presents several algorithms that solve simple tasks in the areas of mathematics and word processing. Our formulation will be in pseudocode as introduced in Section 1.3.

The programming novice should carefully study these examples, simulate execution with concrete values to clearly understand the flow of the algorithms, and try to think through the decisions made in the development of each algorithm. Examples (6), (7) and (8) might not be comprehensible at first for beginners. Therefore, feel free to skip over examples that prove difficult and have another go at them at a later date.

Any problem which is solvable by algorithmic means also has multiple solutions. Each reader should attempt to solve each task in his/her own way.

(1) Computation of the Factorial

A positive integer n is given. Compute fn, the factorial of n ($n!$).

Solution:

```
Factorial(↓n ↑fn):
   objects n, fn, i: integer, ≥0

   fn := 1
   i := 0
   WHILE i<n
      (* fn = i! *)
      i := i+1
      fn := fn*i
   END
End Factorial.
```

(2) Finding Minimum and Maximum

An array a with length n ($a_1 . . a_n$) whose elements are integers is given.

Find the smallest and the largest (min, max) elements in the array a.

Solution:

```
MinMax(↓n ↓a ↑min ↑max):
   objects   n:   integer, ≥0
             a:   array of n integer elements
             min, max, i:  integer

   min := a₁
   max := min
   i := 1
```

```
      WHILE i < n
        (* min in the minimum of a₁...aᵢ *)
        (* max is the maximum of a₁...aᵢ *)
        i := i + 1
        IF aᵢ < min
          THEN min := aᵢ
          ELSE IF aᵢ > max THEN max := aᵢ   END
        END  (* end if *)
      END      (* end while *)
  END MinMax.
```

(3) Testing for Prime Numbers

A positive integer n greater than or equal to 2 is given.

A boolean value `prime`, which indicates whether n is prime, is to be computed.

Solution:

The following algorithm employs the knowledge that for every factor q of a non-prime number n, if q is greater than $\sqrt{n}$, then there must be another number less than $\sqrt{n}$ which is also a factor (namely n/q). Therefore it suffices to test whether n is divisible by two or by an odd number between three and $\sqrt{n}$.

```
PrimeTest(↓n ↑prime):
    objects   n, q:  integer, ≥0
              prime: boolean value

    IF (n modulo 2 = 0) AND (n ≠ 2)
      THEN prime := FALSE   (* n is even and greater than 2 *)
      ELSE
        prime := TRUE (* we assume that it is prime *)
        q := 3
        WHILE (q ≤ √n) AND prime
          IF  n modulo q = 0
              THEN  prime := FALSE    (* n divisible by q *)
              ELSE  q := q+2
          END     (* IF n modulo q=0 *)
        END   (* WHILE *)
    END   (* IF (n modulo 2 = 0) ... *)
END PrimeTest.
```

(4) Eliminating Extraneous Blanks in a Text

An array of characters `text` is given (the length of the array being n, with n≥1). Write an algorithm that changes the array such that each sequence of blanks is replaced by a single blank. The new array length k is also to be computed.

Solution:

In the following algorithm, each sequence of multiple blanks is replaced by a single blank by shifting the remainder of the array of characters to overwrite extraneous blanks.

```
EliminateBlanks(↓n ↕text ↑k):
   objects  n, k, i:  integer, ≥0
                  text:  array of characters
   k := 1
   i := 2
   WHILE  i ≤ n
      (*text₁..textₖ contains no sequence of multiple blanks*)
      IF  (textᵢ = blank) AND (textₖ = blank)
         THEN  (* textᵢ is extraneous blank *)
         ELSE  (* textᵢ is not extraneous—transfer! *)
            k := k+1
            textₖ := textᵢ
      END  (* IF *)
      i := i+1
   END  (* WHILE *)
END  EliminateBlanks.
```

In this example we have our first occurrence of an input object (text) that is not only
used, but also changed, and thus becomes an output object. Such input/output objects are
marked with the double arrow (↕) in the interface description (see above).

(5) Computation of Occurrence Frequency

An array of characters "text" with length n (n ≥ 0) is given. Devise an algorithm that
computes the relative frequency of occurrence (in percent) of each vowel. (We will be
merciful and not consider "y," the sometimes-vowel.)

Solution:

```
Vowels(↓n ↓text ↑fa ↑fe ↑fi ↑fo ↑fu):
   objects  n, i : integer, ≥ 0
                  text:  array of characters
                  fa, fe, fi, fo, fu : real

   i := 1
   fa := 0; fe := 0; fi := 0; fo := 0; fu := 0;
   WHILE  i ≤ n  (* count the vowels *)
      CASE  textᵢ
         "a" :  fa := fa+1
         "e" :  fe := fe+1
         "i" :  fi := fi+1
         "o" :  fo := fo+1
         "u" :  fu := fu+1
         ELSE :   (* do nothing *)
      END
      i := i + 1
   END  (* WHILE *)
   (* compute the relative frequencies in percent *)
   fa := fa/n*100
   fe := fe/n*100
   fi := fi/n*100
   fo := fo/n*100
   fu := fu/n*100
END  Vowels.
```

(6) Text Compression

The following are given:

- an array of characters, `text`, of length m, containing some text, e.g.:

                 `Brevity is the soul of all wit`

- the length n of the target array (`shorttext`), and

- a maximal word length k

Formulate an algorithm that transfers the words in `text` to `shorttext` in such a way
that only the first k characters of each word are transferred. If a word is truncated, it is to
be followed by a period. For k=3, the following should result:

                 `Bre. is the sou. of all wit`

If the abbreviated source array does not fit into the target array, then the source is to be
truncated.

Note: You can assume that 1≤k<n<m.

Solution:

In the following algorithm, each element of the array of characters `text` is
considered sequentially. In transferring to the target array `shortText`, we use a
counter j to keep track of how full the target array is and a counter 1 to record the
length of the last word which was transferred to `shortText`.

```
Compress (↓m ↓n ↓k ↓text ↑shortText) :
   objects   i, j, k, l, m, n :   integer
             text, shortText:   array of character

   i:=0; j:=0; l:=0   (* no characters transferred yet *)
   WHILE (i<m) AND (j<n)   (* text₁..textᵢ is processed;
                          shortText₁..shortTextⱼ is filled *)
       i := i+1
       IF  textᵢ = " "
         THEN
             IF  (j>0) AND (shortTextⱼ ≠ " ") THEN
                 j := j+1
                 shortTextⱼ := " "
                 l := 0
             END
         ELSE
             IF  l≤k  THEN
                 j := j+1
                 IF  l=k
                     THEN  shortTextⱼ := "."
                     ELSE  shortTextⱼ := textᵢ
                 END
                 l := l+1
             END   (* IF  l≤k *)
       END   (* IF  textᵢ = " " *)
   END   (* WHILE *)
```

```
     (* i = m, i.e., entire text has been processed, or
        j = n, i.e., shortText full *)
     WHILE   j<n
        j := j+1
        shortText_j := " "
     END
END  Compress.
```

(7) Application Simplified

A very popular computer science professor had a staggering number of students applying to him for assistantships and graduate work. In seeking a fair way to choose the lucky few to fill the available positions, the professor stumbled upon Knuth's (1973) method described under the title of *"Josephus' Problem"* and decided to proceed in an analogous fashion as follows:

> Each time a position became available, the professor had the n candidates arranged in a circle. Beginning at candidate 1, the professor then counted off the candidates from 1 to m. (The number m was a random number in the range 1 to n provided by his computer's random number generator. The mth applicant was eliminated, and so on. The last remaining candidate got the position. For example, with n=7 applicants and the random number m=3, candidates 3, 6, 2, 7, 5, and 1 are eliminated (in that order) and the overjoyed applicant 4 would be awarded the position.

Design an algorithm that, given m and n, identifies the candidate who receives the position.

Solution:

> The following algorithm is based on the idea of noting for each candidate the number of the next remaining candidate (in the direction of the countoff). We recommend that the reader apply the algorithm to a concrete example in order to understand how it works.

```
SelectFairly(↓m ↓n ↑selected):
   objects   m,n,selected: integer, >0
             hopefuls:   array of n integers
             i,k,x,y:    integer
   i := 1
   WHILE  i < n     (* set up candidates in a circle *)
      hopefuls_i := i+1; i := i+1
   END
   hopefuls_n := 1
   x := n
   i := 1
```

```
WHILE  i<n
  k := 1
  WHILE  k≤m      (* count off *)
    y := x
    x := hopefuls_y
    k := k+1
  END  (* WHILE  k≤m *)
  (* candidate x (= hopefuls_y) is eliminated *)
  hopefuls_y := hopefuls_x
  i := i + 1
END  (* WHILE  i<n *)
selected := hopefuls_y
END SelectFairly.
```

(8) Diagonalization

Diagonalization of a matrix plays an important role in mathematics. The idea is to run through the elements of a matrix along its diagonals as follows:

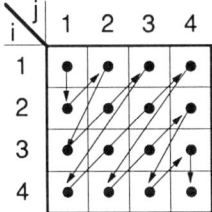

Formulate an algorithm that prints the elements of an $n \times n$ matrix M in the diagonal order shown above for any $n \geq 1$.

Solution:

We use a pair of nested WHILE loops for our diagonalization. The inner loop is responsible for printing out the elements along one diagonal; we leave this loop as soon as one of the indices (i or j) falls outside the matrix. Then i and j are set to the beginning of the next diagonal. This process is repeated until all diagonals have been printed (i.e., until the beginning of the next diagonal would fall outside the matrix).

```
PrintMatrix(↓n ↓M) :
  objects  n, i, j :      integer, >0
           M:   n x n matrix with integer elements

  i := 1
  j := 1
```

```
WHILE   j<n
  (*all diagonals before the one containing M_{i,j} printed*)
  WHILE   (i≥1) AND (j≤n)
    (* all predecessors of M_{i,j} are printed *)
    Print M_{i,j}
    i := i - 1
    j := j + 1
  END  (* inner WHILE *)
  IF   j≤n
    THEN    (* upper triangle *)
      i := j
      j := 1
    ELSE    (* lower triangle *)
      j := i + 2
      i := n
  END  (* IF   j≤n *)
END  (* WHILE   j≤n *)
END  PrintMatrix.
```

The interface description in the above solution has no output object (result). The result is printed out within the algorithm. For this purpose, we use the writing operation Print, which has not yet been introduced. Read and write operations occur in numerous applications and, if the processor is a computer, mean that an input/output unit (scanner, printer, etc.) is activated. We simply use this action without establishing a particular notation for it; its meaning is clear.

1.6 Algorithms and Programs

As we have already mentioned, the formulation of an algorithm depends on whether the processor is a person or a machine (computer). This section discusses the problems that arise when the processor is a computer.

People usually communicate with computers via input of text (e.g., on a keyboard). Algorithms can be expressed in various ways, as shown in Section 1.4. The difficulty is that the computer as processor needs to be able to understand the manner of representation. Therefore the notation used must contain all elements that are necessary for formulating algorithms, and it must have the characteristic that everything expressed in it must be absolutely precise and unambiguously interpretable. Furthermore, the notation needs to be easy for people to read and write so that algorithms can be fluently formulated. In order to meet all these requirements, languages for describing algorithms have been developed since the days of the first computer. These languages often remind us of mathematical formula notation. Such formalisms are called programming *languages* because, similar to natural languages, they employ a vocabulary and grammatical rules that determine exactly how sentences are formed and what these sentences mean.

Programs are algorithms that are formulated in a programming language so that they can be executed on a computer. The act of expressing an algorithm in a programming language is termed *programming*.

Numerous programming languages exist, each with its own vocabulary, and new ones are steadily being developed. The oldest among them, the machine languages, are so constructed that a computer can interpret each command directly. These languages are oriented to the internal architecture of a particular machine and not to the way that the person who uses them thinks. The formulation of algorithms in these languages is very arduous. In order to simplify programming, languages were developed that are oriented to an algorithmic way of thinking rather than to machine architecture. These are called the *high level* or *algorithmic* programming languages.

A computer can directly interpret only the machine language upon which it is based. Any program which is to be executed on a computer must therefore be in the machine language specific to that computer on which it is to be executed. A program written in another programming language must first be *translated (compiled)* before it can be executed. Since algorithms formulated in a programming language represent a *precise, unambiguous* description of an approach to solving a problem, the translation from a higher programming language to machine language can be carried out by a computer program. Such programs are called or *compilers*. In the translation process, a compiler generates *code* in machine language (called *machine code* or *object code*) from the algorithm formulated in a higher programming language. In terms of its meaning, the result of the translation is the original algorithm, yet its outward appearance has changed. The object code can then be interpreted by the computer. Figure 1.6 shows the evolution of such an executable program.

Familiar programming languages today range from the level of machine languages to middle-level languages (Cobol, Fortran, Basic) to a very high level (Ada, Modula-2) that incorporates experience from the development of modern programming techniques. Algorithmically oriented higher programming languages simplify programming and enable the production of high quality program systems, but they complicate the process of program translation. However, since translation can be handled by a computer program, it is clear that simplifying programming at the human end takes priority.

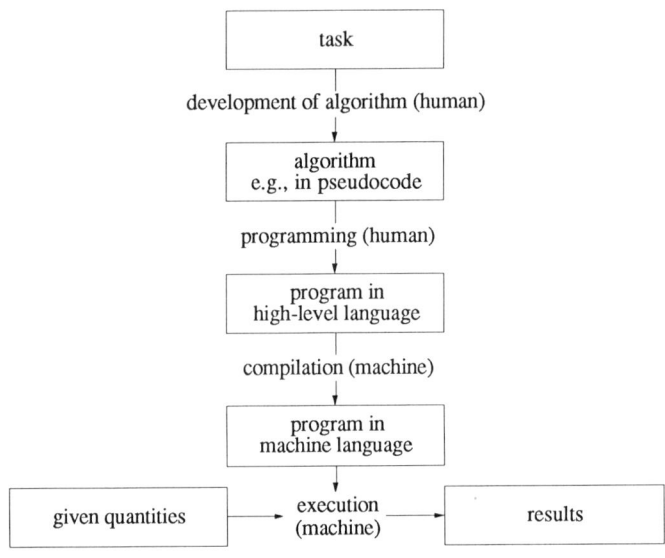

Fig. 1.6 The program development process

Exercises

(1) Nim is a simple game for two persons. 12 matches are distributed in three rows consisting of 5, 4, and 3 matches:

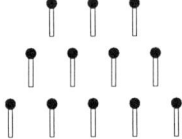

Players alternatingly remove any number of matches from any one row. The player who can pick up the last match wins.
Formulate an algorithm in stylized prose to describe the course of a game.

(2) Use algorithm (3) in Section 1.3 as a basis for an algorithm that computes the first n prime numbers. Document the algorithm in the form of a flow chart.

(3) Formulate an algorithm that determines all prime numbers smaller than a given upper bound n (n>0, n integer). Note the difference with respect to exercise 2.

(4) Two n x n matrices with real elements are given. Write:
1. an algorithm Mult(↓A ↓B ↓n ↑C) that multiplies the two matrices and assigns the result to the matrix C.

$$C_{ij} = \sum_{k=1}^{n} A_{ik}*B_{kj}$$

2. an algorithm Trans($\downarrow$A $\downarrow$n $\uparrow$C) that transposes the matrix A about its main diagonal and assigns the result to matrix C.

(5) An array of characters f with a length n (n$\geq$1) and an index k (1$\leq$k$\leq$n) are given. A word (= sequence of letters) begins at f_k.

Devise an algorithm Move($\downarrow$f $\downarrow$n $\updownarrow$k $\uparrow$word $\uparrow$wl) that transfers the word into an array word, whose length is 8. Afterwards k must point to the last letter that is part of the word, and wl must contain the length of the word (= number of characters).

Note: A word ends at the latest at f_n. A transferred word must not be longer than 8 characters. If it is longer, only the first 8 characters are transferred and the rest are skipped over in such a way that k afterwards points to the last skipped character.

(6) A card file for an arbitrary number of customers contains n$\geq$1 cards for each customer. Each card contains a customer number, his/her name and an unpaid balance for a single transaction. Write an algorithm that tabulates customer numbers, names, and each customer's respective *total* balance. Be aware that before reading another card, the algorithm must test whether there is another card in the card file.

Note: The card file is organized such that all cards for a given customer are located together.

(7) Newton's method for computing a square root functions as follows:

In order to compute $\sqrt{a}$ for a$\geq$0, begin with any estimate x_0>0. Compute a new estimate $x_1=(x_0+a/x_0)/2$. Repeating this process produces better and better estimates $x_2,x_3,..$, which rapidly converge on $\sqrt{a}$.

Formulate an algorithm SQRT($\downarrow$a $\downarrow$e $\uparrow$x) that uses the Newton method in such a way that for given a and tolerance ε>0 the following holds true: $\left| x^2-a \right| \leq \varepsilon$.

(8) The array "numbers" contains n$\geq$0 numeric values. Write an algorithm Sort($\downarrow$n $\updownarrow$numbers) to sort these values in ascending order.

(9) The fields of an n x n chess board are numbered sequentially according to the following scheme:

The field with the number 1 is always white.

Write an algorithm that lists the numbers of all white fields in ascending order.

e.g.,   for n=3:   1 3 5 7 9

for n=4:   1 3 6 8 9 11 14 16

(10) Formulate an algorithm as Nassi-Shneiderman diagram that computes the Fibonacci numbers $F_0..F_n$ for a given n>0. Fibonacci numbers are defined as follows:

$$F_0 = F_1 = 1, \qquad F_i = F_{i-1}+F_{i-2}$$

(11) An array of integers (length n$\geq$3) is given.

Develop an algorithm Max3($\downarrow$L $\downarrow$n $\uparrow$max) that determines an array max (length 3) which contains the three largest elements of the array L in descending order.

(12) In the following fragment of an algorithm, use assumed values for n and L in order to simulate its execution and thereby determine what it does:

```
objects   m, n, i, j :   integers, positive
          L :  array of integers, length n
. . .
m := 1
i := 2
WHILE   i≤n
   j := 1
   WHILE   (j≤m) AND (Lj≠Li)
      j := j+1
   END
   IF   j>m   THEN
      m := m+1
      Lm := Li
   END
   i := i+1
END
n := m
. . .
```

2 Principles of Program Development

The concepts *algorithm* and *program* were introduced in the first chapter. In additon, solutions to simple algorithms were given. More complex problems raise the question: How can we master the complexity and systematically move from the task description to the solution? Unfortunately, there is no algorithm for the design of algorithms. Rather, problem solving is a creative process that demands a broad knowledge of the task at hand and lots of intuition. We can, however, present useful guidelines for the systematic approach to the design of algorithms.

2.1 The Principle of Stepwise Refinement

The key to solving complex problems is *abstraction*. Therefore Wirth (compare Wirth 1971) recommends:

> Reduce the task to *subtasks*. Handle each subtask separately. If a subtask still proves too complex for an immediate solution, reduce it again to subtasks until they become simple enough to be solved with elementary actions. The composite of the subtasks along with a description of how these are to interact forms the solution to the original problem.

This is known as the *principle of stepwise refinement*. It tells us that, when designing an algorithm, we should not immediately attend to handling the details, but should first get a clear idea of how the task can be reduced to its constituent parts. These constituent parts are always less complex than the original task. Repeated application of this principle either leads to elementary actions that cannot be further refined (in which case the stepwise refinement process has been completed) or it turns out that the chosen abstraction does not adequately represent the actual problem structure and impedes further reduction. In the latter case, we have no choice but to backtrack one or more steps and try a different reduction. The worst case leads to a new start from step one. The work up to that point was not in vain, however, since the knowledge gained in the first reduction attempt can be applied in the next try. In order to show the value of the principle of stepwise refinement, we will demonstrate the process in the following example.

Task Description

In word processing we often encounter the requirement that a sequentially written text be output in an optically pleasing form. We want a program that reads a text sequentially from an input medium and prints the text with justified margins (aligned left and right).

The following are given:

- a text consisting of any number of words. Words are sequences of characters and are separated from one another by at least one blank. The end of the text is marked with a special character (in our case "$").

- a line width.

Justification requires that the output line contain as many words as possible, but only complete words. The first word must begin at column 1; the last word in a line ends at column b. Space between words is to be evenly distributed within each line. In the last output line, the words are to be separated by only one blank (i.e., the last line is not justified).

Preconditions: We require every word in the text to be shorter than half of the output line (width/2). This guarantees that each line (with the possible exception of the last line) will contain at least two words. For the sake of simplicity, we shall assume that the input text meets this restriction. Furthermore, although word processing often uses proportional fonts (with each character occupying space according to its width in order to generate a more pleasing optical effect), we will stay with nonproportional printing, i.e., each character occupies exactly one printer column.

We are to design an algorithm that solves the stated task. Each problem has multiple solutions. In practice, the algorithm that delivers the most pleasing optical results in the shortest time would be preferred. Since our goal is limited to showing the principle of stepwise refinement, we will not strive to optimize our algorithm; instead, we want to achieve an algorithm that is as simple as possible.

In solving the problem, we apply the principle of stepwise refinement in such a way that we first design the *overall structure of the algorithm*.

Since the input text consists of a sequence of words terminated with "$," we approach a solution that reads and processes individual words. This process continues until the end of the text is reached. The processing of words leads to the formation of output lines, giving us the following algorithm as a starting point:

```
Algorithm Justify(↓width):
    objects   width: integer
              line:  output line
              word:  word of text
              eot:   boolean value  (* end of text *)
        ClearLine(↑line)      (* start with a blank line *)
```

```
        REPEAT
          ReadWord(↑word ↑eot)
          ProcessWord(↓width ↓word ↕line)
        UNTIL eot
        PrintLine(↓line)     (* print last line *)
     END Justify.
```

In this first, still coarse version, we introduced four abstract actions.

— `ClearLine` returns an empty line containing no characters.

— `ReadWord` reads a whole word from the input source and determines whether the end of text (`eot`) has been reached.

— `ProcessWord` adds the word just read to the output `line`. If this is not possible (i.e., if the resulting `line` would be longer than `width`), then `ProcessWord` justifies the existing `line`, prints it, and begins a new output line.

— `PrintLine` prints `line` without changes.

None of these actions is simple enough to be expressed in the form of elementary actions. However, the problem of justification has already become much simpler because of our first design step. Now we have to stepwise refine each of the four new steps toward a solution. We will begin with the most difficult action, `ProcessWord`, and develop the following subalgorithms:

```
     Algorithm ProcessWord(↓width ↓word ↕line):
        objects   width:    integer
                  word:     word
                  line:     output line
                  fits:     boolean value
        AppendWord(↓width ↓word ↕line ↑fits)
        IF NOT fits THEN
           StretchLine(↓width ↕line)
           PrintLine(↓line)
           StartNewLine
           ClearLine(↑line)
           AppendWord(↓width ↓word ↕line ↑fits)
                          (* this time it fits for sure *)
        END
     END ProcessWord.
```

`ProcessWord` first attempts to append the word to the `line` (`AppendWord`). This attempt fails if the word no longer fits in the line (i.e., if appending would make the line longer than `width`). In this case, the line `line` remains unchanged and the boolean value `fits` is assigned the value FALSE. Since the word does not fit, the line must be padded with sufficient blanks to make the line end at column `width` (`StretchLine`). In addition to these new subalgorithms, we need the two already introduced actions `PrintLine` and `ClearLine` for preparing the next output line.

For the next step in our refinement, we will again take the most difficult action, `StretchLine`.

Our task description requires us to distribute the spaces between words evenly in each line. This can be achieved most easily by progressively inserting spaces from left to right. The stretching process ends when the desired line length is reached. If all white spaces have been increased, but the prescribed line length has not been achieved, the stretching process begins anew:

```
Algorithm StretchLine (↓width ↕line) :
  objects   width: integer
            line:  output line
            c:     current line length
            pos:   integer (*position of white space in line*)
  GetLineLength (↓line ↑c)
  pos := 1
  WHILE c<width
    FindWhitespace (↓line ↑pos)
    (* there is a blank at column pos in the output line *)
    InsertBlank (↓pos ↕line)
    c := c+1
  END
END StretchLine.
```

In refining StretchLine, we again encounter three further subtasks:

- GetLineLength has the sole task of determining the current length c of line.

- Beginning at the current column position pos, FindWhitespace locates the next white space and sets pos to that position.

- InsertBlank stretches the whitespace and thereby the line by inserting one blank at column pos .

By stepwise refining the most difficult subtasks, we have simplified the task without elaborating on the concrete representation of a word or an output line. The following subtasks still need to be refined:

```
ClearLine
ReadWord
PrintLine
StartNewLine
AppendWord
GetLineLength
FindWhitespace
InsertBlank
```

Continuing the refinement process requires that we know more about words and output lines. As you can see, *stepwise refinement* applies not only to actions, but also to the objects which they have to process (principle of *data abstraction*).

Both words and lines can be represented as *arrays of characters*. In addition, we will need to know how many elements of the respective arrays are actually occupied (the length of the word or the output line). Thus we will implement both words and output lines as *structured objects* (refer to Section 1.3 on objects and actions).

Fig. 2.1 Structured objects for `word` and `line`

We will denote the length of a word `word` as `word.length` and its i-th character as `word.text`$_i$. The length of an output line `line` will be designated as `line.length` and its i-th character as `line.text`$_i$. Now we are ready to refine the remaining actions:

```
Algorithm ClearLine(↑line):
   objects  line:  output line
   line.length := 0
END ClearLine.
```

`ClearLine` returns an output line whose length is 0.

```
Algorithm ReadWord(↑word ↑eot):
   objects   word:  word
             eot:   boolean value
             ch:    character
   REPEAT     (* skip blanks *)
      Read(↑ch)
   UNTIL ch≠" "
   word.length := 0
   WHILE (ch≠" ") AND (ch≠"$") (* form word *)
      word.length := word.length+1
      word.text_word.length := ch
      Read(↑ch)
   END
   eot := ch="$"     (* end of text ? *)
END ReadWord.
```

`ReadWord` performs three tasks:

–   At the beginning, blanks are skipped, i.e., the start of a word is located.

–   Further characters are read and combined into a word until either the end of the word (ch=" ") or the end of text (eot, ch="$") is reached.

–   The variable parameter `eot` contains the value TRUE if the end of text has been reached, otherwise `eot`=FALSE.

The situation after the last word has been read is not yet quite clear. The following two examples show which situations can arise:

(a) The end-of-text mark immediately follows the last word:

```
. . . lastword$
```

(b) The end-of-text mark stands alone, that is, it is separated from the last word by at least one blank:

```
. . . lastword     $
```

In the first case, the reading of "lastword" ends with the character "$" (which, because of the construction of the loop, is not transferred to word.text. The parameter eot contains the value TRUE.

In the second case, the end of the text cannot yet be determined with the reading of the last word (eot has the value FALSE). ReadWord is activated again by Justify. Blanks are skipped, then we immediately encounter the end-of-text mark "$". The returned word has the length 0. Since ProcessWord is executed with every word that is read, this special case must be covered in that subalgorithm. ProcessWord uses AppendWord in order to lengthen an output line by one word. We need to determine that nothing is to happen in AppendWord in case word.length=0 (the variable parameter fits is to have the value TRUE).

```
Algorithm AppendWord(↓width ↓word ↕line ↑fits):
   objects   width: integer
             word:  word
             line:  output line
             fits:  boolean value
             c:     integer    (* current line length *)
             i:     integer    (* auxiliary variable *)
   IF word.length = 0
     THEN fits := TRUE
     ELSE
       GetLineLength(↓line ↑c)
       fits := c+1+word.length≤width
       IF fits THEN
         IF c>0 THEN
           AppendChar(↓" " ↕line)  (* generate one blank *)
         END
         i := 1
         WHILE i≤word.length
           AppendChar(↓word.text_i ↕line); i := i+1
         END      (* WHILE *)
       END      (* IF fits *)
   END   (* IF word.length=0 *)
END AppendWord.
```

If the output line already contains words (line.length>0), then before a new word can be appended, a blank needs to be inserted (appended to the output line before the word is appended).

In order to append a character to the output line, we use a new action AppendChar, which we will now refine:

```
Algorithm AppendChar(↓ch ↕line):
    objects   ch:       character
              line:     output line
    line.length := line.length+1
    line.text_{line.length} := ch
END AppendChar.
```

Given our representation of an output line, it is easy to refine the subalgorithm `GetLineLength`:

```
Algorithm GetLineLength(↓line ↑c):
    objects   line:     output line
              c:        integer
    c := line.length
END GetLineLength.
```

The task of finding the next white space is not so easy. `FindWhitespace` must set the value of `pos` at some blank in the whitespace following the next word:

```
Algorithm FindWhitespace(↓line ↕pos):
    objects   line:   output line
              pos:    integer
    WHILE line.text_{pos} = " "
        pos := pos+1
    END
    WHILE line.text_{pos} ≠ " "
        IF pos = line.length
            THEN pos := 1
            ELSE pos := pos + 1
        END
    END
END FindWhitespace.
```

First we must ensure that `pos` points to a word within the output line. Then we look for the end of the word (i.e., a sequence of one or more blanks). Since no blanks may follow the last word in an output line, the search process begins in column 1 again after the end of the output line is attained ($pos = line.length$).

The algorithm `InsertBlank` has the job of shifting the entire contents of the output line from column `pos` to the end of the current output line to the right by one space, making it one character longer:

```
Algorithm InsertBlank(↓pos ↕line):
    objects   pos:     integer
              line:    output line
              i:       integer
    i := line.length
    WHILE i≥pos
        line.text_{i+1} := line.text_{i}; i := i-1
    END
    line.length := line.length+1
END InsertBlank.
```

That leaves us with the refinement of `PrintLine`:

```
Algorithm PrintLine(↓line):
   objects   line:   output line
              i:      integer
   i := 1
   WHILE i≤line.length
      Print(↓line.text_i); i := i+1
   END
END PrintLine.
```

All subtasks have now been elaborated to the point that they cannot be further refined. Aside from control structures and assignment statements, only three actions occur:

`Read(↑x)` reads the next character x from the input device.

`Print(↓x)` outputs the character x on the output device printer.

`StartNewLine` causes the next character output by `Print` to appear on a new line (line feed on a printer).

These are all *elementary actions* in the sense that it is fair to expect that the processor that executes our algorithm can directly "understand" them.

Figure 2.2 depicts the interaction of the various subalgorithms.

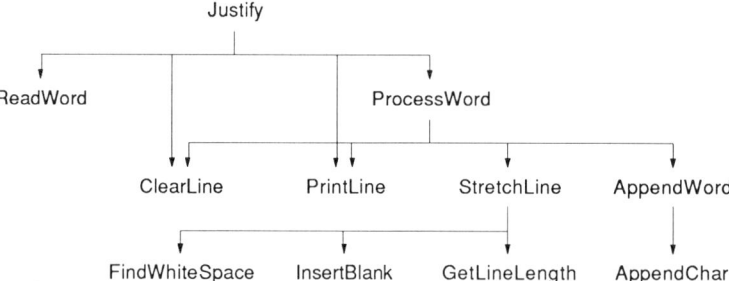

Fig. 2.2 Interconnection of subalgorithms of `Justify`

When the stepwise refinement has been completed, we often discover that some subalgorithms are used at only one location (e.g., `StretchLine`) and others are so simple that they consist of very few simple actions (e.g., `ClearLine` or `GetLineLength`). The actions of these subalgorithms could be inserted at the points where they are used without affecting our solution. However, we would lose some of the reduction gained in stepwise refinement and the longer algorithm which results would, in general, no longer be as easy to understand.

2.2 Data Capsules

Studying the solution for the justification problem developed in the previous section reveals that six subalgorithms (ClearLine, PrintLine, GetLineLength, FindWhitespace, InsertBlank, and AppendChar) all manipulate the same data object (line), that is, *directly* access the object. Furthermore, there are three subalgorithms (ProcessWord, StretchLine and AppendWord) that *indirectly* manipulate the object line by using one of the above six algorithms. This is nothing unique to our exercise and actually occurs quite often. The relationship is shown in Figure 2.3.

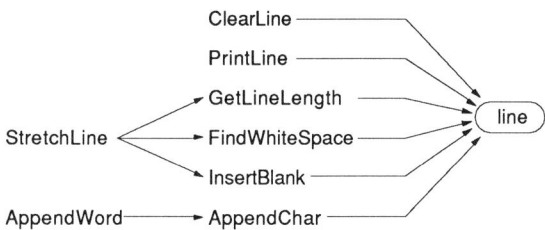

Fig. 2.3 Access to a data object by algorithms

We made this access possible by passing the parameter line to all the algorithms. This means that the output line line must be known in all subalgorithms. This is even true in the main algorithm, although it does nothing with line except pass it to subalgorithms. The following can be observed about our solution thus far:

- The parameter lists became unnecessarily long due to this passing around of parameters.

- The object line must be described in each subalgorithm, even those that do not work directly with it (ProcessWord, StretchLine, AppendWord). This contradicts the principle of data abstraction.

- The representation of an output line with the components length and text was an arbitrary decision in the design process. If we later determine that another representation is more suitable, the change would affect the object descriptions in all the subalgorithms.

Parnas was the first to allude to these disadvantages (see Parnas 1972). He recommends *capsuling* such global data structures off from their environment by writing a set of *access algorithms* for each data structure and combining these algorithms with the data structure itself to a higher-level unit. All other algorithms that want to access this data structure can do so by means of the access algorithms, and they use the access algorithms in order to change the contents of the encapsulated data or to retrieve information about them.

The combination of data structures and access algorithms to a higher-level unit is called a *data capsule*.

We use the following notation in order to represent a data capsule in pseudocode:

data capsule capsule name

    access algorithms :   list of names of access algorithms
        (e.g., ClearLine, PrintLine, InsertBlank)

    objects : description of encapsulated objects
        (e.g.,   line: structure
                       length: integer
                       text: array of characters)

    description of the access algorithms, e.g.:

```
Algorithm InsertBlank(↓pos) :
  objects   pos: integer
            i:    integer
  i := line.length
  WHILE i ≥ pos
    line.text_{i+1} := line.text_i
    i := i-1
  END
  line.length := line.length+1
END InsertBlank.
```

    description of the local auxiliary algorithms (e.g., algorithms that are used by the access algorithms, but are not access algorithms themselves).

```
END name.
```

A data capsule consists of three parts:

1. description of the encapsulated data (those data which are known to all algorithms defined in the data capsule, i.e., to which all the algorithms in the data capsule have access),

2. algorithms that work with the encapsulated data, and

3. a list of algorithms that can be used from outside the data capsule.

In some cases all the algorithms within a data capsule are accessible from outside. In general, however, auxiliary algorithms for the management of encapsulated data are included. These are used only by the access algorithms and are not accessible from outside.

We could write the following data capsule LineManagement for the justification exercise:

data capsule LineManagement

access algorithms : ClearLine, StretchLine, AppendWord, PrintLine

object: line: structure
               length: integer
               text: array of characters

description of access algorithms :

```
Algorithm ClearLine:
  line.length := 0
END ClearLine.

Algorithm StretchLine(↓width):
  objects  width: integer
           pos:   integer
  pos := 1
  WHILE line.length<width
    FindWhitespace(↕pos)
    InsertBlank(↓pos)
    c := c+1
  END
END StretchLine.

Algorithm AppendWord(↓width ↓word ↑fits):
  objects  width: integer
           word:  word of text
           fits:  boolean value
           c,i:   integer
  IF word.length = 0
    THEN fits := TRUE
    ELSE
      c := line.length
      fits := c+1+word.length ≤ width
      IF fits THEN
        IF c>0 THEN
          AppendChar(↓" ")
        END
        i := 1
        WHILE i ≤ word.length
          AppendChar(↓word.textᵢ)
          i := i+1
        END     (* WHILE *)
      END     (* IF fits *)
  END    (* IF word.length=0 *)
END AppendWord.

Algorithm PrintLine:
  objects  i:      integer
  i := 1
  WHILE i ≤ line.length
    Print(↓line.textᵢ)
    i := i+1
  END
END PrintLine.
```

description of local auxiliary algorithms

```
Algorithm FindWhitespace(↕pos):
  object pos:    integer
  WHILE line.text_pos = " "
    pos := pos+1
  END
```

```
        WHILE line.text_pos ≠ " "
          IF pos = line.length
            THEN pos := 1
            ELSE pos := pos+1
          END
        END
      END FindWhitespace.

      Algorithm InsertBlank(↓pos):
        objects  pos:   integer
                 i:     integer
        i := line.length
        WHILE i≥pos
          line.text_{i+1} := line.text_i
          i := i-1.
        END
        line.length := line.length+1
      END InsertBlank.

      Algorithm AppendChar(↓ch):
        objects  ch:  character
        line.length := line.length+1
        line.text_{line.length} := ch
      END AppendChar.
    END LineManagement.
```

We have now combined those algorithms that process our output line into a data capsule. Note that we included the algorithms StretchLine and AppendWord in the capsule because they logically belong in the category of LineManagement. Since the object line is accessible to all algorithms in the data capsule, the subalgorithm GetLineLength became superfluous.

Changing the solution at which we arrived through stepwise refinement to a solution with a data capsule naturally has implications for the algorithms that employ the access algorithms of the data capsule. In each of these algorithms the description of the object line is to be omitted and the line is to be deleted from the parameter list. For example, the algorithm Justify now assumes the following modified form:

```
      Algorithm Justify(↓width):
        objects  width: integer
                 word:  word of text
                 eot:   boolean value
        ClearLine      (* start with a blank line *)
        REPEAT
          ReadWord(↑word ↑eot)
          ProcessWord(↓width ↓word)
        UNTIL eot
        PrintLine      (* print last line *)
      END Justify.
```

The interaction of the individual subalgorithms is shown in Figure 2.4.

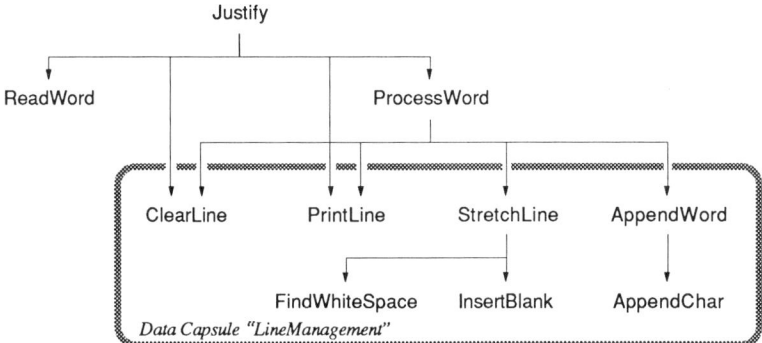

Fig. 2.4 Structure of the algorithm Justify with data capsule

Advantages of data capsules

- The *interfaces* of access algorithms are simplified because encapsulated objects do not need to be listed.

- Encapsulated objects are *protected* from unauthorized access. Only operations defined by the access algorithms can be applied to them.

- The algorithms that use the data capsule do not need to know anything about the representation of the encapsulated objects (principle of *information hiding*). This means that a change in the structure of the encapsulated objects affects only the access algorithms (according to the principle of data abstraction).

The only disadvantage of data capsules is that they can easily contain very simple access algorithms that, for example, do nothing more than make an assignment (in our example, ClearLine). Disguising an assignment or other elementary action in its own algorithm inflates the overall solution. If the number of access algorithms becomes very large, our overview of the situation suffers.

2.3 The Module Concept

In the previous section, several algorithms were combined into a data capsule, thereby following the principle of collecting, in a *data-oriented* way, all algorithms that work with the same objects to a higher-level unit. This is not, however, the only principle by which we can form collections of subalgorithms. We could just as well proceed in a *problem-oriented* fashion and collect all algorithms that contribute to the solution of a self-contained subproblem. In our example, the main work (the justification itself) is accomplished by the subalgorithm StretchLine, which we could combine into a higher-level unit along with GetLineLength, FindWhitespace and InsertBlank. A third possibility is to assemble all algorithms with related functions into a *function-oriented* unit. Classical examples of this approach are collections of algorithms for input/output of data and for string manipulation.

Which of the three combination methods is to be applied in a specific situation depends on the nature of the problem and the interaction of the subalgorithms. There are even solutions for which the three approaches would be equally suitable. Usually, however, one principle of organization seems to assert itself, while others seem unnatural.

The collection of several algorithms into a higher-level unit is called a *module*, defined according to Goos (see Goos 1973) as follows:

> A module is a collection of objects and algorithms with the property that communication with its external environment takes place only via a clearly defined interface. Assembling modules to an overall solution must not require any knowledge of the inner workings of the modules, and the correctness of a module must be testable without any knowledge of its imbedding in the system of which it is to be a part.

This definition shows us that the interface has particular meaning for the module concept. We can divide the interface of a module into two parts:

- The *import interface* identifies which objects and algorithms a module will be needing from its external environment.

- The *export interface* identifies which objects and algorithms a module provides to its external environment.

We will use the following notation for formulating a module in pseudocode:

```
MODULE module name :
   IMPORT list of imported objects and algorithms
   EXPORT list of exported objects and algorithms
   description of the module's objects
   description of the module's algorithms
END module name
```

The *description of the module's objects* serves the purpose of establishing all data types that are either exported or used by several algorithms in the module.

Similarly the *description of the module's algorithms* covers both the exported algorithms and the (local) auxiliary algorithms.

The data capsule is a special case of a module with the property that it exclusively exports algorithms, since all of its defined objects are kept secret from the external environment.

The principle of stepwise refinement gives us not only a technique for mastering complexity, but also an aid in structuring algorithms. The module concept offers another possibility for structuring a solution. In our justification example, the organization of the modules could lead to the following hierarchy:

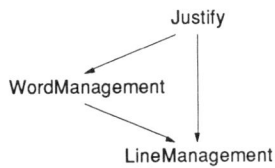

Fig. 2.5 Module hierarchy of the algorithm `Justify`

Our overall solution consists of three modules: the data capsule `LineManagement` (data-oriented unit); the function-oriented module `WordManagement`, containing the algorithms for processing words (`ReadWord` and `ProcessWord`); and the control module `Justify`.

Modularization is one of the most important design principles. Thus we want to summarize the points that are especially to be heeded in the formation of modules:

- *Simplicity.* Each module should form a unit that is clear and comprehensible in and of itself. This requirement does not prescribe a maximal length (lines or pages) for modules. A module that is several pages long can still be clear and comprehensible if it is well organized.

- *Minimization and Comprehensibility of Interfaces.* The interfaces between modules should be kept as simple as possible, which means short parameter lists and few imported and exported objects and algorithms. If a module trades too much information with its environment, there is a danger that clarity and comprehensibility will suffer.

- *Independence.* Modules need to be independent of each other so that changes made in one module or any of its algorithms do not affect the other modules. That is, the set of all assumptions that one module makes about another is restricted to the objects in their respective interface descriptions. Once a module's interface has been specified, the design of the inner structure can be carried out without knowledge of the overall system of which it is to be a part. This is also in line with the principle of stepwise refinement and the definition of the module concept.

- *Self-Containment.* The algorithms in the module should either all work with the same data structure or be necessary and adequate for solving a particular task. A module cannot be simply a collection of miscellaneous algorithms without a logical connection.

- *Testability.* Each module must be constructed so that its correctness can be tested without any knowledge of the overall system in which it is imbedded.

Exercises

(1)   Write an algorithm that constructs an array of 100 elements. Each element is one of three digits (0,
       1, or 2). Arrange the field so that no identical substrings are located next to one another (Rechenberg
       1974, Wirth 1975).
       Examples of erroneous sequences: 0̲0̲1201,   01̲0̲2̲1̲0̲2101.
       Design the algorithm using the principle of stepwise refinement.

(2)   Use stepwise refinement to devise an algorithm WordCount (↓text ↓n):
       A text in the form of an array of characters of any length n (n≥0) is given. The array consists of
       words that are separated from one another by blanks, commas, or periods. Determine the (absolute)
       frequency of each word and list the words along with their respective frequencies at the conclusion of
       the algorithm.
       Example
              The text (and answer to the age-old question)
                     If a woodchuck could chuck wood, a woodchuck would chuck as much wood as a
                     woodchuck could chuck if a woodchuck could chuck wood.
       would lead to:

If	1
a	4
woodchuck	4
could	3
chuck	4
wood	3
would	1
as	2
much	1
if	1

       Restrictions : If a word is longer than 10 characters, only the first 10 characters are considered.
       Multiple delimiters (blanks, commas, periods) that follow one another function as one (the comma
       and several blanks after "wood" in the above example). Only the first 100 different words need to be
       registered. If the text is longer, a message needs to be output to say that further words are not
       processed. For simplicity's sake, "If" and "if" are considered to be separate words.

(3)   Expand the algorithm Justify in Section 2.1 so that the text can be printed in multiple columns: n
       columns with m lines. Justification in each line is to be carried out with a line width of width:
       JustifyColumns(↓n ↓m ↓width).

(4)   Develop an algorithm Columns(↓ncols ↓nlines ↓colsize) that reads an input text characterwise and
       prints out the contained words in columns. Words are separated by any number of blanks. The
       input text is to be output in ncols columns of colsize characters and is to be readable from top to
       bottom in each column. After nlines words, a new column is to be started; after ncols columns, a
       new page. Words that are too long are to be truncated in such a way that at least one blank separates
       the columns.

       Example
              ncols = 3,   nlines = 4,   colsize = 6
              input text:
                     Those who bring sunshine into the lives of others cannot keep
                     it from themselves.

output text:

```
Those into  other       1st page
who    the   canno
bring lives keep
sunsh of    it
-------------------------------
from                    2nd page
thems
```

Develop your algorithm using stepwise refinement. Make careful choices regarding each abstraction level and document each step in the design fully.

(5)   Design a data capsule for managing a waiting line (queue) of length n.
The access algorithm Insert(↓name ↑ok) adds the element name to the end of the queue if there are less than n persons in the queue already. If there was room in the queue, then ok is TRUE, otherwise ok is FALSE. The access algorithm Delete(↓name ↑ok) removes the first element from the queue and returns the respective name and ok=TRUE. IF the queue is empty, then ok=FALSE is returned. The queue can be visualized as follows:

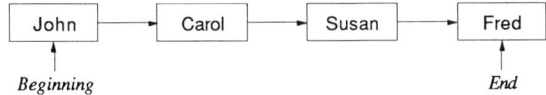

Carefully consider how you will implement the queue and how you can keep track of the beginning and the end.

3 The Programming Language Modula-2

The first two chapters introduced the term algorithm and explained how solutions can be described by means of algorithms. This chapter describes the programming language Modula-2 and gives guidelines for formulating algorithms as Modula-2 programs (the last step in program development by stepwise refinement).

The chapter is organized in such a way that a beginner can stepwise assimilate the vocabulary and grammatical rules of Modula-2, but also so that advanced programmers can use it as a reference. Perhaps some beginners will feel overwhelmed by the many details. Be reassured that it is not necessary to keep all these details in your head right from the beginning. Instead, the beginner should strive for an overview on the basis of the included examples. If questions arise later (during exercises or application of Modula-2), then the handbook character of this chapter should serve well to provide a sure footing in the use of Modula-2.

The first part of this chapter introduces a diagrammatic notation system for describing the elements of a language. Then the syntax and application of all program constructs possible in Modula-2, progressively from simple to complex, are shown. Particular consideration is given the beginner in the form of explicit explanations and numerous examples.

3.1 Notation for Language Description

There are many methods for describing programming languages. Verbal explanations in natural languages have the disadvantage of being long-winded. Furthermore, they are not always free of ambiguity and can be misinterpreted. Thus formal descriptions (so-called *grammars*) in various forms have asserted themselves in computer science. They have the disadvantage of being difficult to understand for the beginner. Believing that a picture is worth a thousand words, we have chosen to represent the language elements of Modula-2 in graphic form. The illustrations used for this purpose resemble those found in the description of Pascal by Jensen and Wirth (1978). All language elements have names and are numbered sequentially. The numbers are intended to help you find a particular language element.

In the following example we present the grammar rules for forming names as we sometimes find them in bibliographies. Our rules specify that a name begins with a last name and ends with a first name. The two parts of the name are to be separated by a comma:

Name$_1$

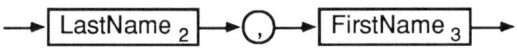

Language elements that are themselves composites, and are consequently explained at some other point, are represented by a rectangular box. A circle denotes self-explanatory language elements, such as the comma in our example. Arrows show the direction in which the illustration is to be read.

A last name consists of a sequence of one or more letters:

LastName$_2$

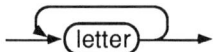

The repetition of a letter is indicated by a fork after letter. The rounded oblong frame indicates that "letter" (like the comma in the above example) is a constituent part that cannot be further reduced. Note, however, that "letter" does not stand for any definite letter, but for an entire class of characters.

A first name is comprised of either a "simple first name" or of two simple first names joined by a hyphen ("double name"):

FirstName$_3$

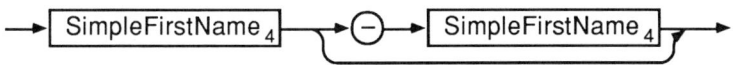

The fact that the hyphen and the second simple first name can be omitted is indicated by the "bypass" arrow.

A simple first name consists, as does a last name, of a sequence of letters. It can, however, be abbreviated by means of a single letter followed by a period:

SimpleFirstName$_4$

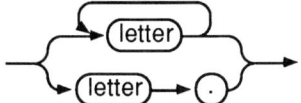

The options for a simple first name are portrayed by arrows that first fork and then merge (as in the case of the omission of the second first name and its preceding hyphen for first name).

According to the rules outlined so far, the following is a valid name:

```
Kennedy,John-F.
```

while this form would not be accepted:

```
Charly Chaplin
```

but not because the first name appears in the first position (a sequence of letters, according to our rules, can be either a first name or a last name). Instead, the error is that the two names are separated by a blank and not a comma.

The language constructs of Modula-2 can be fully described with the illustration elements shown so far. Even if many diagrams look complicated at first glance, they are all to be read in the same fashion, namely by *following the arrows*.

3.2 Lexical Elements of Modula-2

Each Modula-2 program consists essentially of a sequence of *symbols* (such as numbers and names), which in turn consist of individual characters. This section explains the rules of formation for these symbols (known as the *lexical elements* of the programming language).

This section might prove tedious to read; some things will only become clear as they find application in following sections.

3.2.1 Identifiers

Every program works with *objects*. For the purpose of unique identification, these objects can be *named*, that is, the programmer can give them *names*. In the field of computer science, these names are known as *identifiers*. We use the terms name and identifier synonymously.

In Modula-2, identifiers must be constructed according to the following rules:

Ident$_1$

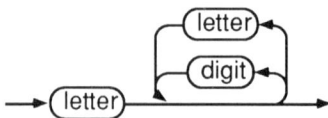

- An identifier can consist of the *letters* A-Z and a-z and the *digits* 0-9.

- The first character *must* be a letter. (The shortest identifier consists of one letter.)

- There is no length limit on identifiers (contrary to older programming languages).

- Upper-case and lower-case letters have different meanings (i.e., the identifiers value, Value, and VALUE are interpreted as distinct and can therefore be used to identify different objects).

Examples

The following are valid identifiers:

```
i
Modula2
George
ThisIsOneVeryLongIdentifier
switch
```

The following are not valid identifiers:

```
4times              (number as first character)
string$             (special character: "$")
George Orwell       (no space allowed)
annual_balance      (no underscore allowed)
```

These rules only define how an identifier must be constructed in order to be recognized by the Modula-2 compiler. Be aware, however, that the *choice of names* (see Section 5.1.2) plays an important role in programming.

In some cases the name alone is insufficient for the unique identification of an object. Then an identifier z would be preceded by an identifier y and a period (y.z). This notation is known as *qualification* of an identifier. y.z is then called a *qualified identifier*.

QualIdent$_2$

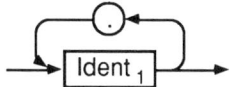

- A qualified identifier can be a single name. (In Modula-2, every identifier that uniquely determines an object is called "qualified.")

- If a single qualification still does not suffice to uniquely determine an object, then the qualification can be repeated.

These rules describe only the formulation of qualified identifiers. A detailed explanation of qualification and its meaning can be found in Section 3.8, "The Module Concept."

3.2.2 Key Words

Every programming language has a number of words with a fixed meaning for the description of actions and objects contained in a program. These are the language's *key words*.

Key words in Modula-2 are made up exactly like identifiers. They are, however, reserved words and cannot be used as names of objects, but only for their intended tasks. The simplicity of Modula-2 can be seen in the fact that, in contrast to many other programming languages, there are only 40 key words, and so they can easily be remembered:

AND	ELSIF	LOOP	REPEAT
ARRAY	END	MOD	RETURN
BEGIN	EXIT	MODULE	SET
BY	EXPORT	NOT	THEN
CASE	FOR	OF	TO
DEFINITION	IF	POINTER	UNTIL
DIV	IMPLEMENTATION	PROCEDURE	VAR
DO	IMPORT	QUALIFIED	WHILE
ELSE	IN	RECORD	WITH

Key words must be written as upper-case letters. Because Modula-2 is case-sensitive, the lower case variations (e.g., Pointer or var) could be used as identifiers, but, to avoid confusion, we recommend not doing so.

3.2.3 Numbers

In Modula-2, as in other programming languages, integers and real numbers are differentiated:

Number$_3$

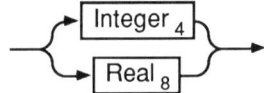

Integers are usually used for counting. In Modula-2, integers can be written in various types of notation, depending on the base (decimal, octal, or hexadecimal):

Integer$_4$

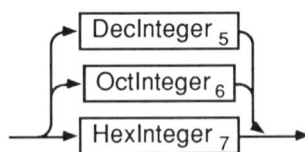

Decimal integers are formulated as usual by a sequence of decimal digits without any special notation:

DecInteger$_5$

They cannot contain a sign or any separating characters.

Octal integers are composed of the digits 0-7 and are marked with the letter B at the end:

OctInteger$_6$

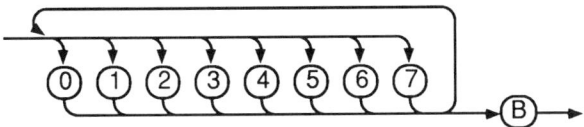

Note: The octal number 123B is equal to the decimal number 83 $(1*8^2 +2*8^1+3*8^0)$.

Hexadecimal integers are formed from the decimal digits and the letters A-F. They must begin with a decimal digit and terminate with the letter H.

HexInteger$_7$

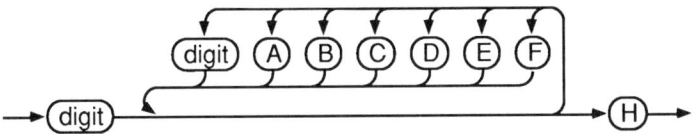

The letters A-F are "digits" in the hexadecimal system and have the values 10 through 15, respectively.

Note: The hexadecimal number 4D2H equals the decimal number 1234 $(4*16^2+13*16^1+2*16^0)$.

The decimal number 4012 must be written as 0EACH in hexadecimal format. The 0 is required in order to show that it is a number. (EACH alone would be a valid identifier according to the rules in Section 3.2.1.)

Real numbers are used to represent numbers with fractional components. They consist of an *integer part*, which is constructed like a decimal integer (DecInteger), followed by a *decimal point*, optionally followed by a *fractional part* (one or more digits), optionally followed by an *exponential part*:

Real$_8$

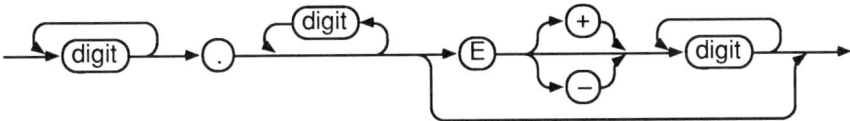

- The integer part of a real number must be terminated by a decimal point, even if no fractional part follows. (100. is interpreted as a real number; 100 is interpreted as an integer. The difference is important because real numbers and integers have different internal representations in a computer and different operations are permitted on the two types.)

- At least one digit must appear before the decimal point. One tenth, for example, must be written with the leading zero as 0.1 (not as .1).

- The letter E can be read as "... times ten to the power of ..." The numbers 1.E3 and 1.E-3 are interpreted as 1000. and 0.001 respectively.

Examples of valid numbers

integers:

```
0
123
0CH                        (12)
77B                        (63)
77BH                       (1915)
```

real numbers:

```
0.
0.0
3.14159
1.5E6                      (1500000.0)
5.E-4                      (0.0005)
```

Examples of improper numbers

integers:

```
5o                         (the letter "o/O" is not equivalent to zero)
1D                         (hexadecimal must end with H)
BEACH                      (hexadecimal must start with a digit)
678B                       (8 is not a valid octal digit)
1 000 000                  (numbers cannot be separated by blanks
1,000,000                  or any other character)
```

real numbers:

```
123,4                      (the European comma is not valid)
1E6                        (decimal point must not be omitted)
.333                       (integer part must not be omitted)
```

3.2.4 Character Strings

As the example "Justify" in Chapter 2 showed, not only numbers, but also *characters* can be processed in a program. A *string* is a sequence of any number of characters. Which characters are allowed in a string depends on the implementation on a particular computer and on the character set available. We will use the *ASCII code* (American Standard Code for Information Interchange) that is used for most microcomputers. It includes upper-case and lower-case letters, digits and special characters (printable characters). In addition, there are certain control characters for various devices (e.g., printers). Appendix D contains an ASCII table.

A character string in Modula-2 takes the following form:

String$_9$

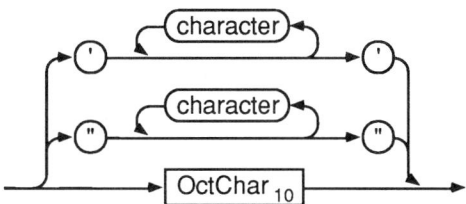

- A character string is bracketed in a pair of apostrophes (') or a pair of quotation marks ("). It must terminate with the same delimiter with which it began.

- A character string can contain any number (including zero) of printable characters. The delimiters are not part of the string.

- The number of characters between delimiters is known as the *length* of the character string. A string of length 1 is also called a single character or simply a character .

- In contrast to other symbols, a character string may contain *blanks*. It may not, however, extend over multiple lines, but is restricted to *one line*.

- If a character string is enclosed in apostrophes, it can contain quotation marks but no apostrophes. The case is analogous for quotation marks as delimiters. This means that a string *cannot contain both* quotation marks *and* apostrophes.

Examples

valid character strings:

```
' '    or   ""              (the empty or null string)
' '    or   " "             (a string containing one blank)
'George'
"George Orwell's Book"
'He shouted, "Careful!" '
```

invalid character strings:

```
'Laurel & Hardy "           (delimiters must match)
'George Orwell's "1984" '   (both " and ' enclosed)
```

For single characters (i.e., strings of length 1), another method of representation is possible:

OctChar$_{10}$

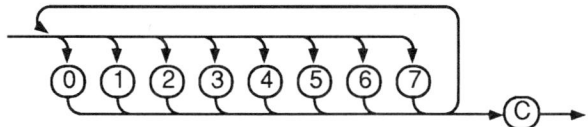

This form resembles the representation of octal numbers with the exception of the C (for character) that replaces the B. The character described by this format is the one at the position in the respective table (e.g., ASCII) as determined by the octal number (see Appendix D). The highest number possible is 377C (decimal 255). This form can be used to describe nonprintable characters.

Examples

12C	(line feed)
40C	(blank)
63C	(digit "3")

3.2.5 Operators and Delimiters

A Modula-2 program contains not only objects that are processed (*operands*), but also *operators* that define what is to be done with the *objects*, and *delimiters* that separate operands.

For the most part, operators are described by special characters or combinations of special characters. However, the key words AND, DIV, IN, MOD, NOT and OR also serve as operators. The following is a list of all special characters that are used as operators and delimiters. Their use will be explained later.

arithmetic and set operators:

+	addition, union of sets
-	subtraction, sign inversion, difference of sets
*	multiplication, intersection of sets
/	division, symmetric difference of sets

logical operators:

&	conjunction (equivalent to AND)
=	equal
<> or #	not equal
<	less than
<=	less than or equal; subset
>	greater than
>=	greater than or equal; superset
~	negation (equivalent to NOT)

brackets:

( )	parentheses in algebraic sense
[ ]	index brackets
{ }	set brackets (braces)

other operators:

:=	assignment
^	pointer dereferencing

delimiters:

,	comma
.	period
;	semicolon
:	colon
. .	range symbol
|	separation symbol (vertical bar)

3.2.6 Separation of Symbols

Unlike some older programming languages such as Cobol and Fortran, Modula-2 has no regulations regarding the outward form of programs. The programmer must simply guarantee that the compiler can interpret the symbols contained in his program. That is, the compiler must know where one symbol ends and the next begins. Some helpful rules are:

- A symbol must be completely contained in one line.

- Symbols cannot contain blanks. The only exception is the character string.

- Any number of blanks can separate two symbols.

- If it cannot lead to any misinterpretation, symbols can be written adjacent to one another without separating blanks, e.g.:

        percent:=value/total*100.0;

Only when the beginning of one symbol can also be the continuation of the preceding one are blanks *required* to separate them. For example, x MOD y represents the modular division of x by y, but xMODy is simply one valid identifier.

3.2.7 Comments

Comments play an important role in programs. They give *explanations* and *notes* for the human reader and are ignored by the compiler (i.e., they do not affect program execution). This also means that comment brackets can be used to render parts of a program nonexistent for the compiler without actually having to erase them. This is called "commenting out" program text.

Comments can be used wherever blanks are permitted. They are enclosed in comment brackets, which consist of the pair of double symbols (* and *). Comments can stretch over multiple lines and can be nested (i.e., comments can themselves include comments). The possibility of nesting comments is particularly important when program text is commented out, since the text could already contain comments.

Examples

valid comments:

```
(*   CAUTION:
     incorrect input can cause the program to crash *)
(*****  New Version:  2.0 *****)
(*This is a (*nested*) comment*)
(* sum := x + y;  (* for test purposes *)*)
```

improper comments:

```
(* end with "*)" *)        (comment brackets must always appear
                                                  in pairs)
( * invalid comment * )    (space between * and ))
```

The rules introduced so far only explain what form comments must have in order to be recognized by a Modula-2 compiler. Really good and useful documentation of a program is an art that is learned only with practice. Documentation is therefore treated in a separate section (5.1.3).

Exercises

(1) Which of the following symbols are valid in Modula-2 and what do they mean? Which symbols are improper and why?

```
VARiable      from1to10        1to10              1-10
1..10         1.10             auxiliaryVariable  capitalization
set           in               IN                 MODUL
OF            468              -468                468.
.468          468B             468H               468E10
468.E10       468EH            FFH                 0FFH
14C           777C             1.0E-6             'characterstring'
"character"   'capitalization'     "          "   ''''
"'''"         '"'"'            :=                 : =
<=            =>               >=                 <>
.             ..               ...                **
```

(2) Below is an excerpt from a Modula-2 program. Reduce it to its individual symbols and explain the meaning of each.

```
PROCEDURE SquareRoot(x:REAL):REAL;
   CONST e = 1.0E-20;
   VAR
      y:  REAL;
      count:  CARDINAL;
BEGIN
   IF  x<0.  THEN
      WriteString("-negative argument in 'SquareRoot'-");
      HALT
   END;
   y := x;
```

```
WHILE (ABS(y-x*x) > e) AND (count<20)  DO
    y := (y*y+x)/(2.*y);
END;
RETURN y
END SquareRoot;
```

3.3 Elementary Program Structure

Its *module concept* distinguishes Modula-2 from other programming languages. In
Chapter 2 we explained how important modules are for the development of large programs.
A Modula-2 program is a particular kind of module known as a *program module.*

The Euclidean Algorithm from Section 1.4 takes on the following form in Modula-2:

```
MODULE GCD;
  FROM InOut IMPORT
    ReadCard, WriteCard, WriteLn, WriteString;
  VAR
    m, n, h, r:  CARDINAL;
BEGIN
  WriteString("m = ");  ReadCard(m); WriteLn;
  WriteString("n = ");  ReadCard(n); WriteLn;
  IF  m < n THEN
    h := m;
    m := n;
    n := h
  END;
  r := m MOD n;
  WHILE  r # 0  DO
    m := n;
    n := r;
    r := m MOD n
  END;
  WriteString("gcd(m,n) = ");  WriteCard(n,1);  WriteLn
END GCD.
```

This program consists of:

- the *module heading* (key word MODULE followed by the name of the module (GCD)
  and a semicolon);

- an *IMPORT statement* which specifies that the following procedures (from an existing
  module InOut) are to be used: ReadCard, WriteCard, WriteLn and WriteString (for
  reading numbers and writing numbers, line feeds, and strings, respectively);

- the *declaration* of the variables m, n, h and r as positive integers (data type
  CARDINAL); and

- several *statements* that establish what actions are to be executed when the program is
  run.

The following diagram describes how Modula-2 program modules are constructed. The
general rule for making up a program module is presented below:

ProgramModule$_{11}$

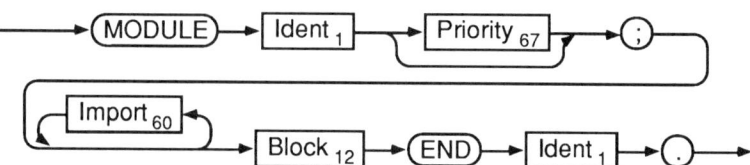

- A program module begins with the key word MODULE followed by a name chosen by the programmer and a semicolon.

- A priority can be designated after the module name (the explanation follows in Section 3.10.2, "Interrupts and Priorities").

- Any number of IMPORT statements can follow the module heading (see also Section 3.8 for detailed explanation).

- The actual contents of the module (i.e., a description of its objects and actions) are termed its *block*.

- Every program module ends with the key word "END" followed by the name of the module and a period.

Block$_{12}$

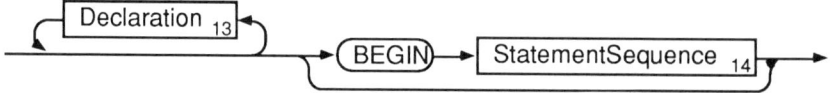

- A block consists of any number of declarations (see Section 3.4) and a sequence of statements.

- Declarations and statements must be separated by the key word BEGIN, which can be omitted if there are no statements. (The meaning of the omission of the statement part is explained in Section 3.8, "The Module Concept.")

Declaration$_{13}$

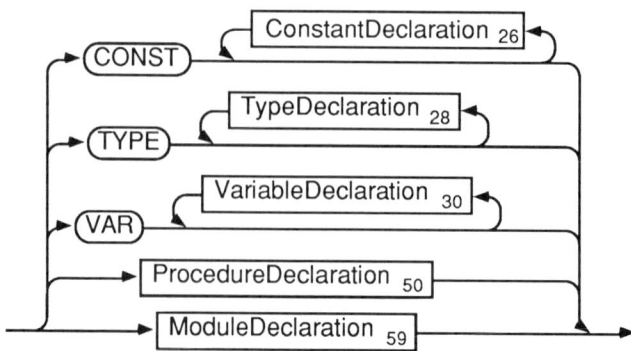

- A declaration can apply to a constant, data type, variable, procedure or module.

- Constant, type and variable declarations begin with the key words CONST, TYPE and VAR, respectively. (The structure of the declaration is explained more precisely in Sections 3.4.2–3.4.4).

StatementSequence$_{14}$

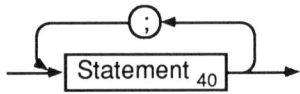

- A statement sequence consists of any number of statements (see Section 3.6) that describe actions in the sense of Chapter 1.

- Statements are *separated* from one another with semicolons. A semicolon is not required to terminate a statement, thus none is needed after the last statement.

A program module executes by carrying out the statements in its block. Execution ends automatically after the last statement has been executed.

Examples

```
MODULE Short;
END Short.
```

The program Short contains neither declarations nor actions. Its execution has no effect.

```
MODULE Welcome;
   FROM InOut IMPORT
      WriteString, WriteLn;
BEGIN
   WriteString("Hello ...");
   WriteLn
END Welcome.
```

The program Welcome imports two procedures, WriteString and WriteLn, from the module InOut (see Section 4.2) and uses these procedures to output a line with the text "Hello ..."

```
MODULE Addition;
   VAR   x, y, sum:   INTEGER;
BEGIN
   x := 123;   y := 1234;
   sum := x + y
END   Addition.
```

The program Addition computes the sum of two integers x and y. It generates no output, since the program terminates right after the sum is calculated.

3.4 Declarations

A program normally works with objects, whether they are integers or real numbers, characters, character strings or any of numerous other possibilities (see Section 1.3, "Objects and Actions"). Modula-2 requires that any object used in a program be declared at the beginning. These declarations have several purposes:

- A declaration links a *name* to a *data type*. The programmer must have a clear idea of what types of objects he/she wants to process. Because the objects have to be declared, this forces the programmer to describe them all explicitly Since different data types permit different operations, the compiler has the possibility of detecting misuse and reporting this as an error before program execution.

- Frequently used *constant values* can be given names that can be used in place of the values in the program (constant declarations). This makes programs easier to change because this constant could be strewn throughout the whole program, but a single change in the declaration makes the change effective wherever the name is used.

- Like its predecessor Pascal, Modula-2 has a type concept that allows *user-defined* (or *custom*) data types. The definition of a new data type occurs with the assignment of a name as a synonym for that data type (type declarations).

- On the basis of declarations, the compiler can *reserve storage* of appropriate size. Furthermore, the compiler can make provisions for testing the validity of the objects' variables (with respect to their data types) at *run time*.

Modula-2's data types (predefined, simple and structured) and the operations permitted with each are explained in the following sections. Then we show how types, constants and variables can be declared and explain the conditions under which data types can be considered equivalent.

3.4.1 Data Types

Each data type defines a range of values and a set of operations that can be applied to its elements. Such definitions are well-known in the field of mathematics, and we use them in everyday life without being aware of it. We know that the operation additon ("+") can only be applied to numbers (e.g., prices) and not to character strings (e.g., names). (BASIC programmers know the operator "+" in conjunction with strings as well. The operation signified in this case, however, is concatenation (appending one string to another), not addition in the mathematical sense.)

3.4.1.1 Predefined Data Types

Modula-2 is equipped with 6 predefined data types (the *standard types*) which are known in every program and can therefore be used without having been declared. These elementary types have six associated identifiers (not key words!) which can be imagined as invisibly and automatically declared in each program (thus the term "predefined types"):

```
INTEGER, CARDINAL, REAL, BOOLEAN, CHAR, BITSET.
```

The **data type INTEGER** encompasses all whole numbers (positive and negative) within a definite range. For 16-bit computers (most microcomputers), this range is –32768 to 32767 (-2^{15} to $2^{15}-1$), while for 32-bit machines we have –2147483648 to 2147483647.

INTEGER objects permit the following operations:

+	addition
–	subtraction or sign inversion
*	multiplication
DIV	integer division
MOD	remainder for integer division (modulus)

• The operators +, *, DIV and MOD are always located between the operands to be combined. The operator – can be located between two operands (subtraction) or before a single operand. In the second case, the unary minus reverses the sign of its one operand.

• Applying these operators to INTEGERs produces results that are INTEGERs. In the execution of an operation, the result must be in the range for integers. Failure to meet this condition causes an *overflow*, which can cause a program to crash.

• The operator DIV carries out integer division (in contrast to /). This means that the operand on the left is divided by the operand on the right, then the quotient is truncated to an integer, for example:

```
0 DIV 3 = 0                4  DIV   3  =  1
1 DIV 3 = 0               (-4) DIV   3  = -1
2 DIV 3 = 0                4  DIV (-3) = -1
3 DIV 3 = 1               (-4) DIV (-3) =  1
```

• The operator MOD is used to produce the remainder for an integer division (DIV). The formal definition is:

```
x MOD y =  x  -  ((x  DIV y) * y)
```

MOD is defined only for positive values of y, contrary to DIV, for example:

```
6 MOD 3 = 0                (-6) MOD 3 =  0
7 MOD 3 = 1                (-7) MOD 3 = -1
8 MOD 3 = 2                (-8) MOD 3 = -2
```

Whole numbers can also be compared to one another. The relational operators =, <> (#), <, <=, >, and >= serve this purpose (see Section 3.2.5 "Operators and Delimiters"). The result of a comparison is always a truth value (TRUE or FALSE—see BOOLEAN data type later in this section).

The **data type CARDINAL** encompasses all positive integers including zero, although a particular implementation is dependent upon the internal representation of numbers on a specific computer. The largest CARDINAL number for 16-bit machines is typically 65,535; for 32-bit machines, 4,294,967,295. This data type should be used wherever negative values are to be precluded. Since whole numbers are primarily used for counting, this is most often the case. We therefore recommend using the data type INTEGER only when negative values can actually occur.

The data type CARDINAL permits the same operations as INTEGER.

Floating point numbers constitute the **data type REAL** (real numbers). Their range and precision vary with the implementation. A floating point number is usually stored internally as an integer (the *mantissa*) and an *exponent* (which indicates the relative placement of the decimal point). The precision of real numbers is determined by the number of significant digits in the mantissa. The bounds of the exponent determine the largest and smallest REAL numbers that can be represented.

The following operations are permissible on REAL objects:

+	addition
−	subtraction and sign inversion
*	multiplication
/	division

In addition to these arithmetic operators, all relational operators can be applied to REAL numbers as they are to INTEGERs.

Because of limited precision in the representation of floating point numbers, rounding errors can occur during computations with REAL numbers. Assuming a precision of six places, the division 1.0/3.0 would yield the quotient 0.333333. If we multiply this result by 3.0, 0.999999 is returned instead of 1.0.

The **data type BOOLEAN** describes values that can be only true or false. In Modula-2, the range of BOOLEAN values is covered in the two predefined constants TRUE and FALSE.

The following operations are permitted on BOOLEAN objects:

AND	conjunction
OR	disjunction
NOT	negation

- x AND y is true if both x and y have the value TRUE.
- x OR y is true if x or y or both have the value TRUE.
- NOT x is true if x has the value FALSE.

Modula-2 evaluates the operations AND and OR in such a way that the second operand is evaluated only if the result cannot be determined by the first operand alone:

x AND y is defined as

- FALSE   if x=FALSE (y disregarded)

- y   if x=TRUE

x OR y is defined as

- TRUE   if x=TRUE (y disregarded)

- y   if x=FALSE

In other words, the order of operands plays a role in the computation of the result (see Section 3.5.3, "Operators").

Boolean values can be compared with one another just like numbers. The expression "x or y, but not both" (*exclusive OR*) can be written as x<>y (or as x#y). The result of the comparison is TRUE if x is TRUE and y is FALSE, or vice versa. Less than and greater than operators can also be applied to boolean values, whereby

FALSE < TRUE

The expression x AND NOT y can be written as x>y (which can only be true if x=TRUE and y=FALSE). Note, however, that in relational operations, both operands are always evaluated. The following table shows the correspondence of relational operations and boolean operations:

x=y	(x AND y) OR (NOT x AND NOT y)
x<>y	(x AND NOT y) OR (NOT x AND y)
x<y	NOT x AND y
x>=y	NOT x OR y
x>y	x AND NOT y
x>=y	x OR NOT y

The **data type CHAR** consists of all individual characters contained an individual computer's character set. Each character is assigned an ordinal number that identifies its position in the character set (see the ASCII table in Appendix D as an example). Still, no arithmetic operations are possible with characters. Individual characters can, however, be compared with one another. In such a relational operation, the ordinal numbers for the characters (i.e., the internal representations of the characters) are compared. The ASCII code was constructed with such relational operations in mind. The letters A to Z (likewise a to z) are ordered alphabetically and the digits 0 to 9 numerically. The boolean expression

"x is a digit"

can thus be formulated as

(x>="0") AND (x<="9").

The **data type BITSET** serves to represent sets of numbers from 0 to some upper bound determined by the implementation (normally 15 for 16-bit machines and 31 for 32-bit machines). In Modula-2, a set is written as a list of its members enclosed in set brackets (braces).

Examples

```
{}                                    (empty set)
{5}
{1,3,5,7,9,11,13,15}
{0,10,4..7}                           (4..7 is equivalent to 4,5,6,7)
```

Set objects can be used with the following operations:

+   set union

−   set difference

*   set intersection

/   symmetric set difference

- u+v is the set of all elements contained either in u or in v or in both.

- u−v is the set of all elements contained in u but not in v.

- u*v is the set of all elements contained in both u and v.

- u/v is the set of all elements contained in u or v, but not in both.

Examples

```
u = {1,2,5,6}         v = {1,3,5,7}

u+v = {1,2,3,5,6,7)

u−v = {2,6}

u*v = {1,5}

u/v = {2,3,6,7}
```

Sets can also be compared to one another. In contrast to numbers and characters, only the operators =, <> (#), <=, and >= are possible, and they have a different meaning:

- u=v is true if u and v contain exactly the same elements.

- u<>v is true if there is at least one element that is contained in either u or v, but not in both.

- u<=v is true if all elements contained in u are also contained in v (in which case we call u a subset of v and v a superset of u).

- u>=v is equivalent to v<=u.

The relational operator IN can be used to determine whether a value (first operand) is contained in a set (second operand). The expression

```
i IN u
```

is true if the element i is contained in the set u.

3.4.1.2 Elementary User-Defined Data Types

In Modula-2, as in Pascal, the programmer can invent data types in order to exactly specify his/her objects and to make programs more readable and easier to change. The simplest possibilities for such user-defined data types are the *enumeration* and the *subrange* types.

Enumeration types can be used to introduce names for non-numeric values. If a programmer has to write a program to manage products made of various materials, conventional languages force him/her to assign each material a unique number. Then the programmer needs to keep in mind which number corresponds to which material, e.g., steel might be 1 and glass 3. Modula-2 permits the introduction of a new data type that encompasses all possible materials:

```
Material = (iron,steel,copper,glass,acrylic,pvc,rubber)
```

An enumeration type is defined by listing within parentheses all values that the type can assume. All names that identify the individual values (the *enumeration constants*) are defined simultaneously with the name of the type. The general rule for declaration of enumeration types is:

Enumeration$_{15}$

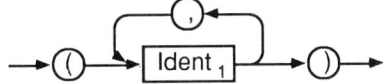

- An enumeration type consists of a list of identifiers in parentheses.

- The identifiers are separated by commas.

- The identifiers must be unambiguous both within the parenthesis and with respect to other objects.

The individual enumeration constants are assigned ordinal numbers in the order in which they are listed. The first constant (iron in our example) is number 0. This allows the values of an enumeration type to be compared with all of Modula-2's relational operators. In the above example, the boolean value of the expression "material <= copper" would tell us whether the material is a metal. (Remember that the type Material and the variable material are distinct because of capitalization in the *case-sensitive* language Modula-2.)

Note : The predefined data type BOOLEAN can be viewed as an enumeration type (FALSE, TRUE).

Subrange types are used to limit the range of types whose elements are assigned ordinal numbers. This includes all enumeration types as well as INTEGER, CARDINAL, BOOLEAN and CHAR. The declaration of a subrange type indicates that the elements of the type can assume values only within the definite bounds given. This information can help someone reading the program to understand it and enables the compiler to generate code for the run-time testing for violations of the programmer's subrange bounds.

The subrange type is declared in Modula-2 as follows:

Subrange$_{16}$

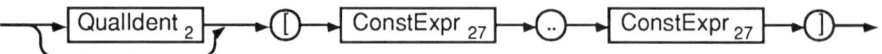

- A subrange type is defined by a lower and an upper bound (see Section 3.4.2 for ConstExpr).

- The two bounds are separated by two periods and enclosed in square brackets. Both values must be of the same data type and the first must not be greater than the second.

- The *base type* of the subange type can be specified by a preceding qualified identifier.

- INTEGER, CARDINAL, BOOLEAN, CHAR and enumeration types are permissible base types.

Every subrange type is assigned a *base type*, that is, the type from whose range the minimum and maximum were chosen. In the case of whole number bounds, this can lead to ambiguity because the data types INTEGER and CARDINAL overlap. [-10..10] clearly has the base type INTEGER since the lower bound is negative; [0..40000] has the base type CARDINAL (for 16-bit computers) because the upper bound lies outside the range of INTEGERs. For subrange types whose bounds are both positive INTEGERs (e.g., [0..10]), the base type CARDINAL is assumed unless the type name INTEGER is explicitly placed in front of the brackets.

Subrange types permit the same operations as their base types.

Examples

Valid subrange types: base types:

```
[0..9]                             CARDINAL
["0".."9"]                         CHAR
[0C..177C]                         CHAR
INTEGER[1..1000]                   INTEGER
[iron..copper]                     Material
[FALSE..TRUE]                      BOOLEAN
```

Improper subrange types:

```
[0 .   . 9]       (periods must not be separated)
["A".."9"]        ("A" is greater than "9" in ASCII code)
[1.5..2.5]        (REAL is not a permissible base type)
[12B..17C]        (bounds must be of the same type)
CHAR[40..50]      (type of bounds conflicts with base type)
```

3.4.1.3 Structured Data Types

The predefined and elementary user-defined data types are self-explanatory in the sense that they do not require other data types for their definition. By contrast, structured data types "contain" other types and are thus dependent on them.

SET types

Normally sets (in the mathematical sense) consist of elements of the same type (in our case, data type). Thus Modula-2 requires the programmer to declare the elements of which the SET type is comprised:

SetType$_{17}$

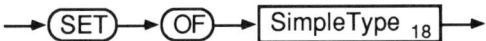

- A SET type is defined by the key words SET and OF followed by a simple data type.

- SimpleType is known as the *base type* of the set and must be either an enumeration type or a subrange type. (BOOLEAN is considered an enumeration type.)

- The ordinal numbers of the set elements must, as with BITSET, fall in the range of 0 to some implementation-dependent upper bound (e.g., 15).

SimpleType$_{18}$

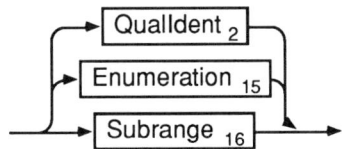

- All data types that can be identified by a *name* (QualIdent) (e.g., predefined data types), enumeration types and subrange types are collectively known as *simple types*.

The standard type BITSET (see Section 3.4.1.1) is defined as

```
SET OF [0..N-1]
```

whereby N is the implementation-dependent maximum number of elements in a set. SETs thus permit all operations that were listed for the data type BITSET in Section 3.4.1.1.

Examples

valid SET types:

```
SET OF [3..5]
SET OF Material              (compare Section 3.4.1.2)
SET OF [iron..copper]
SET OF [0C..17C]             (set of characters)
SET OF BOOLEAN              (set of boolean values)
```

improper SET types:

```
SET OF [-1..+1]              (negative elements not permitted)
SET OF CHAR                 (only enumeration and subrange types)
```

ARRAY types

With the help of ARRAY types, several objects of the same type can be combined into one object. In Modula-2, an ARRAY is an object that consists of a definite numbers of elements, all of the same data type. Each element of the ARRAY is assigned an index (usually a whole number) that can be used to uniquely identify the element. A classical example of an ARRAY is a string of characters that consists of a definite number of sequential individual characters.

ArrayType$_{19}$

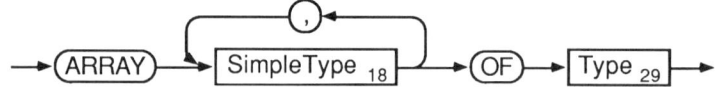

- An ARRAY type is defined by the key word ARRAY, followed by one or more simple data types separated by commas, followed by the key word OF, followed by any data type.

- SimpleType describes an *index type* (the data type to which the indices of the ARRAY belong) and must be an enumeration type, a subrange type, or one of the predefined data types BOOLEAN or CHAR.

- Type identifies the *element type* of the array (i.e., the data type of the individual elements).

- The notation

        ARRAY T1,T2 OF T

  is an abbreviated form of

        ARRAY T1 OF ARRAY T2 OF T

This enables the declaration of multidimensional ARRAYs (matrices). Such multi-dimensional arrays are handled as arrays of arrays in Modula-2.

ARRAY types can be used to implement tables. The specific weights (floating point decimals, thus REAL) of all materials occurring in the enumeration type Material (see Section 3.4.1.2) could be stored in an array with the type declaration

        ARRAY Material OF REAL

The following data type could be used for character strings (e.g., names of persons) with a maximum of 20 characters:

        ARRAY [0..19] OF CHAR

And 100 names (of type ARRAY[0..19] OF CHAR) with 20 characters each can be stored in

        ARRAY [1..100],[0..19] OF CHAR

Examples

valid ARRAY types:

```
ARRAY [-1000..+1000] OF CARDINAL
ARRAY [0..9] OF CHAR
ARRAY CHAR OF [0..9]
ARRAY ["0".."9"] OF CARDINAL
ARRAY BOOLEAN, BOOLEAN OF BOOLEAN
ARRAY [iron..copper] OF SET OF [1..10]
ARRAY CHAR, BOOLEAN, Material, [5..7] OF BITSET
```

improper ARRAY types:	invalid index type:
`ARRAY BITSET OF INTEGER`	`BITSET`
`ARRAY CARDINAL OF INTEGER`	`CARDINAL`
`ARRAY REAL OF BOOLEAN`	`REAL`

RECORD types

While the ARRAY type permits the collection of elements of the same data type, the RECORD type allows elements of various data types to be combined. A classical example of the application of a RECORD type is a date that consists of year, month and day. We could manage that with the data type

```
ARRAY [1..3] OF CARDINAL
```

In using this data type, however, we have to keep in mind that the first index is the year and the third is the day (or vice versa). Another disadvantage is a loss of clarity in that month and day can assume any value within the range of CARDINAL. Both of these disadvantages can be avoided with the following definition of a date:

```
RECORD
  year:  [1900..1999];
  month: [Jan,Feb,Mar,Apr,May,Jun,Jul,Aug,Sep,Oct,Nov,Dec];
  day:   [1..31]
END
```

The individual components (known as fields) are now identified by the names year, month and day instead of the numbers 1 to 3. Furthermore, they are all different data types, which reflects reality. The subrange definitions of year and day establish the respective numeric ranges (in particular, the date is restricted to the 20th century). The enumeration type for month permits (indeed, it requires) the use of names instead of the numbers 1 to 12.

The definition of a RECORD type takes the following form:

RecordType$_{20}$

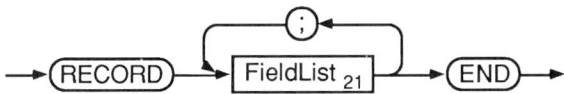

- A RecordType consists of the definitions of its components bracketed between the key words RECORD and END.

FieldList$_{21}$

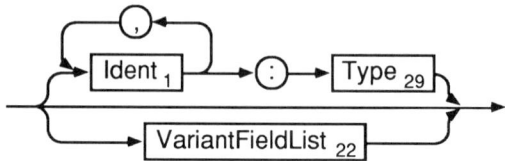

- A FieldList describes RECORD components (fields) that are of the same data type.

- The FieldLists within a RECORD declaration are separated from one another by semicolons.

- A FieldList consists of a sequence of identifiers (the names of the respective RECORD components), a colon and any data type.

- The names of all components within a definition of a RECORD type must be unique. However, identifiers which were used outside the RECORD with a different meaning can be used within the RECORD.

Often RECORDs contain components that can never assume valid values at the same time. This is particularly true if components are used to discriminate various cases, for example:

```
RECORD
    matno: CARDINAL;
    kind: Material;  (* from 3.4.1.2 *)
    color: (white,red,blue,yellow,green);
    frosted, stainless: BOOLEAN;
    specWeight: REAL
END
```

In this RECORD for storing material descriptions, the material number and kind as well as the specific weight are always active, whereas the component stainless is only meaningful if kind = steel. Such case discrimination is handled in Modula-2 with a VariantFieldList within a RECORD:

VariantFieldList$_{22}$

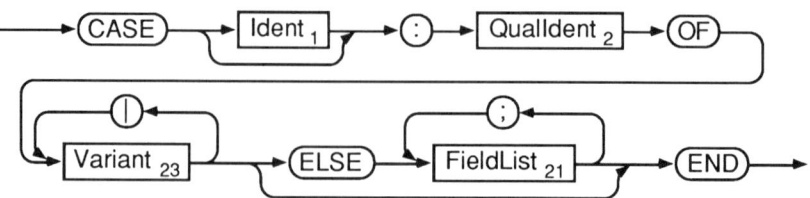

Variant$_{23}$

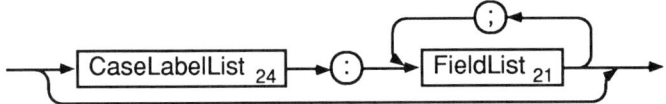

CaseLabelList$_{24}$

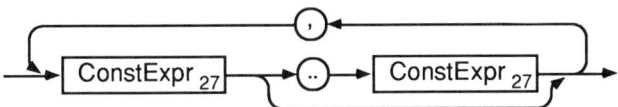

- A VariantFieldList begins with the key word CASE, followed by the name of the RECORD component (Ident) that is to serve as *discriminator*, and its type (QualIdent). In this context, we call the Ident a *tag field*.

- If Ident is omitted, it means that no storage is to be reserved for the tag field. The data type QualIdent, however, still needs to be provided.

- After the key word OF, the respective declarations (variants) are listed for each valid value of the tag field. These variants are separated by vertical bars.

- Each variant begins with a list of all values or ranges of the tag field which are valid for the particular variant (CaseLabelList). The values must be constants (see ConstExpr in Section 3.4.2) and of the same type as the tag field itself. Each value can appear at most once. The notation x..y can be used as with subrange types in place of listing all values from x to y.

- After the key word ELSE, components can be listed that become active if the tag field has a value matched by none of the listed variants.

- A variant can also be empty. This rule permits the insertion of vertical bars before the first and after the last variant in a VariantFieldList.

- A VariantFieldList is terminated with the key word END.

With this possibility, the above example can be reformulated so that the validity of each of the RECORD components is clear:

```
RECORD
   matno: CARDINAL;
   specWeight: REAL;
   CASE kind: Material OF
      steel:
         stainless: BOOLEAN
   | glass:
         frosted: BOOLEAN
   | pvc,rubber:
         color: (white,red,blue,yellow,green)
   END (*CASE*)
END (*RECORD*)
```

Using variant RECORDs has the additional advantage that the compiler can *overlap* variants that cannot simultaneously assume values (i.e., assign them the same storage).

Which components of the RECORD contain valid values can be determined at any time from the value of the tag field. An example is given in Section 3.6.2.2, "CASE Statement." Sometimes the tag field itself is not needed because the context clearly indicates which variant is correct. In such cases, the identifier Ident after the key word CASE can be omitted. For example, if we want to include the elasticity of rubber and the processing of PVC into a foil in the record, it can be handled with the following additional CASE statement:

```
...
| pvc, rubber:
    color: (white,red,blue,yellow,green);
    CASE : Material OF
      pvc: foil: BOOLEAN
    | rubber: elast: REAL
    END
...
```

Here, it would be senseless to store the component kind a second time under a different name because its occurrence in the original RECORD suffices to discriminate PVC and rubber.

POINTER types

The data types introduced so far have in common that their "size" (i.e., the amount of storage they require and thus also the amount of data that they can accomodate) is established in the declaration. This is not always convenient, since we don't always know how much data is to be processed. For example, we used an ARRAY type that could contain 100 names. If our needs grow to exceed 100 names, the array no longer suffices. Or if we use less than 100 names, we waste storage in the unused array elements.

As a solution to this uncomfortable dilemma, Modula-2 offers the POINTER type, with which *dynamic data structures* can be constructed that can change their size and structure. A POINTER itself has no value in the usual sense, but points to a variable that contains the desired data. A POINTER type is declared with the key words POINTER and TO followed by any type:

PointerType$_{25}$

Every POINTER is bound to a definite data type (its *base type*) and cannot be used as a pointer to variables of various types, as was the case in older programming languages.

No arithmetic operations are permitted on variables of type POINTER TO ... ; they can only be tested for equality or inequality.

How powerful the POINTER concept is can easily be seen in that a pointer can point to a RECORD variable that in turn contains one or more pointers, such as to the next variable:

```
Nameptr  = POINTER TO Name
Name     = RECORD
              name:  ARRAY [0..19] OF CHAR;
              next:  Nameptr
           END
```

This declaration enables us to create a *list* of any number of names with 20 characters each by simply linking each name to its successor:

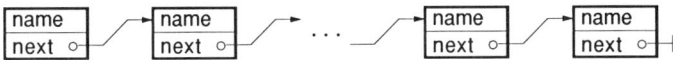

The above illustration shows the end of the list as a vertical line in place of an arrow. This is implemented in Modula-2 in the predefined constant NIL, which can be imagined as pointing nowhere. The end of a list can thus be tested by comparing the component next of a list element to NIL.

3.4.2 Declaration of Constants

The concept of declaration of constants proved itself well in Pascal. Thus it was carried over to Modula-2 in nearly unchanged form. It is possible to assign names to constant values that are used in numerous places throughout a program. This makes programs more amenable to changes since the value of a constant needs to be changed at only one location in order to change it throughout the progam. As shown in Section 3.3, "Elementary Program Structure," constant declarations are introduced with the key word CONST.

ConstantDeclaration$_{26}$

- A constant declaration begins with an identifier followed by an equal sign and a constant expression. It ends with a semicolon.

- A constant declaration causes the declaration of the name Ident as a constant. Ident is known from that point on in the program and is handled as if the value of the constant expression were in its place.

A *constant expression* is a simple or combined expression of any data type that consists exclusively of constant elements. Constant expressions are very similar in construction to expressions in general. Thus we will not enumerate in detail all the conditions that are to be heeded in writing constant expressions, but refer the reader to Section 3.5, "Expressions."

ConstExpr$_{27}$

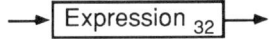

Examples

valid constant declarations:

CONST	data type:
wordSize = 16;	CARDINAL, INTEGER
bytes = wordSize DIV 8;	CARDINAL, INTEGER
minus1 = -1;	INTEGER
version = "V 2.3";	ARRAY [0..4] OF CHAR
listSize = 20000;	CARDINAL, INTEGER
listBytes = listSize*bytes;	CARDINAL
fullSet = {0..wordSize-1};	BITSET
noPtr = NIL;	POINTER TO ...

Note : Every constant belongs to a definite data type. For whole number constants, some cases are not clearly INTEGER or CARDINAL and can thus be interpreted as either. Negative numbers (e.g., minus1) are of course INTEGER and positive numbers that exceed the range of INTEGER (e.g., listBytes) are CARDINAL.

improper constant declarations:

CONST	
x: 64;	("=" instead of ":")
y = n;	(n not yet defined)

3.4.3 Declaration of Types

In Modula-2, names can be assigned to user-defined data types. This makes it possible to define the structure of a data type once in the program and then use it repeatedly. Furthermore, a good choice of a name can add clarity to the program.

Type declarations are introduced with the key word TYPE (see Section 3.3, "Elementary Program Structure") and are constructed as follows:

TypeDeclaration$_{28}$

•   A type declaration begins with an identifier, followed by an equal sign and any data type, and is terminated with a semicolon.

•   The type declaration declares the name Ident as a synonym for the data type to the right of the equal sign.

•   All data types listed in Section 3.4.1 are permissible as Type, as well as the procedure type to be discussed in Section 3.7.9.

Type29

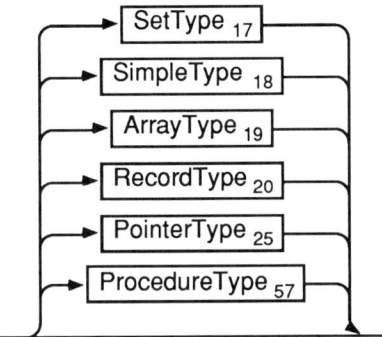

Examples

```
TYPE
   Coordinate =  CARDINAL;
   String =      ARRAY [0..listSize] OF CHAR;
   Index =       [0..10];
   ListPtr =     POINTER TO ListElem;
   ListElem =    RECORD
                    x,y: Coordinate;
                    next: ListPtr
                 END;
```

If the name of another data type occurs in a type declaration, the data type referred to must already have been defined in the preceding text. The only exception to this rule is the declaration of a POINTER, for which the base type need not be known at the time of declaration. Only in this way is it possible, as in the ListElem example above, to declare a POINTER that is also part of the declaration of its own base type. Exchanging the declarations of ListPtr and ListElem would not be permissible. (See also Section 3.4.1.3, "POINTER Types.")

3.4.4 Declaration of Variables

The main purpose of declarations is to establish the names and data types of variables to be used in a program and to make these variables known to the compiler.

Variable declarations are always introduced with the key word VAR (see Section 3.3, "Elementary Program Structure") and are constructed as follows:

VariableDeclaration30

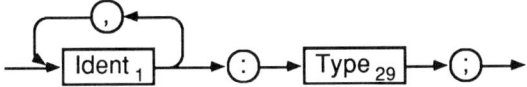

- A variable declaration begins with a list of identifiers separated by commas (as in FieldList in 3.4.1.3). This list of identifiers is terminated with a colon, which is followed by a data type and a semicolon.

- A variable declaration establishes all identifiers preceding the colon as variables with the data type Type.

- If Type is a user-defined name, it must already have been defined in the text preceding the variable declaration.

Examples

```
VAR
  i,j,k: CARDINAL;
  material:   Material;
  header:   ListPtr;
  name:   ARRAY [0..19] OF CHAR;
  error: BOOLEAN;
```

3.4.5 Type Identity Among Objects

In Modula-2, the permissibility of most operations depends on the types of their operands. We will often be making the requirement that two objects be of the *same data type*, and so we need to define what this means:

The two objects x1 and x2 with the data types t1 and t2 have the *same data type* if one of the following conditions is met:

- t1 and t2 are identified by the same name, e.g.:

```
VAR                          VAR
  n: INTEGER;                  material: Material;
  val: INTEGER;                substance: Material;
```

- x1 and x2 are declared within the *same variable list*, e.g.:

```
VAR                          PROCEDURE P(x,y: CHAR);
  n,val: INTEGER;              (* see Section 3.7 "Procedures" *)
  die,dot: [1..6];
```

- t1 and t2 are identified by names that are designated as *synonymous* in a type declaration, e.g.:

```
TYPE                         TYPE
  Minute = [0..59];            t  = (a,b,c);
  Second = Minute;             t1 = t;
VAR                            t2 = t;
  sec: Second;               VAR
  min: Minute;                 x1: t1;
                               x2: t2;
```

- x1 and x2 are constants of the same enumeration type, as low and high or red and yellow in the following examples:

```
VAR                              VAR
   voltage: (low,high);            color: (red,blue,yellow)
```

If none of the above cases applies, the objects are considered to have *different data types*, even if their structure is the same. In the following declarations, the three variables x, y, and z have different data types:

```
TYPE
   t1 =  ARRAY [1..10] OF CHAR;
   t2 =  ARRAY [1..10] OF CHAR;
VAR
   x:  t1;
   y:  t2;
   z:  ARRAY [1..10] OF CHAR;
```

x and y have the types t1 and t2, which, although they look alike, are still distinct. z has an anonymous (unnamed) data type which has the same form.

Note : The *elements* of the ARRAYs x, y and z are of the *same type* (CHAR).

Exercises

(1) Write declarations for data types to represent the following:

  amounts of money

  signs (positive, negative or zero)

  population

  population growth

  dates in the 20th Century

  indication of leap year status

  address (street, number, city, zip, state)

  personal data (e.g., for resident list)

  chess figures

  set of chess figures

  chess board (and which figures are where)

Check whether your data type for personal data really contains all the information necessary to describe a person completely. Use a RECORD type with variants and POINTER types in order to establish relationships (e.g., marriage of x and y).

(2) Which of the following declarations are improper and why?

```
CONST
   max  =  1000;
   min  =  -0;
   String  =  "string";
   pi  =  3.14159;
   pi2  =  2*pi;

TYPE
   range   =  (min, max, medium)
   Name    =  ARRAY [1..10] OF String;
   Number  =  SET OF [min..max];
   circle  =  [0.0..pi];
```

```
Node    =  POINTER TO RECORD
              x:  Node;
              CASE [1..2] OF
                 1:  y:  Element
              |  2:  z:  [max..-max]
              END;
```

3.5 Expressions

Whenever values are to be computed in a program, we use *expressions* to describe how the values are to be formed. Every expression consists of *operands* and *operators* and serves as a set of instructions for how the value of the expression is to be computed from the values of the operands.

This section first explains which classes of expressions exist in Modula-2, which kinds of operands are allowed, and which operations can be applied to them. Then rules for writing expressions are covered. Finally, we discuss which operands can be combined with one another.

3.5.1 Classes of Expressions

Every expression describes a *value*. Since every value is associated with a *data type* in Modula-2, expressions can also be grouped in classes according to their data type:

- *Arithmetic expressions* (data types CARDINAL, INTEGER, REAL)
  describe computations (in a narrower sense) with numbers.

- *Logical expressions* (data type BOOLEAN)
  describe comparisons of values and combinations of logical values according to boolean algebra.

- *Set expressions* (data type BITSET or SET OF ...)
  describe the collection of elements into sets and the combination of sets.

- *General expressions* (all remaining data types)
  are expressions that do not include operators (e.g., RECORDs, ARRAYs).

Certain operators are permitted for each of the classes (except the last) (see Section 3.5.3).

3.5.2 Operands

An expression can contain any combination of constants, variables and function procedure calls (see Section 3.7.4) as operands.

A *constant* can be described by a numeric constant (see Section 3.2.3), a character string (see Section 3.2.4) or an identifier that was declared in a constant declaration (see Section 3.4.2).

A *variable* is described by its name in the simplest case. If the variable is an ARRAY, RECORD or POINTER, then its components (which again are variables) can be described by a *designator* :

Designator$_{31}$

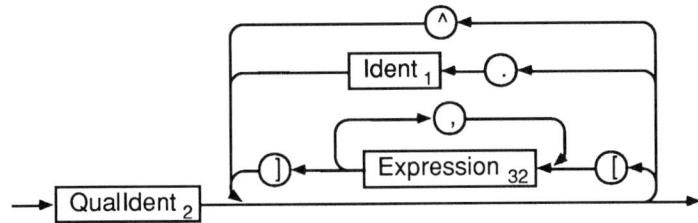

- The simplest designator consists of a qualified identifier.

- If x is the name of an ARRAY, then an element of the ARRAY can be designated as x[y]. This is called *indexing*. The following rules govern indexing:

  - y can be an expression of any complexity, but must be *assignment compatible* (see Section 3.6.1, "Assignments") with the index type of the ARRAY.

  - At run time, the value of y must be in the range of the index type of the ARRAY.

- If the element x[y] of the ARRAY x is again an ARRAY, then the indexing can be repeated. Instead of x[y][z], the shorter and clearer notation x[y,z] can be used.

- If x is the name of a RECORD with a component y, then "x.y" designates the component.

- If x is a POINTER TO T, then the object to which x points can be designated as x^ (*dereferencing*).

Note : Using x^ to dereference a NIL pointer (x=NIL) causes an error because x does not point to any object (see Section 3.4.1.3, "POINTER Types").

Examples

```
TYPE
    PA = POINTER TO A;
    PR = POINTER TO R;
    A = ARRAY [0..10], BOOLEAN OF PR;
    R = RECORD
            x: CARDINAL;
            y: PR;
        END;
VAR
    a: PA;
    b: PR;
    c:  A;
    d:  R;
```

valid designators:	data type:
`a`	PA
`a^`	A
`a^[2,TRUE]`	PR
`c`	A
`c[5]`	ARRAY BOOLEAN OF PR
`d.x`	CARDINAL
`d.y^.x`	CARDINAL
`a^[d.y^.x,b=NIL]^.y`	P

improper designators:

`a[2]`	(a is no ARRAY)
`b.x`	(b is no RECORD)
`d.z`	(z is no component of RECORD d)
`c[1,2]`	(2 not assignment compatible with BOOLEAN)
`a^[20]`	(20 not in range [1..10])
`d.x^.y`	(d.x is no POINTER)

3.5.3 Operators

We can distinguish three classes of operators based on the classification in Section 3.5.1:

- *Arithmetic operators* combine arithmetic operands to an arithmetic result.

- *Logical operators* combine logical operands to a logical result.

- *Set operators* combine set operands to a set result.

What these three classes of operators have in common is that their results always belong to the same class as the operands. There is a fourth class of operators:

- *Relational operators* compare two operands and return a logical result.

The operations permissible in Modula-2 and their meanings were discussed in Section 3.4.1.1, "Predefined Data Types." Only the priority of operators (which defines their order of evaluation) needs to be explained here:

- The multiplication operators *, /, DIV and MOD are evaluated before the addition operators + and -, and the latter are evaluated before relational operators (including IN).

- The conjunction operator (AND, &) is treated as a multiplication operator and the disjunction operator (OR) is treated as an addition operator. Thus AND is evaluated before OR. The evaluation of boolean expressions ends as soon as the result can be determined with certainty (see data type BOOLEAN in Section 3.4.1.1).

- Negation (NOT) has the highest priority and is evaluated before AND.

- Operators with equal priority are evaluated from left to right (e.g., two addition operators).

- Operators in parenthesized (partial) expressions are evaluated before any operators outside the parentheses. That is, parentheses can be used to alter the natural order of evaluation of expressions.

These priority rules lead us to the following conclusions:

- `10-5 DIV 2*2` yields 6 (order of evaluation: DIV, *, -).

- The expression `x>=10 AND x<=20` is improper because the AND operation is evaluated first (`10 AND x`), but AND is valid only for boolean operands. In order to achieve the desired result, parentheses must be used: `(x>=10) AND (x<=20)`.

- The expression `NOT x<10` is improper for the same reason (NOT is evaluated before `<`). Instead, we need to write `NOT (x<10)` or, better yet, `x>=10`.

- The expression `(p<>NIL) AND (p^>0)` with p declared as POINTER TO CARDINAL always returns a valid result ("p points to a number greater than zero"). Reversing the order of the two relational expressions—`(p^>0) AND (p<>NIL)`— leads to an error if `p=NIL` (see Section 3.5.2, "Operands," and "Data Type BOOLEAN" in Section 3.4.1.1).

- In the expression a `AND NOT b`, if a=FALSE, then `NOT b` is no longer evaluated.

3.5.4 Rules for Writing Expressions

The following rules show how expressions are to be written in Modula-2.

Expression$_{32}$

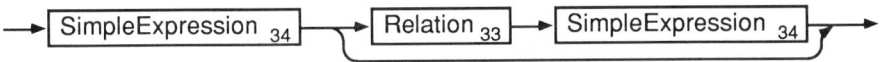

Relation$_{33}$

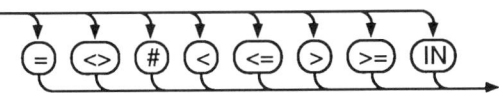

- An expression consists either of a simple expression or of two simple expressions connected by a relational operator.

- If a relational operator is included, then the two combined simple expressions must be *expression compatible* (see Section 3.5.5). That is, their data types must match. The result of the relation is always of type BOOLEAN.

- Only simple expressions of certain data types can be compared to one another:

    - INTEGER, CARDINAL, CHAR, BOOLEAN, enumeration types and subrange types with one of the predefined types as base type

    - REAL

    - BITSET and SET types (sets do not permit the relational operators < and >; <= and >= have a different meaning)

    - POINTER types (can only be tested for equality or inequality)

• RECORDs and ARRAYs cannot be compared as a whole, but only element by element.

• The relational operator IN plays a unique role. Its second (right) operand must be a set (SET types including BITSET); its first operand must be compatible with the base type of the SET type (see Section 3.5.5).

SimpleExpression34

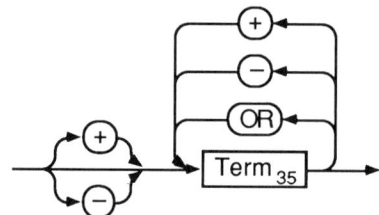

• A simple expression consists of a *term* or of multiple terms connected by addition operators.

• The "addition operator" OR can only be used to combine BOOLEAN terms.

• The operations + and - can be applied to numeric values (INTEGER, CARDINAL, REAL) and to SETs. The terms must be *expression compatible* (see Section 3.5.5).

• A leading + or – sign always relates to the first term, which must be a numeric value.

Term35

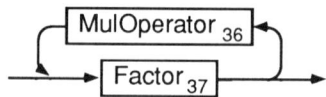

MulOperator36

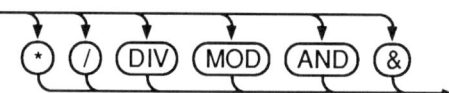

• A term consists of a *factor* or of multiple factors connected by multiplication operators.

• A multiplication operator can be one of the arithmetic operators *, /, DIV and MOD as well as the boolean operator AND (&).

• The "multiplication operator" AND (&) can only connect BOOLEAN factors.

• If a multiplication operator is used, the factors which it connects must be *expression compatible*.

• The operator * can be applied to numeric values (INTEGER, CARDINAL, REAL) and to SETs.

• The operator / can only be applied to REAL numbers and to SETs.

- The operators DIV and MOD are reserved for INTEGERs and CARDINALs.

Factor₃₇

Factor$_{37}$

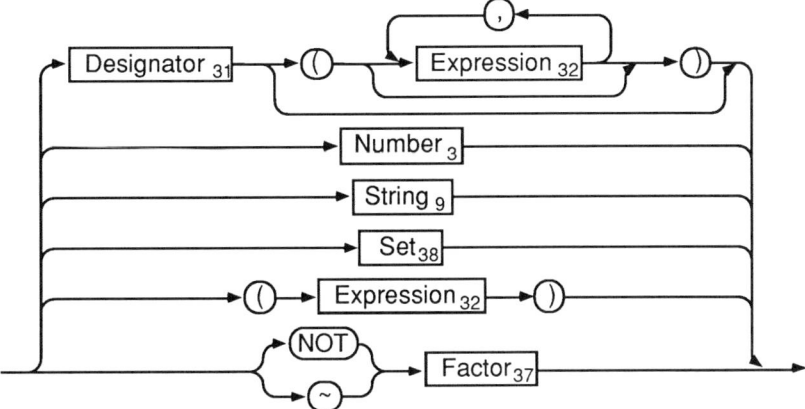

- A factor can be a designator (possibly followed by a parameter list—see Section 3.7 "Procedures"), a number, a character string, a set, an expression in parentheses, or a negated factor.

- A designator can refer to a variable (which might have already been declared) or to a constant (which has been assigned a name in a constant declaration). If the designator is followed by a list of parameters, then it is an invocation of a procedure (which will be handled in detail in Section 3.7.4).

- The unary operator NOT (~) denotes boolean negation and can only appear in front of a BOOLEAN factor.

Set$_{38}$

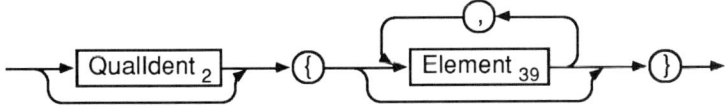

- A set consists of set brackets (braces) enclosing the elements of the set.

- A set can be preceded by a known qualified identifier (the name of a SET type). This is required if a set with a data type other than BITSET is to be the result.

Element$_{39}$

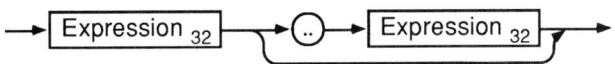

- The elements of a set can be described by means of simple or complex expressions whose values are within the range of the base type of the respective SET type.

- The data types of the elements must be expression compatible with the base type
  ([0..wordsize] for BITSET) of the respective SET type (see Section 3.5.5).

- A range of set elements can be described by its lower and upper bounds separated by
  two *adjoined* periods (range symbol). The second expression must be greater than or
  equal to the first expression upon evaluation.

Examples

For these examples and some to follow, we will use the following declarations:

```
CONST
  stringLength = 20;
  wordSize = 16;   (* assuming a 16-bit computer *)
TYPE
  String = ARRAY [0..stringLength-1] OF CHAR;
  Set = SET OF [0..wordSize-1];
  TextPtr = POINTER TO Text;
  Text = RECORD
              text:  String;
              length:  [0..stringLength];
              next:  TextPtr
          END;
VAR
  i,j: INTEGER;
  n: CARDINAL;
  x,y: REAL;
  ok,error: BOOLEAN;
  bitset: BITSET;
  set: Set;
  string: String;
  text: Text;
  ptr: TextPtr;
```

valid expressions:	data type:
`x`	REAL
`-x*y`	REAL
`(x*y)/2.0`	REAL
`i+j*2^`	INTEGER
`i DIV wordSize*wordSize`	INTEGER
`{0..wordSize-1}/bitset`	BITSET
`ok AND NOT error`	BOOLEAN
`i IN set`	BOOLEAN
`ptr^.text[ptr^.length-1]`	CHAR
`set + Set{i-1..i+1}`	Set
`string`	String
`ptr = NIL`	BOOLEAN

improper expressions:	
`i/j`	(/ permitted only for REALs)
`n+i`	(n and i are not expression compatible)
`string[stringLength]`	(index not in [0..stringLength-1])
`{5..7} < bitset`	(< not permitted for SETs)

3.5.5 Expression Compatibility of Operands

In Section 3.5.4 we repeatedly required that the operands in an operation be *expression compatible*. Since this term will be appearing again in future sections, we need to define what is meant by the term:

Two operands x1 and x2 with data types t1 and t2 are expression compatible if any one of the following conditions is met:

- t1 and t2 are the *same data type* (see definition in Section 3.4.5).

- t1 is a subrange type with base type t2 (or vice versa).

- t1 and t2 are subrange types with the *same base types*.

- t1 is INTEGER or CARDINAL and t2 is a subrange type (or x2 is a constant) in the range [0..MAX(INTEGER)] (or vice versa). The value of MAX(INTEGER) depends on the particular computer used, but in any case it is the largest INTEGER that can be represented, which is also a CARDINAL number.

- x1 is the predefined constant NIL (see POINTER types in Section 3.4.1) and t2 is any POINTER type (or vice versa).

- t1 and t2 are *procedure compatible* (see definition in Section 3.7.9).

Examples (using the declarations in Section 3.5.4)

The following are expression compatible:

```
i, j
text.text[i], "A"
text.length, n
text.length, i
n, 3
i, 3
x, 3.14159
ptr, ptr^.next
ptr, NIL
Set{}, set
{}, bitset
ok, (i IN bitset) OR error
```

The following are not expression compatible:

set, bitset	(different SET types)
set, {0..wordSize-1}	(Set and BITSET, as above)
i, n	(INTEGER and CARDINAL (!))
i, 1.0	(INTEGER and REAL)

Exercises

(1) Write variable declarations for all structured data types you developed in the exercises at the end of Section 3.4. What designators can be used to reference individual components of these variables?

(2) Write arithmetic expressions to represent the following quantities:

> 35% of an amount of money x
>
> the value of x/y rounded to the nearest whole number (x and y CARDINAL)
>
> area of a circle of diameter d (REAL)
>
> boolean value for "year x is a leap year"
>
> boolean value for "x is a factor of y"

(3) When making computations with CARDINAL and INTEGER values, care must always be taken that not only the final result but also intermediate results remain within the respective range. Furthermore, errors from rounding in division are to be avoided as much as possible.

Write an arithmetic expression that computes the value of x*y/z (all CARDINAL) as precisely as possible and without causing an overflow. Assume that the computation is to take place on a 16-bit machine with a maximum CARDINAL number of 65535.

Test your expression by hand to see whether it yields satisfactory results for

$$x = 1000, \quad y = 100, \quad z = 131;$$
$$x = 500, \quad y = 600, \quad z = 777$$

(4) The following declarations are given:

```
TYPE
    P =    POINTER TO R;
    R =    RECORD
                x:    CARDINAL;
                y:    INTEGER;
                z:    P
           END;
    A =    ARRAY [1..10] OF P;
    E  =   (x,y,z);
    S  =   [x..y];
VAR
    a:    A;
    b:    S;
    c:    ARRAY S OF R;
    d:    ARRAY BOOLEAN OF A;
    e:    [5..20];
```

along with the expressions:

```
b = z
c[x].x+e
c[y].y+c[x].x
d[FALSE]
d[TRUE,5]^.y+e
d[FALSE] = d[e=0]
a[e]^
a[e-4]^.z^.x
```

Decide which expressions are correct and determine the data types of their results.

3.6 Statements

In preceding sections, we became acquainted with various objects and data types that can be processed in Modula-2 programs. This section is dedicated to programming in the narrower sense of the word. We want to explain what actions can be undertaken with objects, that is, which *statements* Modula-2 provides for processing objects.

While the declaration part of a Modula-2 program (see Section 3.3) serves "only" to define the necessary constants, data types and variables (as well as procedures and internal modules, which will be described in Sections 3.7 and 3.8), the statement part (the StatementSequence$_{14}$ after the key word BEGIN) details what is to happen in the execution of the program. (Sometimes the term "executable statements" is used in this context.)

Modula-2 provides only *eleven* kinds of statements, which makes them easier to keep in mind than the variety of statements in other programming languages. In particular, Modula-2 has no special statements for input and output of data. Instead, library procedures are used for this purpose (see Section 4.2, "Input/Output").

Statement$_{40}$

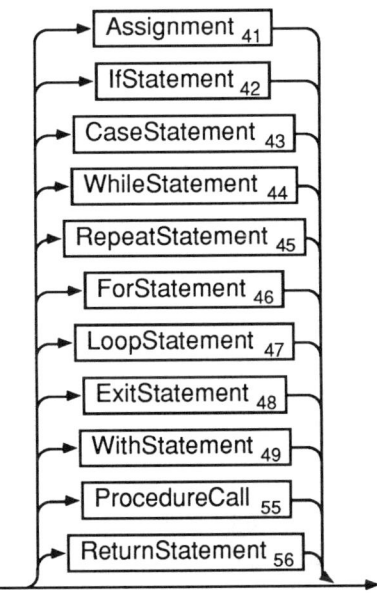

A statement can be one of the following (compare to the actions established in Section 1.3):

- an assignment statement (Assignment; Section 3.6.1)

- a conditional statement (IfStatement, CaseStatement; Section 3.6.2)

- a loop control statement (WhileStatement, RepeatStatement, ForStatement, LoopStatement; Section 3.6.3)

- a scope control statement for RECORDs (WithStatement; Section 3.6.4)

- a procedure invocation statement (ProcedureCall; Section 3.7.2)

- a statement to terminate loops or procedures (ExitStatement and ReturnStatement; Sections 3.6.3.4 and 3.7.3)

A statement can also be empty, that is, within a StatementSequence, two semicolons can appear in succession. The empty statement can, among other things, be used to place a semicolon after the last statement in a StatementSequence, as it was required in many older programming languages (e.g., PL/I).

3.6.1 Assignment

The simplest statement is the *assignment*. It serves to give a variable a (new) value.

Assignment$_{41}$

- An assignment consists of a designator (Section 3.5.2) and an expression, separated by ":=" (the *assignment operator*).

- The expression on the right side of the assignment can be of any data type, which expressly permits the assignment of entire RECORDs or ARRAYs.

- The designator must be *assignment compatible* (see the definition below) with the expression.

Execution of an Assignment

First the designator on the left side of the assignment is evaluated (i.e., its address in memory is determined). Then the expression on the right side of the assignment is evaluated. Finally, the value of the expression is assigned to the designator. The original value of the designator is lost in the process. The designator maintains its new value until another assignment statement changes it.

The assignment

```
i := 5*2
```

gives the variable i the value 10. The succeeding statement

```
i := i+1
```

increments the value of i by 1. (First $i+1 = 10+1 = 11$ is computed, then the computed value is assigned to i.)

If two variable values are to be swapped, the following statement sequence will not deliver the desired result:

```
i := j; j := i
```

because with the execution of the first assignment, i := j, the original value of i is lost. In order to avoid this, an auxiliary variable h can be used to temporarily store the original value of i:

```
h := i; i := j;   j := h
```

Assignment Compatibility

As with the combination of operands and operators (expression compatibility), assignments are governed by rules for permissibility of data types. For the assignment d:=e, we will call the designator d with data type t d and the expression e with data type t e *assignment compatible* if one of the following statements applies:

- The designator d and the expression e are *expression compatible* (see Section 3.5.5).

- t d is INTEGER (or a subrange thereof) and t e is CARDINAL (or a subrange thereof), or vice versa. In the execution of the assignment under these conditions, we must guarantee that the value of the expression e is in the range determined by t d, otherwise the result of the assignment is undefined.

- t d is an ARRAY [0..n-1] OF CHAR (i.e., a character field with length n) and e is a character string constant of length l with l<=n. (If l<n, the string e is stored in d[0] to d[l-1] and d[l] is assigned the null character OC.

3.6.2 Conditional Statements

Every programming language has statements that make it possible to control program flow based on certain conditions, for example:

(a) absolute value computation:

```
if x<0 then replace x with -x
```

(b) minimum and maximum determination:

```
if x<y
    then set min := x and max := y
    else set min := y and max := x
```

(c) comparison of two values:

```
if x=y then print "x=y"
if x<y then print "x<y"
else (x>y) print "x>y"
```

(d) forming powers of 2 (with 0<=x<=4)

```
if x=0, then set pot :=  1
if x=1, then set pot :=  2
if x=2, then set pot :=  4
if x=3, then set pot :=  8
if x=4, then set pot := 16
```

Modula-2 has two conditional statements: the IF statement and the CASE statement.

3.6.2.1 The IF Statement

The IF statement affords conditional control of program flow on the basis of the boolean value of a condition. It takes the following form:

IfStatement₄₂

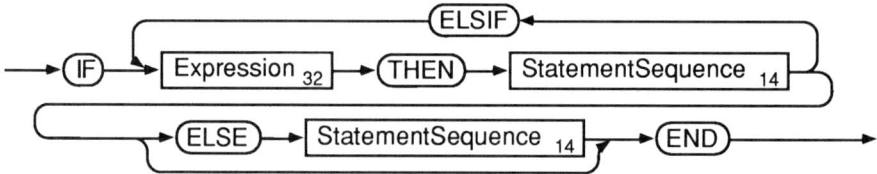

- An IF statement always begins with the key word IF followed by an expression and the key word THEN.

- The statement sequence following THEN (called the THEN branch) can be followed by any number of ELSIF clauses (each with an expression, the key word THEN, and a statement sequence).

- After the THEN branch or (if ELSIF is used) after the last ELSIF clause, the key word ELSE followed by a statement sequence (the ELSE branch) can be added.

- Each expression following IF or ELSIF must be of data type BOOLEAN.

- The statement sequence following THEN or ELSE can contain any number of statements.

- An IF statement is always terminated with the key word END.

Execution of the IF Statement

The expressions after IF and ELSIF are evaluated in the order of their occurrence.

As soon as the evaluation of an expression produces TRUE (i.e., when such a condition is fulfilled), the statement sequence following the respective key word THEN is executed. Program flow then continues after the key word END.

If all the expressions are FALSE (i.e., none of the conditions are fulfilled), the statement sequence following ELSE is executed and program flow continues after the key word END. If the key word ELSE is omitted, then, after the conditions have been tested, program execution resumes after END.

Note : The effects of the following two statement sequences are identical:

```
     IF x1                          IF x1
        THEN ss1                       THEN ss1
        ELSIF x2 THEN ss2              ELSE
        ELSE ss3                          IF x2
     END                                     THEN ss2
                                             ELSE ss3
                                             END (*IF x2*)
                                       END (*IF x1*)
```

We recommend always using the shorter and clearer form with ELSIF whenever more than two alternatives are possible. (Special cases of the multiway decision can be formulated even more clearly with the CASE statement.)

The examples at the beginning of Section 3.6.2 can be formulated as follows with the help of IF statements:

```
(* a:  absolute value computation *)
IF x<0 THEN x := -x END

(* b:  minimum and maximum determination *)
IF x<y
   THEN  min := x; max := y
   ELSE  min := y; max := x
END

(* c:  comparison of two values *)
IF x=y
   THEN WriteString ("x=y")
   ELSIF x<y THEN WriteString ("x<y")
   ELSE WriteString ("x>y")
END

(* d:  forming powers of 2  (with 0<=x<=4) *)
IF x=0
   THEN pot := 1
   ELSIF x=1 THEN pot := 2
   ELSIF x=2 THEN pot := 4
   ELSIF x=3 THEN pot := 8
   ELSIF x=4 THEN pot := 16
END
(* If x<0 or x>4, then the value of pot remains unchanged *)
```

3.6.2.2 The CASE Statement

With the help of the CASE statement, *multiway decisions* that are all based on the value of *one* expression can be formulated shorter and more clearly and can be executed more quickly.

CaseStatement$_{43}$

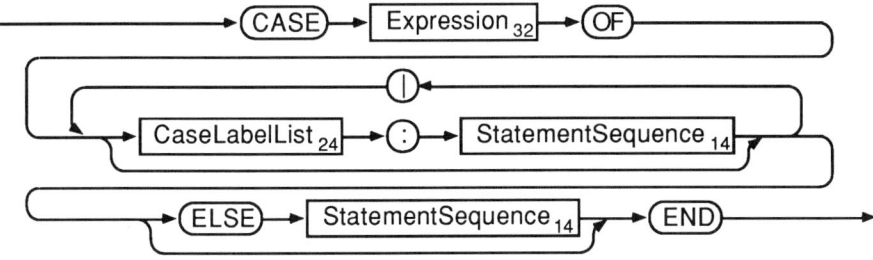

- A CASE statements begins with the key word CASE followed by an expression and the key word OF.

- The expression (called the *CASE expression*) can be any of the data types INTEGER, CARDINAL, BOOLEAN, CHAR, an enumeration type or a subrange type. The data type REAL is not permitted.

- The key word OF is followed by a list of all cases (statement sequences) that are to be executed, dependent on the value of the expression. The cases are separated from one another by vertical bars.

- Individual cases can be empty. Thus vertical bars can also be inserted before the first or after the last case.

- Each case begins with a list of constant expressions or ranges (CaseLabelList). Each constant expression must be *expression compatible* with the CASE expression. No value may appear more than once within a CASE statement. (The structure of a CaseLabelList was discussed in 3.4.1.3 under the subtitle "RECORD Types.")

- Each CaseLabelList as well as the key word ELSE (which can be omitted) can be followed by any number of statements.

- A CASE statement is terminated with the key word END.

Execution of a CASE Statement

First the CASE expression is evaluated. Then that particular statement sequence whose CaseLabelList contains a value that matches the expression's value is "sought" and executed. After execution of the statement sequence, the program resumes after the key word END.

If no CaseLabelList is found to match the value of the CASE expression, then the statement sequence following ELSE is executed.

Caution : If the ELSE branch is omitted in the latter case, the effect of the CASE statement is undefined, i.e., its execution can lead to a program crash.

Examples

The last example (d) at the beginning of Section 3.6.2, which was coded as an IF statement in Section 3.6.2.1, can be formulated shorter and more clearly as a CASE statement:

```
CASE x OF
   0: pot := 1
 | 1: pot := 2
 | 2: pot := 4
 | 3: pot := 8
 | 4: pot := 16
ELSE
END
```

This formulation has the additional advantage of a shorter execution time. Searching for the appropriate CaseLabelList generally occurs very quickly and is not dependent upon the value of the CASE expression, whereas the IF statement requires five tests for $x=4$.

The empty ELSE branch is necessary in order to guarantee that the CASE statement operates as does the IF statement for $x<0$ or $x>4$. It simply means that no statement is to be executed if x is not between 0 and 4.

There is a great deal of outward similarity between a CASE statement and a RECORD declaration with variants. This is no accident. It simply shows that the CASE statement is especially suitable for processing RECORDs with variants because it is the best method for choosing the matching variant.

```
(* declarations from Section 3.4.1, "Data Types" *)

   TYPE
      Material = (iron,steel,copper,glass,acrylic,pvc,rubber);
      Substance = RECORD
                       matno:  CARDINAL;
                       specweight: REAL;
                       CASE kind: Material OF
                          steel:
                              stainless: BOOLEAN
                        | glass:
                              frosted: BOOLEAN
                        | pvc,rubber:
                              color: (white,red,blue,yellow,green)
                          END (*CASE*)
                       END (*RECORD*)

   VAR part: Substance;
    ...
   BEGIN
    ...
     WriteString("Material Number: ");
     WriteCard(part.matno,5);
     WriteString(", specific weight: ");
     WriteReal(part.specweight,5,1);
     WriteString(", kind: ");
     CASE part.kind OF
        iron: WriteString("iron")
      | steel:
           WriteString("steel");
           IF part.stainless THEN WriteString(" (stainless)") END
      | copper: WriteString("copper")
      | glass:
           IF part.frosted
              THEN WriteString("frosted")
              ELSE WriteString("clear")
           END;
           WriteString(" glass")
      | acrylic: WriteString("acrylic")
      | pvc, rubber:
           IF part.kind = pvc
              THEN WriteString("PVC/")
              ELSE WriteString("rubber/")
           END;
           CASE part.color OF
              white: WriteString("white")
            | red: WriteString("red")
            | blue: WriteString("blue")
            | yellow: WriteString("yellow")
            | green: WriteString("green")
           END (*CASE part.color*)
```

```
        END   (* CASE part.kind *)
    ...
```

Note : The above program segment outputs the contents of the variable part with the data type Substance. The procedures WriteString, WriteCard and WriteReal are called in order to output strings, CARDINAL and REAL numbers, respectively. For a detailed description of these procedures, refer to Section 4.2, "Input/Output."

CASE statements in the form

```
CASE x OF
      1: ...
|   100: ...
|  1000: ...
END
```

should be avoided. We recommend that such conditional statements be formulated as IF statements with ELSIFs and that the CASE statement be reserved for situations where the case labels are not too far apart.

Exercises

(1) Write a program segment that assigns the values of three variables a, b and c to three other variables x, y and z in such a way that x<=y<=z. Use comparisons and assignments.

(2) Write a program segment that computes the rental costs of a communications line as follows: the first 10 miles, $3 each; the next 15 miles at $2 each; each additional mile, $1. Use only comparisons and assignments.

(3) Write a CASE statement for the computation of the number of days in a given month. Try to find other solutions to the problem and compare the various solutions.

3.6.3 Loops

All the statements we have discussed so far were executed either sequentially or conditionally. We also need language elements that allow us to form *loops*. Some examples:

(a) Find the smallest whole number p with $2^p>=y$ (dual logarithm):

```
set p:=0 and s:=1. (s=2^p)
repeat as long as s is smaller than y:
  increment p by 1.
multiply s by 2.
```

(b) Print the elements of an array x until the first value is 0 (inclusively):

```
set i:=0.
repeat :
  increment i by 1.
  print x[i].
until x[i]=0.
```

(c)   Add up all the elements of an array x: ARRAY [1..100] OF CARDINAL:

```
set s:=0.
repeat for all i from 1 to 100:
  increase s by x[i].
```

(d)   Read and print the character ch to the first blank (exclusively):

```
repeat:
  read ch.
  if ch is a blank
    then terminate loop.
  print ch.
```

Modula-2 has four different statements for loop control (corresponding to the four basic forms of loops depicted in the examples above): WHILE, REPEAT, FOR and LOOP.

3.6.3.1   The WHILE Statement

The WHILE statement serves to repeat a statement sequence *while* a certain condition is met. It takes the following form:

WhileStatement$_{44}$

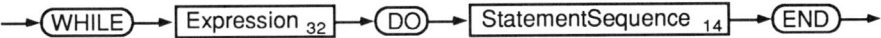

*   A WHILE statement begins with the key word WHILE followed by an expression and the key word DO.
*   The WHILE expression (the *loop control condition*) must be of type BOOLEAN.
*   Any number of statements can follow the key word DO.
*   A WHILE statement is always terminated with the key word END.

Execution of a WHILE Statement

First the loop control condition is evaluated. If the value TRUE results, then the statement sequence between DO and END (the *body* of the loop) is executed. Thereafter, the WHILE statement is again executed (again beginning with the evaluation of the loop control condition). If the evaluation yields FALSE, then the body of the loop is not executed (again) and program control passes to the statement following the END of the WHILE loop.

Since the loop condition is always tested *before* the execution of the body of the loop, it is possible that the body of the loop might not be executed at all.

The examples at the beginning of Section 3.6.3 can be formulated with the help of WHILE statements as follows:

```
(* a:  dual logarithm *)
  p := 0;   s := 1
  WHILE  s<y  DO
    p := p+1;   s := s*2
  END

(* b:  printing an array *)
  i := 1;
  WHILE  x[i] <> 0  DO
    WriteCard(x[i],6);
    i := i+1
  END;
  WriteCard(x[i],6)     (* print last element, with x[i]=0 *)

(* c:  sum of elements of array *)
  s := 0;   i := 1;
  WHILE i<=100  DO
    s := s + x[i];
    i := i+1
  END
  (* i now has the value 101 *)

(* d:  reading and printing characters *)
  Read(ch);       (* read first character *)
  WHILE  ch<>" "  DO
    Write(ch);
    Read(ch)      (* read next character *)
  END
```

3.6.3.2 The REPEAT Statement

The REPEAT statement permits the repetition of a loop *until* a certain condition is met. It takes the following form:

RepeatStatement$_{45}$

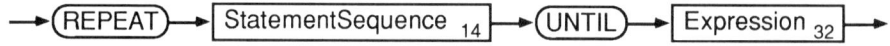

- A REPEAT statement begins with the key word REPEAT, which is followed by any number of statements.

- A REPEAT statement ends with the key word UNTIL followed by an expression. (Note: The REPEAT statement is the only complex statement in Modula-2 that does not end with END. Its key word UNTIL serves the bracketing function and suffices for recognition of the end of the statement.)

- The expression after UNTIL (*loop control condition*) must be of type BOOLEAN.

Execution of a REPEAT Statement

First the statement sequence between REPEAT and UNTIL (the *body of the loop*) is executed. Then the BOOLEAN expression after UNTIL is evaluated. If the value TRUE results, then the program resumes with the statement following the REPEAT statement, otherwise the REPEAT statement is executed again (i.e., beginning with the body of the loop).

The loop control condition is always tested *after* execution of the statement sequence. This guarantees that the body of a REPEAT loop is always executed *at least once*.

Comparison of the WHILE and REPEAT Statements

Both WHILE and REPEAT statements form *iterative loops* that are executed until a certain *termination criterion* is achieved. There are only two differences that need to be taken into account in programming:

- The WHILE loop terminates when the loop control condition is FALSE; the REPEAT loop, when it is TRUE.
- The body of the REPEAT loop is executed at least once; the WHILE loop might not execute at all.

WHILE loops can be transformed into REPEAT loops and conversely.

The WHILE loop

```
WHILE c DO s END   (* c = condition, s = statement sequence *)
```

can be transformed into a REPEAT loop by enclosing the REPEAT statement in an IF statement that tests the value of the loop control condition, and by negating the condition in the REPEAT statement:

```
IF c THEN
    REPEAT s UNTIL NOT c
END
```

The REPEAT loop

```
REPEAT s   UNTIL   c
```

can be transformed into a WHILE loop in either of two ways:

- *code duplication* : The body of the loop is executed once unconditionally before the WHILE statement (and the loop control condition is negated):

```
s;
WHILE NOT c DO s END
```

This transformation is only practical if the code to be duplicated is short.

- *switch variable* : A boolean auxiliary variable (which we will name looping) is introduced as a loop control variable to indicate whether another execution of the loop is necessary. In order to force at least one execution, the variable looping is initialized with TRUE:

```
looping := TRUE;
WHILE looping DO
    s;
    looping := NOT c   (* covers the negation *)
END
```

The examples at the beginning of Section 3.6.3 can be formulated with REPEAT statements as follows (compare the WHILE statements in Section 3.6.3.1):

```
(* a:  dual logarithm *)
  p := 0;
  IF y>0 THEN
    s := 1;
    REPEAT
       p := p+1;   s := s*2
    UNTIL s>=y
  END  (* IF *)

(* b:  printing an array *)
  i := 0;
  REPEAT
    i := i+1;
    WriteCard(x[i],6)
  UNTIL x[i] = 0

(* c:  sum of elements of array *)
  s := 0;   i := 1;
  REPEAT
    s := s + x[i];
    i := i+1
  UNTIL i>100
  (* i now has the value 101 *)

(* d:  reading and printing characters *)
  REPEAT
    Read(ch);
    IF ch<>" " THEN Write(ch) END
  UNTIL ch = " "
```

3.6.3.3   The FOR Statement

The FOR statement executes loops with a fixed number of iterations. We have not yet used this kind of loop. FOR loops take the form:

ForStatement$_{46}$

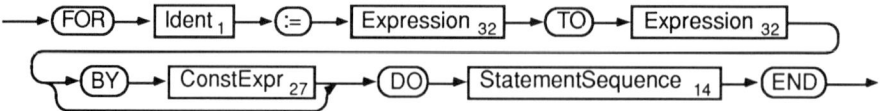

- A FOR statement begins with the key word FOR followed by the loop control clause.

- Ident is the name of a variable (the *loop control variable*) whose data type is INTEGER, CARDINAL, BOOLEAN, CHAR, an enumeration type, or a subrange type. Ident must be a simple variable (no element of an ARRAY or RECORD) and can be neither IMPORTed (see Section 3.8.2 on the scope of identifiers) nor a formal parameter (see Section 3.7, "Procedures").

- The expressions after := and TO must be *expression compatible* with Ident.

- The BY clause (BY followed by a constant expression) can be omitted. The constant expression must be of one of the types INTEGER or CARDINAL and cannot result in 0.

- The key word DO can be followed by any number of statements.

- The FOR statement is always terminated with the key word END.

Execution of a FOR Statement

The body of a FOR statement is (normally) executed repeatedly, with the loop control variable assuming a new value with each run. The expression after the := determines the *initial value* ; the constant expression after TO is the *target expression* (end value); and the constant expression after BY determines the *step size* (*increment* or *decrement*) by which the loop control variable is increased or decreased. If the BY clause is absent, then the loop control variable is incremented by one each time the loop repeats. Incrementation of the loop control variable works as follows:

```
FOR  i:=b  TO  e  BY  s  DO
    ...        (* i=b, b+s, b+2*s,... b+n*s  *)
               (* whereby b+n*s<=e and b+(n+1)*s>e for s>0 *)
               (* or      b+n*s>=e and b+(n+1)*s<e for s<0 *)
END
```

The initial value and the target value are computed only once at the beginning of the FOR statement. If b>e and s is positive (or b<e and s<0) then the loop body is not executed at all and program execution continues after the END of the FOR statement (behaving similarly to a WHILE loop). Otherwise the variable i.is assigned the value b and the loop body is executed.

After each run (i.e., after each execution of the loop body), the loop control variable is automatically incremented by the value of s (or the default of 1) and, as long as i is still within the range set by b and e, the loop body is executed again.

Warnings :

- The value of the loop control variable after execution of the FOR statement depends upon the particular compiler implemented on a particular computer. Thus this value should be viewed as undefined outside the loop and should not be used.

- It is possible to alter the value of the loop control variable within the loop body of a FOR statement, but this is strongly discouraged. Modifying this variable completely destructures the loop and leads to incomprehensible programs. Depending on the particular compiler, it can even lead to totally unpredictable results.

Examples

Example (c) at the beginning of Section 3.6.3 can be formulated with a FOR statement as follows (the other three examples are not suitable for coding with FOR loops because the number of iterations cannot be determined in advance):

```
(* c:   sum of elements of array *)
s := 0;
FOR  i:=1  TO  100  DO
   s := s + x[i]
END
(* the value of i is now undefined! *)
```

A series of n asterisks can be output using a FOR loop. (The loop control variable is used only for counting and has no meaning within the loop body.)

```
FOR  i:=1  TO  n  DO
   Write("*")
END
```

Inserting a value y at position n in the array x can be accomplished with the following FOR statement:

```
FOR  i:=100  TO  n+1  BY  -1  DO
   x[i] := x[i-1]
END;
x[n] := y
```

Note : In order to shift the elements x[n] to x[99] each to the right by one position (x[n+1] to x[100]), we need to start with the higher indices with an increment of -1.

3.6.3.4   The LOOP and EXIT Statements

The LOOP statement and the EXIT statement can be used to construct general loops that could be formulated only with difficulty using WHILE and REPEAT statements. They take the following form:

LoopStatement47

ExitStatement48

• A LOOP statement begins with the key word LOOP and ends with the key word END.

• Any number of statements can appear between LOOP and END.

• An EXIT statement consists of the key word EXIT alone.

• EXIT statements can be used only within LOOP statements.

Execution of LOOP Statements

A LOOP statement creates an *infinite loop*. The statement sequence contained in the LOOP statement is repeated forever.

An EXIT statement causes a LOOP statement to terminate, with program execution resuming after the key word END of the LOOP.

LOOP statements can be nested, i.e., the LOOP body can contain further LOOP statements. When an EXIT statement is encountered, only the *innermost* LOOP statement terminates.

LOOP Statements and Other Loop Constructs

The LOOP statement is the most general statement for constructing loops. It has two advantages compared to the relatively rigid WHILE and REPEAT statements:

- A LOOP statement can terminate anywhere in the LOOP body, not just at the beginning or end.

- A LOOP statement can contain multiple EXIT statements. In this way, several termination criteria can be provided at various locations within the LOOP.

Because LOOP statements are more general, WHILE and REPEAT statements can also be formulated as LOOP statements:

```
WHILE c DO          corresponds to          LOOP
  s                                            IF NOT c THEN EXIT END;
END                                            s
                                             END


REPEAT              corresponds to          LOOP
  s                                            s;
UNTIL c                                        IF c THEN EXIT END;
                                             END
```

Note : For the sake of readability, we recommend using WHILE and REPEAT statements wherever a single test at the beginning or end of a loop is required. LOOP statements should only be used in cases where other loop constructs fail.

The examples at the beginning of Section 3.6.3 can be formulated with LOOP statements as follows:

```
(* a:  dual logarithm *)
p := 0;  s := 1;
LOOP
  IF s>=y  THEN EXIT END;
  p := p+1;  s := s*2
END

(* b:  printing an array *)
i := 1;
LOOP
  WriteCard(x[i],6);
  IF x[i] = 0  THEN EXIT END;
  i := i+1
END
```

```
(* c:  sum of elements of array *)
s := 0;   i := 1;
LOOP
   s := s + x[i];
   IF i=100 THEN EXIT END;
   i := i+1
END
(* i now has the value 100 *)

(* d:  reading and printing characters *)
LOOP
   Read(ch);
   IF ch=" " THEN EXIT END;
   Write(ch)
END
```

Exercises

(1) In Section 3.4.1.3 we declared a RECORD data type for a date in the 20th Century. Use this data type to write a program segment that computes the number of days between two given dates.

(2) Write a program segment that inverts an array of characters of length n (maximum 80), that is, swaps the first with the last, the second with the $n-1^{st}$, and so on. Use the following declarations:

```
VAR
   array: ARRAY [1..80] OF CHAR;
   n: [1..80];
```

(3) The following LOOP statement is given:

```
s := 0;   i := 1;
LOOP
   s := s + x[i];
   IF x[i]=0 THEN EXIT END;
   i := i+1
END
```

Transform this LOOP statement into

   (a) a WHILE loop

   (b) a REPEAT loop

3.6.4 The WITH Statement

In Section 3.5.2, "Operands," we showed that a component y of a RECORD x is designated as "$x.y$". This notation is required to ensure that the component y of RECORD x is unambiguously identified (since the variable y could occur elsewhere, as in other RECORDs). If, however, a program segment frequently uses the same RECORD variable again and again to qualify a field identifier or identifiers, the additional written work for the programmer is not welcome (see the example for the CASE statement in Section 3.6.2.2). In order to simplify work with RECORDs, Modula-2 supplies the WITH statement:

WithStatement49

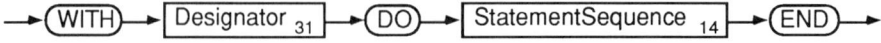

- A WITH statement begins with the key word WITH, followed by a designator and the key word DO.

- Designator must be a variable of type RECORD.

- The key word DO can be followed by any number of statements.

- A WITH statement is always terminated with the key word END.

Execution of the WITH statement

All statements between DO and END can use the components (field identifiers) of the RECORD named by Designator without the need to dereference first with the RECORD name and a period as prefix (i.e., the unqualified field identifiers can be used). The WITH statement does no algorithmic work; it merely shortens the formulation and can help the compiler to optimize the generated code.

Example

```
TYPE
  Name = ARRAY [0..19] OF CHAR;
  PersonnelNumber = [1..1000];
  Person = RECORD
                firstName, lastName:  Name;
                female:  BOOLEAN;
                supervisor:  PersonnelNumber;
                status: (manager,salaried,worker,apprentice);
                marStatus: (single,married,divorced,widowed);
             END;
VAR
  personnelFile:  ARRAY PersonnelNumber OF Person;
  status: CARDINAL;   (* number of personnel *)
  i:  CARDINAL;
```

The statement sequence

```
personnelFile[i].female := FALSE;
personnelFile[i].status := apprentice;
personnelFile[i].marStatus := single
```

can be written as follows using the WITH statement:

```
WITH  personnelFile[i]  DO
   female := FALSE;
   status := apprentice;
   marStatus := single
END
```

Note that status inside the WITH statement signifies

```
personnelFile[i].status.
```

The variable status alone, which represents the number of personnel, cannot be used inside the WITH statement.

To further clarify the concept of scope control by means of the WITH statement, here is an example that prints the names of all unmarried female salaried employees and their managers. Output of the character strings is again handled by the procedure WriteString. WriteLn starts a new line on the output medium.

```
FOR i:= 1 TO status DO      (* for all personnel *)
    WITH personnelFile[i]   DO
        IF female AND (status=salaried) AND (marStatus=single)
        THEN
            WriteString(firstName); WriteString(lastName);
                                    (* employee's name *)
            WITH personnelFile[supervisor] DO
                WriteString(firstName); WriteString(lastName);
                                    (* supervisor's name *)
            END;   (* WITH *)
            WriteLn;
        END (*IF*)
    END (*WITH*)
END (*FOR*)
```

Exercises

(1) The following declarations are given:

```
TYPE
    Date = RECORD
               day: [1..31];
               month: [1..12];
               year: CARDINAL
           END;
    Name = ARRAY [0..29] OF CHAR;
    Employee = RECORD
                   name: Name;
                   children: CARDINAL;
                   soleProvider: BOOLEAN;
                   hired: Date
               END
VAR
    employee: Employee;
    name: Name;
    searchName: Name;
```

   (a) Formulate a WITH construct that makes it possible to automatically dereference the components of the complex variable hired in the complex variable employee.

   (b) Explain which objects are designated in the operations in the following program segment:

```
IF employee.name = name THEN
    WITH   employee   DO
        name := searchName;
        ...
    END; (*WITH*)
    searchName := name;
END
```

3.7 Procedures

In Section 2.1, "The Principle of Stepwise Refinement," we showed how a problem can be solved by reducing it to its constituent subproblems. The result of this design process is a collection of subalgorithms, some of which require other subalgorithms for their execution. We will now discuss how these subalgorithms can be combined into a Modula-2 program. In our text justification problem, the rough structure of the algorithm took the following form:

```
Algorithm Justify(↓b):
          eot:  boolean value
   . . .
   ClearLine(↑z)
   REPEAT
     ReadWord(↑w ↑eot)
     ProcessWord(↓b ↓w ↕z)
   UNTIL  eot
   PrintLine(↓z)  (* print last line *)
END  Justify.
```

Once the refinement of the subalgorithms ClearLine, ReadWord, ProcessWord and PrintLine has been completed, they can be inserted in their respective places in Justify. The result is the overall algorithm for the solution of the problem. However, this would sacrifice the clarity that was gained from stepwise refinement. Furthermore, individual subalgorithms are often required in multiple locations throughout the main algorithm, and so they would have to be inserted repeatedly. Thus most programming languages afford a mechanism that permits the writing of separately designed subalgorithms as separate program segments (called *procedures*) that can be used (activated, invoked or called) at various locations.

3.7.1 Declaration of Procedures

As we established in stepwise refinement in Section 2.1, every algorithm consists of four parts:

- the *name* of the algorithm,
- the description of its *parameters* (i.e., input and output objects),
- the description of its *local objects* (those used only within the algorithm), and
- the *actions* that are to be executed when the algorithm is activated.

When the algorithm is formulated as a procedure, all four of the above parts need to be present. This occurs in the *declaration* of the procedure, which, like constant, type and variable declarations, must be located at the beginning of the program in which it is to be used (see Section 3.3, "Elementary Program Structure").

ProcedureDeclaration$_{50}$

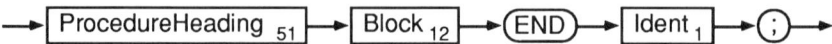

ProcedureHeading$_{51}$

- A procedure declaration begins with a ProcedureHeading, which establishes the name of the procedure and the names and data types of its parameters.

- A procedure heading begins with the key word PROCEDURE followed by the name of the procedure.

- After the procedure name, the *formal parameters*, if present, are listed to specify the input and output objects of the procedure.

- The procedure heading is terminated with a semicolon.

- The procedure heading is followed by a block (see Section 3.3) containing the declarations of the *local objects* of the procedure and the *statement sequence* to be executed when the procedure is activated.

- A procedure declaration is terminated with the key word END followed by the procedure name and a semicolon.

FormalParameters$_{52}$

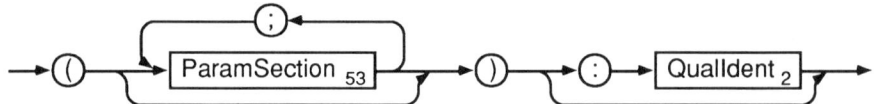

- A procedure's parameter description consists of two parts:

  - a list of its *formal parameters*

  - information about whether the procedure is a *function procedure* and what data type it returns (function procedures are discussed in detail in Section 3.7.4)

- The parameter list of a procedure is enclosed in parentheses, which can enclose any number of parameter sections (ParamSection) separated by semicolons.

- After the parameter list, the name of an already defined data type (QualIdent) can occur. This defines the procedure as a function procedure that returns a value whose data type is described by QualIdent.

ParamSection$_{53}$

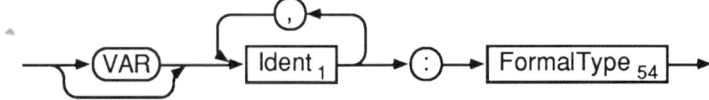

- A parameter section consists of a list of identifiers (the names of the formal parameters of the procedure) followed by a colon and a description of a data type (FormalType).

- The key word VAR can appear in front of the list of names of the formal parameters to establish that they are output (*variable*) parameters.

  − A parameter without VAR means that the parameter is an input (*value*) parameter. (Input parameters were denoted in Chapter 1 with a downward arrow ↓.)

  − Output and input/output parameters (VAR parameters denoted by ↑ or ↕) are defined by means of the key word VAR. The effect of this definition is discussed in Section 3.7.2, "Invocation of Procedures."

FormalType$_{54}$

- For every parameter section, a data type has to be given. In the simplest case, this occurs by means of a qualified identifier (QualIdent).

- The phrase "ARRAY OF" can be used to process arrays with any number of elements (see Section 3.7.7, "ARRAY Parameters").

Examples

(a) computation of the square of a real number:

```
PROCEDURE ComputeSquare(x: REAL; VAR y: REAL);
BEGIN
   y := x*x
END ComputeSquare;
```

This procedure multiplies the input parameter x by itself and assigns the result to the output parameter y (designated by the key word VAR).

(b) computation of 2 raised to an integer power:

```
PROCEDURE BuildPowerOf2(n: CARDINAL; VAR power: CARDINAL);
VAR  i:  CARDINAL;
BEGIN
   power := 1;
   FOR  i:=1  TO  n  DO
     power := power*2
   END
END BuildPowerOf2;
```

This procedure uses a local variable i for counting the number of loops necessary for the power n.

(c) determining the position `pos` of a character `ch` in a character array `s` with length
     `len`:

```
TYPE
   String = ARRAY [1..1000] OF CHAR;

PROCEDURE Search(s:String; len:CARDINAL;
                 ch:CHAR; VAR pos: CARDINAL);
BEGIN
   pos := len;       (* search the list from back to front *)
   WHILE (pos>0) AND (s[pos]<>ch)   DO
      pos := pos-1
   END
   (* if ch occurs in s, then pos specifies its last occurrence;
      if ch does not occur, pos has the value 0 *)
END Search;
```

At the end of Section 1.4 we presented an example of a procedure that computes the
greatest common divisor.

3.7.2 Invocation of Procedures

A procedure that is declared within a program can be activated at an arbitrary number of
locations. To do so, we use a special kind of statement known as a *procedure call*. Like
other statements, procedure calls can occur anywhere within a statement sequence.

ProcedureCall$_{55}$

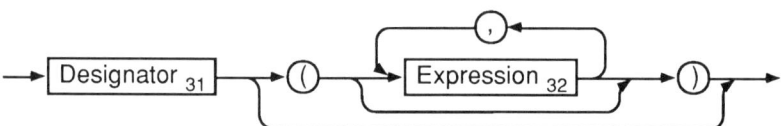

•   A procedure is invoked by specifying its procedure name.

•   The procedure name can be followed by a list of actual parameters.

•   A procedure's actual parameters must be enclosed in parentheses and separated by
    commas.

•   The *formal parameters* (from the declaration of the procedure) and the *actual parameters*
    (in the procedure call) must match with repect to data type, i.e.:

    -   For VAR parameters (output and input/output parameters), the data types of the
        formal and actual parameters must be *the same* (see Section 3.4.5).

    -   For input parameters (without VAR), the formal parameter (x) and the actual
        parameter (y) must be *assignment compatible* (see Section 3.6.1), i.e., the
        assignment $x:=y$ must be permissible.

•   If a formal parameter is labelled with VAR (*VAR parameter*), then the corresponding
    actual parameter must be a variable (designator).

Execution of a Procedure Call

A procedure call causes the activation of the statement sequence contained in the declaration of the invoked procedure.

Depending on the type of parameter, value or VAR, its use within the called procedure has different effects:

* *value parameter* (input)

  When the procedure is called, the value of the actual parameter is computed and assigned to the formal parameter, i.e., a *copy* of the actual parameter is made. Each time the formal parameter is used within the invoked procedure, only the copy of the actual parameter is affected. This is even true if the formal parameter is on the left side of an assignment, in which case only the copy is altered. The value of the actual parameter remains unaffected. This has to be the case, since constants and arbitrary expressions can occur as actual parameters.

* *VAR parameter* (output or input/output)

  When the procedure is invoked, no copy of the actual parameter is made (as with value parameters); instead, the *address* of the actual parameter is passed to the invoked procedure. If the formal parameter is changed within the invoked procedure, this means that the actual parameter is changed as well. For this reason, only variables, not constants or combined expressions, are permitted as VAR parameters.

The execution of the invoked procedure (i.e., its statement sequence) ends either with the last statement in the procedure or with the execution of a RETURN statement (see Section 3.7.3).

After execution of the procedure, program control returns to the first statement following the procedure call, as shown in Fig. 3.1.

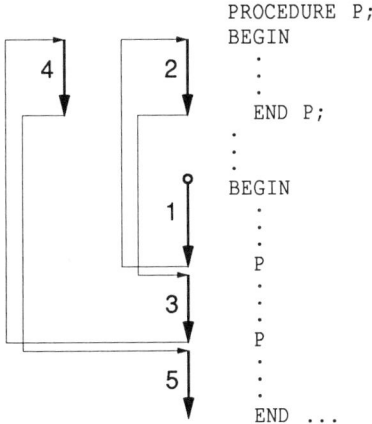

Fig. 3.1 Execution of a program with two procedure calls

3.7.3 The RETURN Statement

During the execution of a procedure, conditions might arise that make further execution
unneccessary or even senseless. In such cases the procedure is to be terminated at once
and program execution is to resume with the statement after the procedure call.

Consider, for example, the algorithm FindDouble, which has the task of determining
whether some character occurs twice in succession in a character array of type

```
String = ARRAY [1..100] OF CHAR.
```

If that is the case, then the index pos of the first character of such a double is returned,
otherwise pos=0 is returned. We use the value parameter len (length of the character
array) in order to tell the algorithm how far to search in the array.

The problem can be solved as follows:

```
FindDouble(↓s ↓len ↑pos):
  IF len>100  THEN
    (* specifications not met; senseless to continue *)
    pos := 0;   end of algorithm
  END
  i := 1
  WHILE i<len
    IF  s[i]=s[i+1]  THEN
      (* double found; continuation superfluous *)
      pos := i;   end of algorithm
    END
    i := i + 1
  END
  (* no doubles found *)
  pos := 0;   end of algorithm
END FindDouble.
```

The execution of the algorithm can terminate at any of three locations, depending on its
parameters. In order to manage this with the statements familiar to us so far, we need to
employ an IF statement and a complex loop control condition:

```
PROCEDURE FindDouble(s:String; len:CARDINAL; VAR pos:CARDINAL);
  VAR i:  CARDINAL;
BEGIN
  IF len>100
    THEN  pos := 0
    ELSE
      i := 1;
      WHILE  (i<len)  AND  (s[i]<>s[i+1])  DO
        i := i+1
      END;
      IF i<len
        THEN  pos := i
        ELSE  pos := 0
      END
  END
END FindDouble;
```

In order to enable (early) termination of such procedures, Modula-2 provides the RETURN statement:

ReturnStatement₅₆

- A RETURN statement consists of the key word RETURN, which can be followed by an expression.

- If the procedure in which the RETURN is contained is a function procedure, then an expression *must* be included and must be *assignment compatible* (see Section 3.6.1, "Assignment") with the data type of the function.

- If the procedure is not a function procedure, then any included RETURN statement consists of the key word RETURN alone.

Execution of a RETURN Statement

A RETURN statement can occur anywhere in a statement sequence in a procedure (or module). It causes the immediate termination of procedure execution and the passing of program control to the statement after the procedure call in the calling program. If a RETURN statement is encountered in a module (e.g., the main program), the immediate termination of the module results.

In function procedures, the RETURN statement, in addition to returning program control to the invoking routine, causes the value of the function to be established. Function procedures are treated in Section 3.7.4 in detail.

Our search algorithm can be reformulated with two RETURN statements as follows:

```
PROCEDURE FindDouble(s:String; len:CARDINAL; VAR pos:CARDINAL);
  VAR i:  CARDINAL;
BEGIN
  IF (len=0) OR (len>100)  THEN
    pos := 0;
    RETURN
  END;
  FOR  i:=1  TO  len-1  DO
    IF s[i]=s[i+1]  THEN
      pos := i;
      RETURN
    END
  END;
  pos := 0
END  FindDouble;
```

Note : The test len=0 in the first IF statement is necessary in order to avoid an error in the procedure caused by len-1 (leading to a negative number in a CARDINAL data type).

3.7.4 Function Procedures

Many procedures return exactly one output parameter as a result. Such procedures are termed *functions* in the mathematical sense. In mathematics, we are accustomed to a function f with arguments (i.e., parameters) x and y, and we regularly use such an object as part of an expression (e.g., f(x,y) + 1). In order to maintain this comfortable notation in programming as well, Modula-2 provides *function procedures*. We referred to them in past sections, so let's first summarize what we already know about function procedures:

• The *procedure heading* of a function procedure must contain the data type of the function value (the domain in the mathematical sense).

• Each RETURN statement in a function procedure must contain an expression representing the function value, which must be *assignment compatible* with the function type in the procedure declaration (see Section 3.6.1).

In addition, the following points need to be observed in writing and using function procedures:

• Every function procedure *must contain at least one RETURN statement*. A function procedure cannot simply end after its last statement has been executed, for that would leave the value of the function undefined.

• The data type of the function value cannot be ARRAY, RECORD or SET.

• A function procedure is invoked not by a special procedure call, but by the occurrence of its name in an expression (see Section 3.5.4, "Rules for Writing Expressions"). If the function procedure has no parameters, then empty parentheses () must be used to indicate that it is a procedure invocation (rather than a variable name).

Examples

(a) The procedure ComputeSquare from Section 3.7.1 as function procedure Square consists of only a single RETURN statement:

```
PROCEDURE Square(x: REAL) : REAL;
BEGIN
    RETURN x*x
END Square;
```

Invocation examples:

```
VAR  x,y,z: REAL;
...
x := Square(3.0);                        x := 3.0²
y := 2.0 * Square(x+1.0);                y := 2.0 * (x+1.0)²
z := Square(Square(x) + Square(y));      z := (x² + y²)²
```

(b) The procedure BuildPowerOf2 from Section 3.7.1 takes the following form as function procedure PowerOf2:

```
PROCEDURE PowerOf2(n: CARDINAL) : CARDINAL;
  VAR
     i, power:  CARDINAL;
BEGIN
  power := 1;
  FOR  i:=1 TO n DO
    power := power*2
  END;
  RETURN power
END PowerOf2;
```

Note : power must be declared as a local variable, whereas in the original version computations were made directly with the VAR (output) parameter.

Invocation examples:

```
VAR  i,j:  CARDINAL;
. . .
i :=  PowerOf2(3);            (*i := 2³*)
j :=  PowerOf2(j*3) - 1;      (*j := 2^{j*3} - 1*)
```

(c) The procedure FindDouble in Section 3.7.3 can be reformulated as a function procedure DoublePos as follows:

```
PROCEDURE DoublePos(s:String; len:CARDINAL) : CARDINAL;
  VAR i: CARDINAL;
BEGIN
  IF (len=0) OR (len>100) THEN RETURN 0 END;
  FOR i := 1  TO  len-1  DO
    IF s[i] = s[i+1] THEN RETURN i END;
  END;
  RETURN 0
END DoublePos;
```

Invocation examples:

```
VAR
   string:  String;
   ch:      CHAR;
   i, len:  CARDINAL;
. . .
i := DoublePos(string,len-10);
IF DoublePos(string,50)>0 THEN
   string[DoublePos(string,50)+1] := " "
END
```

Note : The name changes in transforming the procedures to function procedures were deliberate! The original names accent the actions performed by the procedures, while the new names characterize the values returned by the function procedures. (Compare Section 5.1.2, "Choice of Names").

3.7.5 Scope and Lifetime of Objects in Procedures

In most of the examples presented so far, we made use of the possiblilty of declaring local variables. We now need to explain exactly what effect the declaration of these local variables has. Several questions need to be answered:

- Can one only work with local variables and parameters within procedures?

- Are the declarations of local variables known only in the procedures in which they occur?

- What values do local variables have at the beginning of the execution of a procedure?

- What happens to local variables after the procedure terminates?

These can be reduced to two basic questions:

- scope of declared objects:

   In which program segments are which objects known?

- lifetime of variables:

   In which time periods during the execution of a program do which variables "exist"?

Scope Rules

Every declared object can be assigned a scope that is based upon the position of the declaration in the program.

- The *scope* of an object (range in which it is known) is always the *block* of the procedure or module in which the declaration of the object occurs. This means that every object that is declared in a given procedure is known in all statements and subsequent declarations in that procedure, but not outside of the procedure.

- A procedure declaration can contain any number and kind of further declarations (not just variables, but also constants, types, procedures and local modules). If procedure P contains the declaration of a second procedure Q, we term Q an *internal procedure* of P. The scope of the name Q extends throughout the procedure P, but not outside of P (i.e., Q is not known outside of P and cannot be called there).

- All objects known in a procedure are also known in its internal procedures.

- Identical names can be used for distinct objects in different scopes. If both procedure P and its internal procedure Q declare objects with the name x, then only the object declared in Q itself is known within Q. Because the names are identical, the x declared in P is known only in P and not (as usual) in the internal procedure Q as well. The declaration of x in Q hides the x declared in P.

- Every object x declared in a procedure P is known in all declarations following that of x and in all statements in P as well as in internal procedures that are declared before x. The exception is internal procedures in which x is declared anew.

- Predefined identifiers (e.g., names of predefined data types) are "magically" visible everywhere as long as there is no other declaration of an object of the same name.

Figure 3.2 shows which identifiers are known in which program segments of a module. In order to prevent confusion between objects with identical names, we mark their scopes by indention. For the sake of clarity, the declaration of each object is marked with a circle.

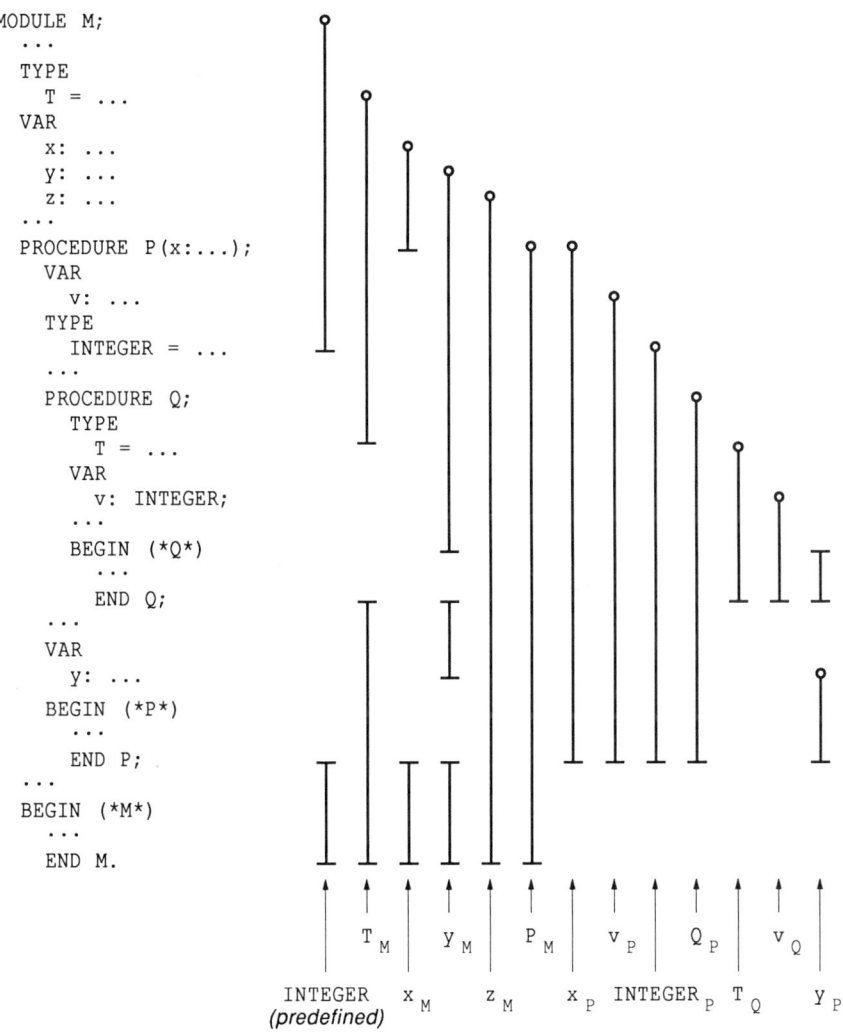

```
MODULE M;
  ...
  TYPE
    T = ...
  VAR
    x: ...
    y: ...
    z: ...
  ...
  PROCEDURE P(x:...);
    VAR
      v: ...
    TYPE
      INTEGER = ...
    ...
    PROCEDURE Q;
      TYPE
        T = ...
      VAR
        v: INTEGER;
      ...
      BEGIN (*Q*)
        ...
        END Q;
    ...
    VAR
      y: ...
    BEGIN (*P*)
      ...
      END P;
  ...
  BEGIN (*M*)
    ...
    END M.
```

Fig. 3.2 Scopes of names in procedures

Lifetime

Scope is a purely *static* characteristic of objects. For any point in the source code of a Modula-2 program, the identifiers that are known and can be used can be determined. The lifetime of these identifiers is another question. This is a *dynamic* characteristic and is defined only for variables:

- With the beginning of the execution of a procedure, storage is reserved for the local variables declared therein (as well as for formal value (no VAR) parameters).

- The value of local variables is *undefined* at the beginning of execution. They need to be initialized with valid values before they are used.

- The formal parameters have the same values at the start of a procedure as the actual parameter in the procedure call. The values of formal parameters (e.g., VAR parameters to be computed) can also have undefined values at the start of the procedure, depending on whether values were assigned to them before invocation.

- The storage reserved for local variables and value parameters is maintained as long as the procedure is active. A procedure is considered active even while another procedure invoked by it is executing (i.e., several procedures can be active simultaneously).

- As soon as execution of a procedure is terminated (regardless of whether after the last statement or via a RETURN statement), all reserved storage for its local variables and value parameters is freed (deallocated). This means that

  (a) the values of the local variables are lost forever, and

  (b) the freed storage can be used for other purposes (e.g., other procedure calls).

3.7.6 Data Exchange Between Procedures and Invoking Program Units

Every procedure describes an algorithm for the solution of a certain problem. Since, as a rule, procedures compute desired (output) objects from given (input) objects, we want to describe all mechanisms for providing a procedure with input objects and for receiving the computed output objects. These mechanisms are:

- parameters,
- function values, and
- nonlocal variables.

In order to show these mechanisms clearly, we will use an example to compute the arithmetic meancontinuously:

In a series of test measurements, for each value `val` the arithmetic mean `ave` of all measurements up to that point is to be computed. We will need the auxiliary objects `sum` for the cumulative total and `num` for the number of readings:

```
input object:      val: REAL
output object:     ave: REAL
auxiliary objects:    sum, num: REAL          (input/output)
sum :=   sum + val;
num :=   num + 1.0;
ave :=   sum/num
```

Parameters

Data exchange by means of parameters is the most general and most flexible solution:

- All objects to be exchanged appear both in the procedure declaration and in the procedure call in the parameter lists.

- Output and input/output objects are recognizable as such (key word VAR) in the procedure declaration.

- Parameter data types are not restricted.

- Different actual parameters can be used with each procedure call.

However, if a procedure has numerous parameters, then the use of a parameter list can be clumsy on account of its length. In addition, care must be taken to match the *order of parameters* in the actual parameter list to those in the formal parameter list.

Example

Procedure declaration:

```
PROCEDURE ComputeAverage(x:REAL; VAR sum,num,ave: REAL);
   BEGIN
      sum := sum + x;
      num := num + 1.0;
      ave := sum/num
   END ComputeAverage;
```

Procedure invocation:

```
sum := 0.0;   num := 0.0;
ComputeAverage(val, sum, num, ave);
ComputeAverage(val*val, sum, num, ave);
```

Function Values

If a procedure returns only *one* output value, it can be formulated as a function procedure with the function value as output object. This has the following advantages:

- If the result of the procedure is needed in an expression, then the procedure invocation can be used directly at the appropriate position in the expression.

- The procedure name can be selected so that it suggests the meaning of the function value.

The disadvantage of function procedures is that ARRAYs, RECORDs and SETs are excluded as function types.

Example

Procedure declaration:

```
PROCEDURE Average(x: REAL; VAR sum, num: REAL): REAL;
BEGIN
   sum := sum + x;
   num := num + 1.0;
   RETURN sum/num
END Average;
```

Procedure invocation:

```
sum := 0.0;  num := 0.0;
ave := Average(val, sum, num);
IF Average(val*val, sum, num) > 1000 THEN ...
```

Nonlocal Variables

If a procedure employs numerous objects that remain the same from invocation to invocation and are common to the procedure's environment, it can be advantageous to declare them outside the procedure (nonlocally) instead of listing them in a long parameter list with each invocation. This method has the disadvantage of a procedure/environment interface (the input and output objects) that is no longer clearly recognizable in the procedure declaration or in the procedure invocation, which makes the procedure less understandable.

Example

Procedure declaration:

```
VAR
   sum, num:  REAL;    (* nonlocal objects *)
.  .  .
PROCEDURE Average(x: REAL): REAL;
BEGIN
   sum := sum+x;    num := num+1.0;
   RETURN sum/num
END Average;
```

Procedure invocation:

```
sum := 0.0;   num := 0.0;
ave := Average(val);
IF Average(val*val) > 1000 THEN ...
```

Our exemplary procedure in its last form uses all three possibilities of data exchange:

- The measurement value to be processed is passed to the procedure as a value parameter.

- The resulting arithmetic mean is returned as a function value.

- The auxiliary objects `sum` and `num` are nonlocal variables and are thus maintained automatically from one invocation to another.

Such hybrid forms are to be used with caution. Above all, the "hidden" nonlocal variables can often lead to undesirable *side effects*. Consider these statement sequences:

```
a)    sum := 0.0;   num := 0.0;
      ave := Average(1.0) + Average(num);

b)    sum := 0.0;   num := 0.0;
      ave := Average(num) + Average(1.0);
```

At a glance, it would seem that the value of ave is the same in both cases because of the commutativity of addition. Since, however, the function procedure Average changes the value of num with each invocation, the upper statement sequence returns ave=2.0, while the second one returns ave=0.5 (assuming that the left invocation is executed first, which depends on the compiler).

We thus recommend using function procedures only when they do nothing but compute a function value.

3.7.7 ARRAY Parameters

One of the most important characteristics of Modula-2 is that objects that are combined or assigned to one another must match in terms of data type. This allows the compiler to catch many careless errors made in the design of a program. On the other hand, this limitation leads to some inconveniences in programming. If, for example, these three data types

```
Name       = ARRAY [0..19] OF CHAR;
Address    = ARRAY [0..99] OF CHAR;
Text       = ARRAY [1..1000] OF CHAR;
```

are contained in a Modula-2 program, we would have to write three procedures to check whether a particular character occurs in three variables using the three data types Name, Address and Text:

```
PROCEDURE IsInName(x: Name; ch: CHAR): BOOLEAN;
PROCEDURE IsInAddress(x: Address; ch: CHAR): BOOLEAN;
PROCEDURE IsInText(x: Text; ch: CHAR): BOOLEAN;
```

The statement sequences in the three procedures are basically the same. They differ only in that the character ch is searched for in one case between x[0] and x[19] (IsInName) and in another case between x[1] and x[1000] (IsInText).

In Section 3.7.1, "Declaration of Procedures," we noted (in explaining the formal parameter list of a procedure) that the data type of a formal parameter can be preceded by the key words ARRAY OF. This mechanism makes it possible to formulate a general-purpose procedure that takes array arguments: from invocation to invocation, various ARRAYs with identical element types but different index types can be passed as parameters. For a procedure with the formal parameter specification

ARRAY OF T

any actual parameter can be used which has the data type

ARRAY I OF T

whereby the index type I plays no role.

The above problem with array parameters can now be solved with an open array parameter that is valid for any character array:

```
PROCEDURE IsInString(x:ARRAY OF CHAR; ch:CHAR): BOOLEAN;
```

Within the procedure, the formal parameter x is handled as though it had the data type

```
ARRAY[0..maxIndex] OF CHAR;
```

The value of the highest valid index (maxIndex) depends on the number of elements in the actual parameter. The standard procedure HIGH (see Section 3.7.8) can be used in the procedure to determine the highest index of the formal parameter x for the respective actual parameter. HIGH(x) always returns a number one less than the number of elements in the actual parameter:

type of the actual parameter	HIGH(x)
Name	19
Address	99
Text	999

The formal ARRAY parameter x in IsInString can only be referenced element by element (i.e., indexed) or again passed as an actual parameter in a further procedure invocation (whereby the respective formal parameter of a successively invoked procedure must again be an open parameter with the same element type).

We can now formulate the procedure IsInString as follows:

```
PROCEDURE IsInString(x:ARRAY OF CHAR; ch:CHAR): BOOLEAN;
VAR  i: CARDINAL;
BEGIN
  FOR i := 0 TO  HIGH(x)   DO
    IF x[i] = ch THEN RETURN TRUE END
  END;
  RETURN FALSE
END IsInString;
```

Note that indices of open ARRAY parameters always begin with 0.

3.7.8 Standard Procedures

Just as there are predefined identifiers for the elementary data types that can be used in any Modula-2 program, predefined (standard) procedures are also provided to solve certain often recurring problems. Some of these procedures could be written in Modula-2; others permit parameters of various data types or even a variable number of parameters, thus breaking through the syntax for normal procedures.

We will group the Modula-2 standard procedures according to their applications:

Conversion Functions

    r := FLOAT(c)

> converts the CARDINAL expression c to a REAL number with the same numeric
> value (FLOAT(2+3) returns 5.0).

    c := TRUNC(r)

> converts the REAL expression r to a CARDINAL number. Any decimal portion
> is truncated (cut off) (TRUNC(7.0/3.0) results in 2). The value of r must be in
> the CARDINAL range (e.g., it must be positive), otherwise the result of TRUNC is
> undefined.

    c := ORD(x)

> returns the ordinal number (of type CARDINAL) of the expression x, which can
> be INTEGER, CARDINAL, CHAR, or BOOLEAN as well as a subrange or
> enumeration type. In the enumeration type (red,blue,yellow,green), for
> example, ORD(yellow) would return 2 and ORD(red) would return 0.

    v := VAL(T,c)

> converts the CARDINAL expression c to a *target type* T with the same value.
> Note that T must be the *name of a type*, which can be INTEGER, CARDINAL,
> CHAR, BOOLEAN, or a subrange or an enumeration type. VAL(E,2) with
> E=(e1,e2,e3,e4) returns e3; VAL(E,0) returns e1. VAL(T,ORD(x)) returns x
> itself if the data type of x is T.

    ch := CHR(c)

> converts the CARDINAL expression c to the character ch that has the ordinal
> number c.

> Using the ASCII character set as a basis, we have

        CHR(65) = "A"   (ORD("A") = 65)
        CHR(12) = 14C   (ORD(14C) = 12)
    CHR(c) returns the same character as VAL(CHAR,c).

    ch1 := CAP(ch2)

> converts the letter ch2 to an upper-case letter. If ch2 is not a letter, the value of
> CAP(ch2) is undefined.

        CAP("g") = "G"   CAP("E") = "E"

Arithmetic Operations

    INC(x)

> increments (raises) the value of x by 1. The data type of x can be INTEGER,
> CARDINAL, CHAR, BOOLEAN, or a subrange or enumeration type.

> If INC is applied to a CHAR type, then the returned value is the character whose
> ordinal number is one more than that of x. That is, INC(x) returns the same

character as x:=CHR(ORD(x)+1); the statement sequence x:="F"; INC(x) returns x="G".

If INC is applied to an enumeration type, then after the execution of INC(x), x is the enumeration constant that is the immediate successor to the original value of x. That is, INC(x) returns the same value as x:=VAL(E,ORD(x)+1) for an enumeration type E.

INC(x,n)

increments the variable x by the value of the expression n. The data type of n must be CARDINAL.

INC(x,n) returns the same value as FOR i:=1 TO n DO INC(x) END.

DEC(x)

decrements (reduces) the value of x by 1. DEC(x) has the inverse effect of INC(x), i.e., the statement sequence INC(x); DEC(x) returns x.

DEC(x,n)

decrements the value of x by n. DEC(x,n) has the inverse effect of INC(x,n), i.e., the statement sequence INC(x,n); DEC(x,n) returns x.

The standard procedures INC and DEC can prove advantageous for modifying values of complex variables. The statement

```
x[i*2,j+1] := x[i*2,j+1]+1
```

can be written more simply as

```
INC(x[i*2,j+1])
```

which has the additional advantage that x[i*2,j+1] need not be evaluated more than once.

y := ABS(x)

returns the absolute value of the expression x (data type INTEGER, CARDINAL, or a subrange thereof; or REAL). y:=ABS(x) has the same effect as the statement IF x>=0 THEN y:=x ELSE y:=(-x) END.

b := ODD(x)

returns a boolean value that specifies whether expression x (data type INTEGER or CARDINAL or a subrange thereof) is an odd number. It returns the same result as x MOD 2 <> 0.

Ranges of Data Types

x := MIN(T)

returns the smallest value that can be represented by the data type T, whereby T can be INTEGER, CARDINAL, REAL, CHAR, BOOLEAN, or a subrange or enumeration type.

$$\begin{aligned}
&\text{MIN(INTEGER)} = -32768 \quad \text{(16-bit machine)}\\
&\text{MIN(CARDINAL)} = 0\\
&\text{MIN(CHAR)} = 0C\\
&\text{MIN(BOOLEAN)} = \text{FALSE}
\end{aligned}$$

x := MAX(T)

returns the largest value that can be represented by data type T under the same conditions as with MIN.

$$\begin{aligned}
&\text{MAX(INTEGER)} = 32767 \quad \text{(16-bit machine)}\\
&\text{MAX(CARDINAL)} = 65535\\
&\text{MAX(CHAR)} = 377C \quad\quad (= \text{CHR}(255))\\
&\text{MAX(BOOLEAN)} = \text{TRUE}
\end{aligned}$$

Set Operations

INCL(s,e)

includes the element described by the expression e in the SET s. The variable s must be a SET type (including BITSET). The data type of e must match the element type of s. INCL(s,e) returns the same result as s:=s+S{e}, whereby S=SET OF E and E is the data type of e.

EXCL(s,e)

excludes (removes) the element determined by the expression e from the SET s. EXCL(s,e) returns the same result as s:=s-S{e}, whereby S=SET OF E and E is the data type of e.

Determination of Array Bounds

c := HIGH(a)

returns the ordinal number (a CARDINAL type) of the upper bound of an ARRAY a. If a is declared as ARRAY [min..max] OF T, then HIGH(a) returns the same value as ORD(max).

Program Termination

HALT

terminates program execution. If HALT is invoked within a procedure, then not just the procedure but *all active procedures* and the *main program* are terminated.

Dynamic Memory Allocation

NEW(p)

allocates a region of memory for an object of data type T and assigns its starting address to the POINTER variable p, whereby p is defined as POINTER TO T and

T can be any data type. After execution of NEW(p), the newly allocated region of memory can be accessed with the help of the designator p^.

NEW(p,t1,t2,...)

allocates a region of memory for a RECORD with variants. p must be declared as POINTER TO RECORD ... , and t1,t2,... must be constants that are used to discriminate among variants. If p is declared as

```
POINTER TO RECORD
  a: CARDINAL;
  CASE b: BOOLEAN OF
    TRUE: c: CHAR;
  | FALSE:
      d: INTEGER
      CASE e: Enum OF      (*with Enum=(x,y)*)
        x: f: BOOLEAN
      | y: g,h: CARDINAL
      END (*CASE e*)
    END (*CASE b*)
END (*RECORD*)
```

then NEW(p,TRUE) stipulates that only enough memory be allocated to contain a RECORD with b=TRUE, i.e., with the three components a, b and c. The second parameter of NEW serves to determine which variant of the outer CASE construct is to be allocated. The invocation NEW(p) allocates enough memory to cover even the largest variant. NEW(p) has the same effect as NEW(p,FALSE). If further differentiation is to occur within a variant, this can take place with further parameters in NEW. The invocation NEW(p,FALSE,x) causes the allocation of memory that is just large enough to contain a, b, d, e and f. The invocation NEW(p,FALSE,y) allocates (as NEW(p) and NEW(p,FALSE)) the maximum amount of memory that needs to be allocated (components a, b, d, e, g, and h).

Caution! Invoking NEW(p) with specification of a certain variant *does not cause the initialization of its corresponding tag fields..*

DISPOSE(p)

frees (deallocates) the memory allocated by NEW(p), i.e., p^ cannot be used again.

DISPOSE(p,t1,t2,...)

frees the memory allocated by the corresponding NEW(p,t1,t2,...). The parameter lists of NEW and DISPOSE must match, otherwise memory other than that allocated for the variable will be freed, which can lead to unpredictable run time errors.

During compilation, invocations of the procedures NEW and D ISPOSE are transformed into two procedures named ALLOCATE and DEALLOCATE as follows:

```
NEW(p)                  ALLOCATE(p,TSIZE(T))
NEW(p,t1,t2,...)        ALLOCATE(p,TSIZE(T,t1,t2,...))
```

```
DISPOSE(p)                      DEALLOCATE(p,TSIZE(T))
DISPOSE(p,t1,t2,...)            DEALLOCATE(p,TSIZE(T,t1,t2,...))
```

This means that the procedures ALLOCATE and DEALLOCATE must be accessible to the program. The easiest way to handle this is to import the library procedures ALLOCATE and DEALLOCATE from Storage, the module responsible for dynamic memory allocation, by means of the following line:

```
FROM Storage IMPORT ALLOCATE, DEALLOCATE;
```

Note : The procedure TSIZE returns the size in memory of any given data type. It is discussed further in Section 3.9.1, "The Module SYSTEM."

Detailed examples for working with dynamic memory allocation can be found in Section 4.3, "Dynamic Data Structures."

3.7.9 PROCEDURE Types and Procedure Variables

In some cases, certain data structures have to be processed in several ways, each differing only minimally from the others. One such example is the sorting of a personnel file for a company. It could be sorted alphabetically by name, or in ascending order by personnel number, or in descending order by salary. We will use the following declaration for the personnel file:

```
TYPE
   Employee = RECORD
                 personnelNo:  CARDINAL;
                 name:         ARRAY[1..30] OF CHAR;
                 salary:       REAL;
                 ...
              END;
   PersonnelFile = ARRAY [1..1000] OF Employee;
VAR
   file: PersonnelFile;
   count: CARDINAL;    (* number of employees *)
```

We will use the *selection method* in order to sort the file. In the process, the array file is divided into a sorted and an unsorted part. The sorted part is repeatedly increased in size by one by "selecting" the smallest element in the unsorted part and swapping it with the first element in the unsorted part.

```
PROCEDURE Sort(VAR file: PersonnelFile; count: CARDINAL);
   VAR
     n:      CARDINAL;   (* length of sorted part *)
     min:    CARDINAL;   (* index of smallest element *)
     h:      Employee;   (* auxiliary for swaps only *)
     i:      CARDINAL;
```

```
BEGIN
  FOR  n:=1  TO  count-1  DO
    (* find smallest element in file[n..status] *)
    min := n;
    FOR  i:=n+1  TO  count DO
      IF  Smaller(file[i], file[min])  THEN  min:=i  END
    END;
    (* swap the smallest element with file [n] *)
    h := file[n]; file[n] := file[min]; file[min] := h;
    (* file[1..n]  are now sorted *)
  END
END Sort;
```

In order to determine the smallest element in the unsorted part of the array, we use the function procedure Smaller, whose boolean value determines whether the employee given by the first parameter is to be ordered before the second. This means that the order of the sorted array is not dependent upon the sorting algorithm itself, but upon the comparison procedure Smaller.

However, in order to fulfill the original task of sorting according to three different criteria, we need to write three different function procedures that can be invoked by the procedure Sort.

Modula-2 permits an elegant solution to such problems using *procedure variables*. A procedure variable describes a procedure rather than an object as we have been accustomed to thus far. Once a procedure P has been assigned to the procedure variable pv, pv can be invoked as a procedure. This invocation has the same effect as the invocation of the procedure P.

Procedure variables have to be declared as any variable does. Their type must be PROCEDURE (see Section 3.4.3, "Type Declarations").

ProcedureType$_{57}$

FormalTypeList$_{58}$

- The description of a PROCEDURE type begins with the key word PROCEDURE, which can be followed by a description of the data types of the formal procedure parameters (FormalTypeList). If the FormalTypeList is omitted, then ProcedureType describes a procedure without parameters.

- FormalTypeList establishes

  - how many parameters are associated with a PROCEDURE type, their data types (FormalType—see Section 3.7.1, "Declaration of Procedures"), and whether they are value or VAR parameters;

  - whether the PROCEDURE type describes a function procedure and, if so, the type of its resultant function value.

Examples

```
TYPE
    RealProc  =   PROCEDURE (REAL, VAR REAL);
    RealFunc  =   PROCEDURE (REAL) : REAL;
    MeanProc  =   PROCEDURE (REAL, VAR REAL, VAR REAL, VAR REAL);
    FindFunc  =   PROCEDURE (ARRAY OF CHAR, CHAR) : BOOLEAN;
```

RealProc describes a procedure with two REAL parameters, of which the first is a value parameter and the second is a VAR parameter (compare ComputeSquare in Section 3.7.1).

RealFunc describes a function procedure with a REAL parameter and a function value of type REAL (compare Square in Section 3.7.4).

MeanProc describes a procedure with a REAL value parameter and three REAL VAR parameters (compare ComputeAverage in Section 3.7.6).

FindFunc describes a function procedure with one ARRAY parameter with element type CHAR and one CHAR parameter; it returns a boolean function value (compare IsInString in Section 3.7.7).

A procedure variable pv, for example, which is declared as

```
VAR pv: RealFunc;
```

could be used as follows:

```
pv := Square;  (*assignment of procedure Square to pv*)
...
q := pv(x);    (* invocation of the procedure Square *)
```

The following points are to be noted:

- Only procedures that are *not declared locally in other procedures* can be assigned to a procedure variable. This restriction is necessary in order to avoid attempted invocations of internal procedures at points where they are unknown.

- No standard procedure may be assigned to a procedure variable.

- The procedure variable and the procedure assigned to it must be *procedure compatible* (see the definition below).

- In an assignment statement, the assigned procedure can only be referenced by its name, i.e., no parameter list may follow. Square(x) represents an invocation of the procedure, while Square is the procedure itself.

Note: When a parameterless function procedure is invoked, empty parentheses must be added for exactly this reason—to show that it is a procedure invocation.

Procedure compatibility between a procedure variable pv and a procedure P means that:

- pv and P have the same number of formal parameters.

- The formal parameters of pv and P match one to one; that is, the ith parameter in pv and the ith parameter in P must

  – be of the same data type (FormalType), and

  – both be value parameters or both be VAR parameters.

- pv and P must either not be function procedures, or their function values must be of the same type.

Beyond being assigned to procedure variables, procedures can be used as actual parameters in procedures invocations, assuming that the corresponding formal parameter is of the type PROCEDURE. This leads us to a solution to our sorting problem. Here are the necessary steps:

(1) declaration of a PROCEDURE type for comparisons:

```
TYPE Comparison = PROCEDURE(Employee,Employee):BOOLEAN;
```

(2) inclusion of the comparison procedure Smaller in the parameter list of Sort:

```
PROCEDURE Sort(VAR file: PersonnelFile; count: CARDINAL;
               Smaller: Comparison);
```

(3) writing the comparison procedures:

```
PROCEDURE ByName(e1,e2: Employee) : BOOLEAN;
  VAR i: [0..30];
BEGIN
  i := 0;
  REPEAT
    INC(i)
  UNTIL (e1.name[i] <> e2.name[i])   OR   (i=30);
  RETURN  e1.name[i] < e2.name[i]
END ByName;

PROCEDURE ByNumber(e1,e2: Employee) : BOOLEAN;
BEGIN
  RETURN  e1.personnelNo < e2.personnelNo
END ByNumber;

PROCEDURE BySalary(e1,e2: Employee) : BOOLEAN;
BEGIN
  RETURN e1.salary > e2.salary
END BySalary;
```

Each of these procedures returns TRUE if employee e1 is to be ordered before employee e2. Otherwise (if e2 is to be ordered before e1, or if the two are the same, as, for example, with equal salaries) FALSE is returned. In comparing names alphabetically, identical characters at the beginning of a pair of names are simply skipped. The result of the test thus depends on the first pair of characters that are not the same, or on the 30th letter if the two names are identical.

(4) invocation of the procedure Sort with various comparison procedures as actual parameters:

```
Sort(file,count,ByName);
Sort(file,count,ByNumber);
Sort(file,count,BySalary);
```

Since procedures without parameters are often used as procedure variables, Modula-2 provides the predefined data type PROC, which is defined as

```
TYPE PROC = PROCEDURE;
```

We will be encountering this type again in Section 3.10, "Processes and Coroutines," since parameterless procedures play an important role in programming parallel processes.

Exercises

(1) Write a procedure that converts a measurement given in meters to feet and inches (1 inch = 2.54 cm). Use the following procedure heading:

```
ConvertMetricToEnglish(meter:REAL;
                        VAR feet: CARDINAL; VAR inches: REAL);
```

(2) A typesetter is to number the x pages of a book. First, the number of each of the digits 0-9 needed for the numbering job is to be calculated. Write a procedure to handle this job. The number of digits needed is to be returned to the invoking procedure in the form of an array. Use the following procedure heading:

```
Digits(x: CARDINAL; VAR count: ARRAY OF CARDINAL);
```

(3) Write a procedure that inserts the character string string2 with length len2 at position pos in character string string1 with length len1. Both strings have a maximum length of 80 characters. If the insertion of string2 in string1 extends string1 past 80 characters, it is to be truncated after the 80th character. Use the following procedure heading:

```
PROCEDURE Insert(VAR string1:ARRAY OF CHAR; VAR len1: CARDINAL;
                 pos: CARDINAL;
                 string2:ARRAY OF CHAR; len2: CARDINAL);
```

(4) A character string w with length 2 which contains an abbreviated name of a weekday is to be converted to a number n as follows:

W	SU	MO	TU	WE	TH	FR	SA	otherwise
n	1	2	3	4	5	6	7	0

Write a function procedure to solve this problem. Use the following procedure heading:

```
PROCEDURE Day(w: ARRAY OF CHAR):CARDINAL;
```

(5) Write a function procedure that counts how often the character `ch` occurs in the character string `k` of length `len`. Use the following procedure heading:

```
PROCEDURE Count(k:ARRAY OF CHAR; len:CARDINAL; ch:CHAR): CARDINAL;
```

(6) Formulate the standard procedures CAP and FLOAT in Modula-2.

(7) The task at hand is to test whether a given array with length `len` is a palindrome, that is, whether the contents read the same forwards and backwards. If the phrase is a palindrome, then the output parameter `correct` has the value TRUE, otherwise it is FALSE. The following procedure is supposed to solve the problem:

```
PROCEDURE Palindrome(string: ARRAY OF CHAR; len: CARDINAL; correct: BOOLEAN);
  VAR I:  INTEGER;
BEGIN
  i := 1;  DEC(len);
  WHILE i<len AND correct DO
    correct := string[i] = string[len];
    INC(i)
  END;
  RETURN correct
END Palindrome;
```

Check the procedure and correct any errors.

3.8 The Module Concept of Modula-2

Section 2.3 introduced the concept of a module. This concept is one of the most important aspects of the programming language Modula-2 (hence the name). This section is dedicated to showing in detail how modules can be implemented in Modula-2.

Section 3.3 established that each Modula-2 program can be viewed as a module. This is what is known as a *program module*. To implement modules in the sense of Section 2.3, Modula-2 provides two further kinds of module: one that facilitates separate compilation of program and another (the *local* module) that is enclosed in such program units.

3.8.1 Local Modules

Local modules can be defined in any block, i.e., in any program module and in any procedure (see Section 3.3, "Elementary Program Structure") and must be constructed according to the following rules:

ModuleDeclaration$_{59}$

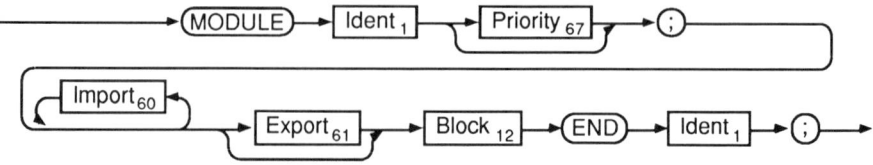

- A module begins with the key word MODULE, followed by the name of the module and a semicolon.

- An optional priority can follow the module name. The meaning of this priority will be explained in detail in Section 3.10.2, "Interrupts and Priorities."

- Any number of IMPORT statements and a single EXPORT statement can follow the module heading. Note that the order (first the IMPORTs, then the EXPORT) must be maintained.

- As was the case with program modules and procedures, the content of the module is described in a block that contains the declaration of local objects and procedures as well as a statement part.

- Every module is terminated with the key word END, the module name, and a semicolon.

IMPORT and EXPORT statements

Import$_{60}$

There are two forms of the IMPORT statement—with and without a preceding FROM. We are introducing them separately because the conditions governing them are quite different:

IMPORT without FROM

- The IMPORT statement consists of the key word IMPORT followed by a list of identifiers that are defined outside the module and used inside it. We term this the *import list*.

- All identifiers enumerated in the import list must be known in the block in which the module is declared.

- There are no restrictions on the kinds of identifiers that can be imported, i.e., they can be constants, data types, variables, procedures or modules.

- If a module name M is imported, then all identifiers that are exported from module M can be used within the importing module. However, they must be qualified with the name of the module (i.e., a procedure P exported from module M can only be invoked with M.P).

IMPORT with FROM

- The IMPORT statement begins with the key word FROM, followed by the name of a module M.

- The module M must be known in the block in which the importing module is declared.

- The key word IMPORT follows immediately, along with an import list with those identifiers that are exported by module M and used in the importing module.

- The key word FROM serves to qualify identifiers in the import list. That is, if procedure P is to be imported from module M, then the statement FROM M IMPORT P; already qualifies P by linking it to the module M. The procedure P can be used without the qualifying module name M.

Export61

- The EXPORT statement begins with the key word EXPORT followed by a list of all identifiers to be exported, the *export list*.

- The EXPORT statement makes all identifiers contained in its export list known to the immediate environment of the exporting module (i.e., the block in which the exporting module is declared), hence they can be used there.

- If an EXPORT statement contains the key word QUALIFIED, then the exported identifiers must, when used outside the module, be qualified with the name of the exporting module. We call this *qualified export* (in contrast to unqualified export without the key word QUALIFIED), and we use it to avoid name conflicts (e.g., if an exported identifier is declared in the enclosing block, or if several modules export identifiers with the same names).

- All identifiers in the export list must be declared in the block of the exporting module or be exported unqualified from an enclosed local module.

- There are no restrictions on the kinds of identifiers—i.e., constants, data types, variables, procedures, and modules—that can be exported.

Execution of a Module

Since a module represents a collection of objects and procedures, it cannot be invoked like a procedure. Constants, data types and variables exported by it can be used and procedures exported by it can be invoked. Since a module contains a block and a block consists of declarations *and statements*, a module can, like a procedure, contain a statement sequence (the *module body*). The statements contained therein are executed before the beginning of execution of the block in which the module is declared. The body of a local module within a program module (or an implementation module—see Section 3.8.3.2) is thus executed only once, whereas the body of a module within a procedure is executed each time the procedure is invoked. If a program module or a procedure contains several local modules, they are executed in the order of their declaration.

The module body can be used to assign initial values to local and exported variables in the module before the procedures and variables exported by the module are used. This is called *initialization* of the module. If no initialization is necessary in order to use a module, then the body of the module (and the key word BEGIN) can be omitted. In this case, the module contains only declarations (of constants, data types, variables procedures, and further local modules).

Example

We will show the implementation of local modules in the example of a *stack*. Stacks have the following general properties:

- A stack is a (possibly empty) list of elements. For the sake of simplicity, we assume that all elements are of the same type.

- The operation Push ($\downarrow$x) adds an element to the end of the stack.

- The operation Pop ($\uparrow$x) removes an element from the same end of the stack to which Push adds on. The stack is thereby made smaller by one element.

```
MODULE Stack;
  IMPORT WriteString;
  EXPORT Push, Pop, empty, full;

  VAR
    stack: ARRAY [1..100] OF CARDINAL;
    length: [0..100];
    empty, full: BOOLEAN;

  PROCEDURE Push(x: CARDINAL);
  BEGIN
    IF full THEN
      WriteString("stack full"); HALT
    END;
    INC(length);   stack[length] := x;
    empty := FALSE;   full := length=100
  END Push;

  PROCEDURE Pop(VAR x: CARDINAL);
  BEGIN
    IF empty THEN
      WriteString("stack empty");   HALT
    END;
    x := stack[length];   DEC(length);
    empty := length=0;   full := FALSE
  END Pop;
BEGIN    (* initialization of the module Stack *)
  length := 0;   empty := TRUE;   full := FALSE
END Stack;
```

If an error condition arises in Push or Pop (e.g., trying to remove an element from an empty stack), the procedure WriteString is used to output an error message. This procedure is known outside the module Stack and is imported by Stack.

In addition to the two procedures Push and Pop, Stack exports the two boolean variables empty and full, which indicate whether the bottom (0) or top (100) of the available stack has been reached. Before the module can be used, the exported variables and the local variable length have to be initialized.

Utmost care must be taken when variables are exported. In most applications, such variables serve only to provide the environment with information about the state of the module. They are not to be changed from the outside, since that could lead to faulty operation of the module. For example, were we to change the values of the exported variables empty or full (e.g., changing the value of the variable empty to FALSE when the stack is actually empty), an error in the management of the stack would result.

3.8.2 Scope and Lifetime of Objects in Modules

We have drawn attention to the central importance of IMPORT and EXPORT statements. Now we will take a closer look at the effects modules have on the scope of identifiers and at the lifetime of identifiers in modules.

Scope

For a procedure, any identifier in the enclosing block (that is not redeclared again in the procedure itself) is also automatically known in the procedure. By contrast, modules form an impenetrable wall that insulates the module from its enclosing environment. The following rules govern the communication of modules with their environment:

Import

- Within a module, only the following identifiers are known: those declared in the module itself, those explicitly or implicitly imported, and those exported by contained local modules.

- Explicitly imported identifiers are all those that are enumerated in the import list.

- If the name of a RECORD type is imported, its internal structure becomes visible. This means that components of such a RECORD can be accessed using their names.

- If the name of an enumeration type is imported, the names of its enumeration constants are implicitly imported.

- If the name of a module M is imported, the identifiers exported from M (whether qualified or unqualified) are *not* implicitly imported. The names exported by M can, however, be accessed via qualification with the module name. The notation FROM M EXPORT ... can be used if the names exported by M are to be accessed without qualification.

- Imported identifiers cannot be redefined within the importing module.

Export

- All identifiers exported by a local module are made known to its environment (the block in which the module is declared) by means of the EXPORT statement. Therefore, they must not already be known in that enclosing block.

- All identifiers exported by a module must either be declared in that module or exported unqualified by an enclosed module ("forwarding" export).

- In the case of a qualified export, all exported identifiers used outside the module have to be qualified with the module name. This permits identical names to be used in the enclosing block without conflict with the exported names.

- If a module uses only unqualified export, the exported names cannot be otherwise known outside of the module; i.e., they can neither be declared within the enclosing block nor exported by another module within the scope of the enclosing block.

- If the name of a RECORD type is exported, the names of its components become visible to the environment. If the name of an enumeration type is exported, the names of all its enumeration constants are exported, too.

- If the name of a module M is exported, all identifiers exported by M (whether qualified or unqualified) can be accessed in the enclosing block.by qualifying them with the module name M.

Lifetime

Compared to procedures, whose local variables exist only as long as their respective procedures are active, local variables in modules have a longer lifetime. They exist as long as the local variables in the block in which the module is declared.

- Memory is reserved for the local variables in a module M (including the exported ones) before the execution of the enclosing block in which M is declared.

- Immediately after this reservation of memory, the body of module M is executed.

- The lifetime of the local variables in module M ends once the last statement in the enclosing block in which M was declared has been executed.

Local variables in a module within a procedure have a lifetime that matches the lifetime of the variables in the procedure itself. Local variables in a local module enclosed immediately in a program module have a lifetime that extends throughout the entire program execution (and likewise for implementation modules—see Section 3.8.3.2).

3.8.3 Modules and Separate Compilation

We are thus far familiar only with program modules, which consist of executable statements and declarations of constants, data types, procedures, and modules. This allows us to solve many small problems in Modula-2. But as soon as we are confronted with a task whose solution requires thousands of statements, a huge Modula-2 program results, along with certain disadvantages in programming:

- The larger a program is, the harder it is to understand and to modify. The probability of a programming error increases more than proportionally with the length of the program. The trouble involved in finding and correcting an error proves to be disproportionately high.

- Compilation time increases with the length of the program. This means uncomfortably long waits for even small changes.

- Large projects are usually handled by teams whose members work on distinct subtasks. If all members have to work on a single program, coordination becomes an additional problem.

Modula-2 facilitates the development of large programs by encouraging their division into modules (compilation units) that are separately programmed and compiled. This is therefore known as *separate compilation*.

The communication of the various modules with one another is governed by a (precisely defined) module interface. A module can use (import) objects and procedures that are provided (exported) by another module.

During the compilation of a module M1 that uses objects and/or procedures from module M2, the identifiers that are exported by M2 and their meaning must be known to the compiler. The compilation of M1 does not require the entire module M2, but only a description of the exported identifiers. For this reason, a module is split into a *definition module* (the module's export interface) and an *implementation module* (the actual contents of the module). The two parts can (indeed, they must) be compiled separately, whereby the compilation of the definition module yields an interface description that the compiler can use in the compilation of the implementation module and other modules that import from this module.

The implications of separate compilation for the development of large program systems are discussed in detail in Section 6.4.

3.8.3.1 Definition Modules

A definition module has the task of describing how a module can be used "from the outside." It must therefore define all exported identifiers. Furthermore, it must define what meaning each identifier has. Hence a definition module contains the definition of all exported identifiers.

DefinitionModule$_{62}$

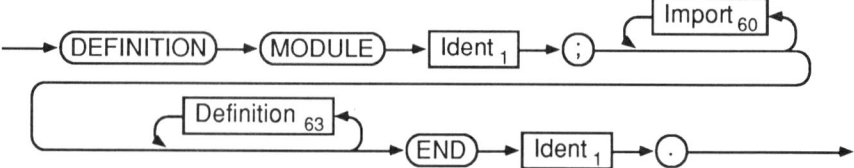

- A definition module begins with the key words DEFINITION MODULE and the name of the module followed by a semicolon.

- A definition module contains any number of IMPORT statements and a sequence of definitions of all exported identifiers.

- Every definition module terminates with the key word END, the module name, and a period.

The definition of identifiers is similar to their declaration:

Definition$_{63}$

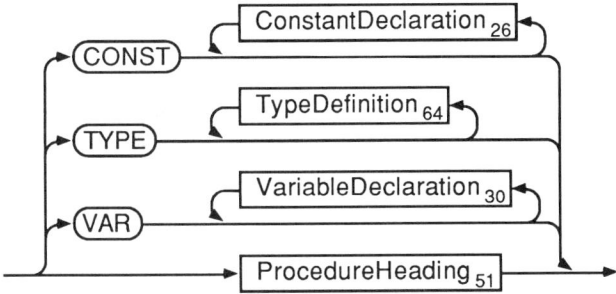

- A definition module can contain definitions of constants, data types, variables, and procedures.

- Definitions of constants and variables are constructed exactly like declarations of the same.

- A procedure definition consists of the procedure heading alone. This establishes how the procedure can be invoked (name of the procedure, parameter list, function type if necessary). Local declarations and the statements of the procedure body are not required for the export.

TypeDefinition$_{64}$

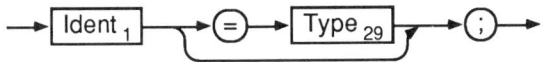

- A type definition is constructed like a type declaration (see Section 3.4.3). It normally consists of a name followed by an equal sign and the description of the data type.

- In contrast to a type *declaration*, the description of the data type can be omitted in a type *definition*. In such a case, the name Ident is merely defined as a type name; the exact data type remains hidden. We call such an export *opaque*. If an opaque type is imported by another module, it can be used in the declaration of variables. This allows us to use opaque data types for the implementation of *abstract data types* whose actual construction is known only to the exporting module. Variables with abstract data types permit only assignments, tests for equality/inequality and those operations that are provided as procedures by the exporting module.

Example

In order to show how a definition module and the corresponding implementation module are made up, we will use a stack as an example once again. We will require that the module `Stacks` be capable of managing multiple stacks. To accomplish this, we introduce the abstract data type `Stack`:

```
DEFINITION MODULE Stacks;

    TYPE Stack;

    PROCEDURE CreateStack(VAR s:Stack);
    PROCEDURE Push(VAR s: Stack; x: CARDINAL);
    PROCEDURE Pop(VAR s: Stack; VAR x: CARDINAL);
    PROCEDURE Empty(s: Stack): BOOLEAN;

END Stacks.
```

The definition module `Stacks` contains no IMPORT statements, which are necessary only if constants or data types that are exported by another module are needed for the definition of the exported names in the given module.

If we want multiple stacks, we will need a function that creates new stacks. Our procedure for this purpose, called `CreateStack`, returns an empty stack.

In addition to the element x to be added to or removed from the stack, the procedures `Push` and `Pop` require the additional parameter s, which identifies which stack is to be manipulated.

The module `Stacks` could be used by another module as follows:

```
    ...
    FROM Stacks IMPORT Stack, CreateStack, Push, Pop, Empty;
    ...
    VAR
       s, t: Stack;
       x: CARDINAL;
    ...
    BEGIN
       ...
       CreateStack(s);
       CreateStack(t);
       Push(s,125);
       Push(t,x*2);
       ...
       IF NOT Empty(s) THEN
          Pop(s,x); Push(t,x)
       END;
```

3.8.3.2   Implementation Modules

The definition module establishes which names are exported and what they mean. The task of the corresponding implementation module is to complete the incomplete declarations in the definition module, i.e.:

- The implementation module must contain the complete declarations of all opaque data types contained in the definition module.

- The actual declaration of an opaque data type is limited to POINTER types (according to language definition). Some Modula-2 implementations permit other data types as well.

    Note : The limitation to POINTER types might seem restrictive at first glance. Remember, however, that POINTER variables can point to objects of any data type.

- The implementation module must contain a complete procedure declaration for each procedure definition.

- All other names contained in the definition module cannot be declared again in the implementation module. They are automatically known because a definition module and its implementation module form a conceptual unit.

- An implementation module can contain any number of local (i.e., not exported) auxiliary variables and procedures (refer to Section 2.3, "The Module Concept").

An implementation module is constructed with the same rules as a program module (see Section 3.3, "Elementary Program Structure"). The only difference is that it begins with "IMPLEMENTATION MODULE" instead of just "MODULE."

ImplementationModule$_{65}$

An implementation module M can contain a statement part (module body) for the initialization of local variables, as was the case with local modules and program modules. If a module M1 imports module M, the body of M is executed before the body of M1. If several modules import M, the body of M is executed only once (before any of the importing module bodies).

Note : Modules can import each other (e.g., A imports B and B imports A). In this case, the order of execution of the module bodies is undefined. This can lead to unexpected results if, for example, the body of A invokes a procedure in B whose execution requires the initialization of module B.

Example

Let us now complete the implementation module Stacks. We first need to define what the data type Stack looks like. In order to avoid establishing an arbitrary maximum stack size (as in the example in Section 3.8.1, "Local Modules," we will use a linked list (see "POINTER Types" in Section 3.4.1.3 and Section 4.3, "Dynamic Data Structures"):

Every element in the stack consists of a value (val) and a pointer to its predecessor in the list. Thus a stack can be described fully by a pointer s to the top element in the stack. The bottom element in the stack is marked by the lack of a predecessor (pred = NIL). A stack is empty if s has the value NIL.

```
IMPLEMENTATION MODULE Stacks;

   FROM Storage IMPORT
      ALLOCATE, DEALLOCATE;
   FROM Terminal IMPORT WriteString;

   TYPE
      Stack = POINTER TO StackElem;
      StackElem =    RECORD
                        val: CARDINAL;
                        pred: Stack
                     END;

   PROCEDURE CreateStack(VAR s: Stack);
   BEGIN
      s := NIL
   END;

   PROCEDURE Push(VAR s: Stack; x: CARDINAL);
      VAR top: Stack;
   BEGIN
      NEW(top);  (* create new top stack element *)
      WITH top^ DO  val := x; pred := s  END;
      s := top
   END Push;

   PROCEDURE Pop(VAR s: Stack; VAR x: CARDINAL);
      VAR top: Stack;
   BEGIN
      IF Empty(s) THEN
         WriteString("stack empty"); HALT
      END;
      top := s;
      WITH top^ DO  x:=val;  s:=pred  END;
      DISPOSE(top)   (* remove topmost stack element *)
   END Pop;

   PROCEDURE Empty(s: Stack): BOOLEAN;
   BEGIN
      RETURN s=NIL
   END Empty;

END Stacks.
```

Exercises

(1) Write a module to simulate functions of an on-board computer for an automobile. Include procedures for initialization, for computation of the distance driven, and for computation of average speed for the trip. Use the procedure headings:

```
Start(miles: CARDINAL;  time: Time);
Distance(miles: CARDINAL; VAR dist: CARDINAL);
Speed(miles: CARDINAL;  time: Time;  VAR average: CARDINAL);
```

The data type Time is to be a RECORD. The procedure Start initializes the data capsule with the odometer reading and the current time (start time). Distance computes the distance covered since the start and Speed computes the average speed for the trip.

3.9 System-Dependent Language Properties

Thus far we have discussed only the kinds of Modula-2 language elements that are needed for application programs (for solving a particular problem). These language elements are problem-oriented, i.e., accomodating the way a programmer thinks. For practical use, we also need operations with which we can address the hardware of the computer. *Systems programming* has the job of providing those operations that extend beyond the range of a particular programming language.

Someone who writes system software must be able to access all parts of a given computer. For example, he has to be able to read the value of a particular storage cell and determine the storage requirement of variables. Since various computers have different properties, these operations do not function in the same way on every machine. They are therefore deliberately *not contained in the language definition*.

This section deals with the elements of Modula-2 that are dependent on the computer used. This list is not exhaustive and some implementations of Modula-2 may deviate herefrom (see Wirth 1985).

3.9.1 The Module SYSTEM

Every implementation of Modula-2 includes a fictive module SYSTEM, which exports several system-dependent data types and procedures. The Module SYSTEM can be imported as a global module. However, it does not consist of definition and implementation modules; instead, it is an imaginary module that is part of the compiler. This means that when the compiler encounters data types and procedures imported from SYSTEM while a program is being compiled, it already knows what they mean and how they are to be translated. This is necessary because the data types and procedures exported from SYSTEM cannot be expressed in Modula-2 itself, and they more or less represent a *language extension*.

The following definition module shows the kind of language elements that can be provided by SYSTEM. Elements that cannot be expressed in Modula-2 are written in italics:

```
DEFINITION MODULE SYSTEM;

  TYPE
    WORD;
    ADDRESS;
    PROCESS;

  PROCEDURE ADR(x:anytype ): ADDRESS;
  PROCEDURE SIZE(x:anytype ): CARDINAL;
  PROCEDURE TSIZE(anytype,tagconst,agconst,...):CARDINAL;
  PROCEDURE NEWPROCESS(P:PROC; a:ADDRESS; n:CARDINAL; VAR p:PROCESS);
  PROCEDURE TRANSFER(VAR from, to: PROCESS);

END SYSTEM.
```

The data type **WORD** designates one word of storage in the computer. Depending on the processor, this can have various lengths. No operations are possible on objects of type WORD. They can only be used in assignments and parameter lists. A variable that is assigned an object of type WORD must occupy exactly one word of storage (the data type WORD is assignment compatible with all types that require one word of storage).

If we assume a 16-bit machine and one word (2 bytes) of storage for the types CARDINAL, INTEGER and BITSET, then the following assignments are permissible:

```
VAR
  c:  CARDINAL;
  i:  INTEGER;
  b:  BITSET;
  w:  WORD;

BEGIN
  c := w;   w := c;
  i := w;   w := i;
  b := w;   w := b;
```

Note that the assignment b:=c is not permissible (BITSET and CARDINAL are not assignment compatible), yet the assignment sequence w:=c; b:=w is valid. This causes the bit pattern representing the CARDINAL number c to be assigned to the variable b without testing and without conversion. A programmer using such an assignment sequence must understand the internal representation of each of the data types in main memory.

The data type WORD has special meaning as a formal parameter in procedures. It allows, for example, the implementation of a stack for any data type that requires one word of storage:

```
PROCEDURE Push(x: WORD);
PROCEDURE Pop(VAR x: WORD);
```

The above declarations make the following invocations possible:

```
Push(c);  Push(i);  Push(b);
Push(i+3);  Push({1..7});
Pop(b);  Pop(i);  Pop(c);
```

ARRAY parameters with element type WORD are unique. Any data type can be passed to a formal parameter with type ARRAY OF WORD. We can produce a very general stack that can store not only simple objects (e.g., CARDINAL) but also structured objects (e.g., ARRAYs and RECORDs) simply by declaring the procedures Push and Pop as follows:

```
PROCEDURE Push(x: ARRAY OF WORD);
PROCEDURE Pop(VAR x: ARRAY OF WORD);
```

The data type **ADDRESS** designates a storage address in the computer. It can be considered as having the following declaration:

```
TYPE ADDRESS = POINTER TO WORD;
```

If a is a variable whose type is ADDRESS, then a^ designates the word of storage to which the address in a points.

The data type ADDRESS is *assignment compatible* with any POINTER type. Calculations can be made with ADDRESS variables as though they were CARDINALs. These properties allow the data type ADDRESS to be used in address computation in memory management modules (e.g., the module Storage; see Section 4.5, "Modules for Memory Management").

The following example shows a procedure that copies n words of storage starting at address from into a region of memory starting at address to:

```
PROCEDURE Copy(from, to: ADDRESS; n: CARDINAL);
  VAR i: CARDINAL;
BEGIN
  FOR  i:=1 to n DO
    to^ := from^ ;
    INC(from);  INC(to)
  END
END Copy;
```

The procedure **ADR** returns the address of a variable of any data type. It could be used to assign the contents of one structured variable to another structured variable:

```
TYPE  Rec =  RECORD
                a, b:  CARDINAL;
                c, d:  INTEGER;
             END;

VAR
  x: ARRAY[1..10] OF Rec;
  y: ARRAY[1..40] OF BITSET;

BEGIN
  Copy(ADR(x), ADR(y), 40)
```

Note : In this example, we assume that the data types INTEGER, CARDINAL, and BITSET all occupy one word of storage. The variables x and y thus are the same size. If this condition is not met, regions of memory can be overwritten, which can have unpredictable results.

The procedure **SIZE** returns the number of storage words occupied by a variable of any data type. With the help of SIZE, the procedure Copy in the above example can be reformulated as:

```
Copy(ADR(x), ADR(y), SIZE(y))
```

The procedure **TSIZE** can be used to determine how many words of storage a variable of a given data type occupies. The first parameter in TSIZE must be an identifier representing a data type. Based on the above declaration, the invocation TSIZE(Rec) returns the value 4.

If the first parameter of TSIZE is the name of a RECORD with variants, further parameters can be listed. These parameters must be constants and valid CASE values (see "RECORD Types" in Section 3.4.1.3). Such additional parameters serve to select a specific variant of the RECORD.

Consider, for example, the following RECORD type R:

```
TYPE R = RECORD
            a: CARDINAL;
            CASE b: BOOLEAN OF
               FALSE:  c: INTEGER
            | TRUE:    d,e:  CARDINAL
            END;    (* CASE b *)
            f: CARDINAL;
            CASE g:  BOOLEAN OF
               FALSE:  h,i:  CARDINAL
            | TRUE:      j:  BITSET;
                     CASE k:  CARDINAL OF
                        1:  l:  ARRAY [1..3] OF INTEGER
                     |  2:  m,n:  CARDINAL
                        ELSE  (* nothing *)
                        END  (* CASE k *)
            END  (* CASE g *)
        END;  (* RECORD *)
```

A variable of this data type could have the following appearance in the main memory of a computer (for a specific implementation):

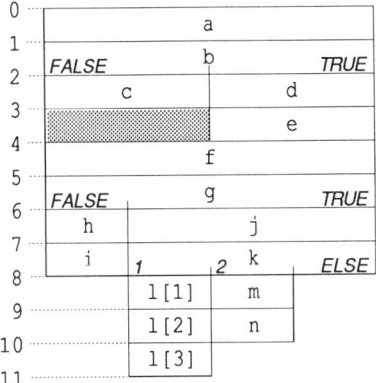

Fig. 3.3 Internal representation of a RECORD with variants

The components c and d overlap one another, as do the components h and j, i and k, l[1] and m, l[2] and n. Regardless of whether the CASE expression b is TRUE or FALSE, the component f must be stored at a fixed location within the RECORD. If b is FALSE, then c is followed by a void, and the size of the RECORD is not altered. Starting at g, however, values assumed by CASE expressions can influence the number of words of storage occupied by a RECORD with data type R (if g is FALSE, 8 words; if g is TRUE, a maximum of 11).

The second parameter of TSIZE corresponds to the *first CASE construct within the RECORD that is not followed by further components*. The invocation TSIZE(R,FALSE) returns the value 8; TSIZE(R,TRUE) returns 11. If a variant again contains a CASE construct that is not followed by further components, an additional parameter can produce further differentiation. In our example, TSIZE(R,TRUE,1) returns 1 (as do TSIZE(R,TRUE) and TSIZE(R)), while TSIZE(R,TRUE,2) returns 10, and TSIZE(R,TRUE,25) returns 8.

Note that the invocation TSIZE(R,FALSE,1) is not valid because the variant with g=FALSE has no successive CASE constructs. Likewise, TSIZE(R,1) is not valid because the first CASE construct that is not followed by further components requires a BOOLEAN value for selection of the variant.

Invocation of the standard procedures NEW and DISPOSE causes the compiler to generate the invocation of TSIZE (see Section 3.7.8, "Standard Procedures"). This means that memory can be saved in reserving storage for RECORDs with variants. This is particularly true if the variants have significant differences in storage requirements.

The data type **PROCESS** and the procedures **NEWPROCESS** and **TRANSFER** are for programming parallel processes. They are explained in detail in Sections 3.10, "Processes and Coroutines," and 4.6, "Parallel Processes."

3.9.2 Type Transfer Functions

Modula-2's strict type checking proves a big help in the development of application programs because it catches numerous errors during compilation. In systems programming, however, situations often arise that require a bit pattern to be read and processed in different ways (e.g., at one point as a CARDINAL number and at another as a BITSET).

For example, if we construe a CARDINAL variable *x* as a BITSET variable and want to test whether the element 4 is contained in the set, we have two possibilities for circumventing the type checking at our disposal so far:

(a) with the help of a RECORD with variants:

```
VAR
   x:  CARDINAL;
   convert:  RECORD
                  CASE:  BOOLEAN OF
                     FALSE: c:  CARDINAL
                     | TRUE:  b:  BITSET
                  END
              END;
BEGIN
   ...
   convert.c := x;
   IF 4 IN convert.b THEN ...
```

The variable x is stored in the component c of the conversion RECORD `convert`. Since the components c and b overlap (i.e., they occupy the same storage space), the bit pattern of the CARDINAL number `convert.c` can than be used as the BITSET `convert.b`. This assumes that `TSIZE(CARDINAL) = TSIZE(BITSET)`.

(b) with the help of the data type WORD:

```
VAR
   x:  CARDINAL;
   b:  BITSET;
   w:  WORD;
BEGIN
   ...
   w := x;  b := w;
   IF 4 IN  b  THEN ...
```

Assuming that `TSIZE(CARDINAL) = TSIZE(WORD) = TSIZE(BITSET)`, the CARDINAL number x can be assigned to a WORD w, which can in turn be assigned to the BITSET variable b. Type checking does not take place in either of these assignments, so b ends up with the same bit pattern as x.

In both cases, additional variables and assignments are necessary for the type transfer. This decreases the readability of the program. Since system progamming also depends on especially short run time, we want type conversion functions that do not depend upon additional statements.

Modula-2 allows such type conversions in a simple fashion by using the name of the target data type like a function procedure:

TypeTransfer$_{66}$

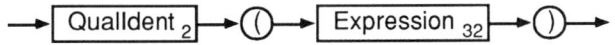

* QualIdent is the name of any data type t1.

* Expression is of data type t2, and TSIZE(t1) = TSIZE(t2) must be fulfilled.

* A type transfer function converts the bit pattern given by Expression to the data type given by QualIdent at compilation time, so run time is not affected.

Examples

```
VAR
    x:    CARDINAL;
    i,j:  INTEGER;
BEGIN
    ...
    IF 4 IN BITSET(x)   THEN ...
    i := j * INTEGER(x+1);
    x := CARDINAL(i);
    x := CARDINAL({0..15});
```

As the second example shows, type transfer functions can be used to combine INTEGER and CARDINAL numbers within an expression. (Remember that the data types INTEGER and CARDINAL are *not expression compatible*.)

The third example uses a type transfer function in order to assign an INTEGER value to a CARDINAL variable. Since the data types INTEGER and CARDINAL are *assignment compatible*, this assignment could be made without the help of a type transfer function in the form x:=i. Observe the following differences between the two approaches:

* x:=i first tests whether the variable i is positive. Only if this restriction is met is the value assigned to the variable x. Otherwise an error has occurred and execution terminates. This means that every assignment containing both INTEGERs and CARDINALs consumes time required for checking the sign.

* x:=CARDINAL(i) interprets the bit pattern in the variable i as a CARDINAL number and assigns this to variable x without testing whether i is positive. Even if the value of i is negative, its bit pattern represents a valid (positive!) CARDINAL number.

Type transfer functions depend upon the internal representation of the various data types in the computer. They should only be used with utmost caution and with exact knowledge of the computer being used.

Transfer functions do not need to be declared or imported. They could occur in a program, hidden in some "harmless" module, while the names imported from SYSTEM have to appear expressly in the import list of a module. Type transfer functions are thus easy to overlook when a program is being implemented on another computer. If the target computer uses other representations for data types, the results are unpredictable. For this reason, many Modula-2 compilers prohibit this form of type transfer, but rather provide a procedure VAL (or CAST) for this purpose that must explicitly be imported from SYSTEM.

3.9.3 Absolute Addressing of Variables

When we write a Modula-2 program, we normally cannot influence which storage cells (i.e., addresses) are to contain the declared variables at run time. Memory is allocated for variables during compilation; however, the final addresses are determined only when the program is loaded into memory for execution. Naturally, this is true only for global variables declared in the block of a module. The addresses of local variables in a procedure are established only when the procedure is invoked.

As long as we only write application programs, the addressing of variables is of no importance since we only use their values and do not need to know their location in memory.

Systems programming is another story. In order to be able to directly access operating system components or even to write parts of the operating system, direct access to certain memory cells is often required:

- In many operating systems, certain values reflecting states are stored at definite addresses (e.g., interrupt vectors, time).

- Some computers interface with peripheral devices by means of memory-mapped I/O. Certain memory addresses are linked to particular devices, so that reading such storage cells represents an input operation, while storing a value at such an address sends the value to the connected device.

We are familiar with one method of accessing particular memory addresses. For example, to store the value 255 at the address 36, we could use the data type ADDRESS:

```
VAR a: ADDRESS;
BEGIN
   ...
   a:= 36;   a^ := 255
```

Modula-2 has a construct designed to permit the specification of the absolute address of a variable when it is declared: after the name of the variable, one simply has to write the desired address enclosed in square brackets:

```
VAR  x[36]:  CARDINAL;
BEGIN
   x := 255
```

Note : Since the absolute addressing of variables is system-dependent and thus not part of the language definiton, it does not appear in the syntax diagram for VariableDeclaration.

The following example shows how a procedure for reading a character from the keyboard can be formulated with the help of absolute addressing of variables. We assume that the keyboard is connected to a serial port. The address 42 is associated with the data register of that port (and that is where we will find the respective character after a key has been pressed.) The status register (whose bit number 1 indicates whether a key has been pressed) is located at address 40; it is reset as soon as the respective character is retrieved from the data register.

```
...
VAR
   status[40]:  BITSET;
   key[42]:  CHAR;
...
PROCEDURE ReadKey(VAR ch: CHAR);
BEGIN
   REPEAT UNTIL 1 IN status;    (* wait for key *)
   ch := key                    (* return the key *)
END ReadKey;
```

3.10 Processes and Coroutines

We are now familiar with all the language elements necessary for the formulation of Modula-2 programs (which can consist of multiple modules). When a compiled program is executed by a certain computer (i.e., *processor*), we denote this as a process, which, once begun, continues to run undaunted until it reaches its end. Everyday life includes many examples of processes. Whether we are driving a car, writing a letter or making a telephone call, we can interpret all of our activities as individual processes and ourselves as processors. Processes in everyday life often occur simultaneously (i.e., in *parallel*). A pair of processes is termed parallel if, at a given point in time, both have begun and neither has terminated. We need to differentiate two types of parallelism:

- Two or more processors are working on various processes simultaneously (e.g., division of labor in a team).

  In this case we have *parallel processes in the actual sense of the term.* Problems arise because the processors usually do not work on strictly isolated tasks, but on related subtasks. They tend to be mutually dependent in such a way that one processor can only continue its work when another processor has completed a part of its task. A processor (and thus the process being executed by it) sometimes has to wait until another processor (process) provides some intermediate results. Therefore the processes periodically have to be brought back into harmony (i.e., they must be *synchronized*). In a programming team, one team member writing a Modula-2 program might have to wait for another team member to complete a procedure required by the former. Each of the programmers can only begin his/her work after the interfaces have been defined, and the program can only be executed when all parts are completed.

- A single processor "simultaneously" works on several processes (e.g., a simultaneous chess game).

If a single processor is to handle multiple tasks, this can only occur by *alternating* attention to the various tasks. There is no actual parallelism, which leads to the term *quasi-parallel* processes. The problems which arise concern *process transfer*, i.e., when the processor is to leave the process now being handled in order to attend to another process, and which process is next in line to be handled.

Most mainframes nowadays work with quasi-parallel processes. A powerful processor is connected to its users via multiple terminals (whose tasks represent processes for the computer). Once the processor has worked on one process "long enough," that process is suspended and processing resumes with another process in such a way that service to all users is as fair as possible.

One way to switch among processes is to allow processes to voluntarily release the processor, thus allowing the processor to resume with other processes. This special case of quasi-parallel processes is known as *coroutines* since the processes work together and surrender the processor at exactly defined points. An example is the simultaneous chess player who is released by one of his opponents and passed to the next opponent as soon as he has made a move.

Literary references to a multitude of mechanisms for process transfer can be found. Most of these concepts hover at a very high level, i.e., they require complex actions for the synchronization of processes. None of these mechanisms is general enough to solve all the problems related to parallel processes.

Therefore Modula-2 provides the programmer only the simple concept of coroutines. Surprisingly, this proves to be no limitation in the programming of parallel processes. Moreover, all the common methods of synchronization of processes can be reproduced with the help of coroutines (Section 4.6, "Parallel Processes," gives an example). The following sections discuss only (parallel) *processes*. We prefer this term because of its succinctness; the reader should remember that coroutines are actually meant.

3.10.1 Creation and Synchronization of Processes

The implementation of parallel processes is extremely dependent upon the particular computer being used. Therefore, all Modula-2 language elements that have to do with coroutines are defined in the module SYSTEM (see Section 3.9.1).

A process in Modula-2 is described by the data type PROCESS, which can be seen as an opaque data type (see Section 3.8.3.1, "Definition Modules"):

```
TYPE PROCESS;
```

The only actions permitted with processes are provided by the procedures NEWPROCESS and TRANSFER.

```
PROCEDURE NEWPROCESS (P: PROC;   a: ADDRESS; n: CARDINAL; VAR p:
PROCESS);
PROCEDURE TRANSFER (VAR from, to: PROCESS);
```

The procedure **NEWPROCESS** creates a new process p. It requires three parameters for the description of a process:

- a parameterless procedure P that contains the actions to be carried out by the process p;

- a start address a of a region of memory (*workspace*) that can be used by the process;

- the size n (number of words of memory) of the workspace.

An invocation of NEWPROCESS only creates the process p; it does not activate it. The process is put in a wait state.

Every process requires work space in which the local variables of the process and its invoked procedures can be stored. If only one process p1 (a main program) is running in a system, then all the computer's free space is available to it. As soon as a second process is added, part of this free memory has to be delineated for use by p2 alone (i.e., p1 cannot have access to it). The choice of the size of this region of memory for p2 (the parameter n) is a matter of fine-tuned intuition. n must be large enough to meet the memory requirements of all procedure invocations in the course of the execution of p2 (caution if there are recursive procedures!). On the other hand, memory available to p1 must not be too restricted. A rule-of-thumb lower limit for n is 100.

The procedure **TRANSFER** serves to explicitly switch processes. Within a process p1, the invocation of TRANSFER(p1,p2) causes process p1 to be suspended and process p2 to be resumed where it was last suspended or at the beginning of p2 if p2 was only created with NEWPROCESS but not yet activated.

A given process can be either *active* or *suspended*. A process created by NEWPROCESS and not yet activated counts as suspended. If only one processor is available, only one process can be active at a given time. The state of a suspended process is stored in a variable of type PROCESS. It is described by a series of system-dependent quantities (next command to be executed, register contents, interrupt mask, etc.). The process variable for the active process is meaningless since these quantities change continuously.

The invocation TRANSFER(p1, p2) means that

(1) the currently active process is suspended and all the parameters depicting its state are stored in the variable p1; and

(2) the process described by p2 is activated (i.e., the process is resumed at the state that was stored in p2).

While the process p2 is active, TRANSFER(p2, p1) can switch back to the original process p1; or TRANSFER(p2, p3) can switch on to another process.

When an active process ends (e.g., by encountering its last statement, a RETURN, or a run time error), it is not possible to resume processes currently in an interrupted state because this can only be attained by the invocation of TRANSFER. Thus the end of a process means the end of the whole program.

Since the actions of a process are determined in the statement part of a parameterless procedure, the question arises of how several processes can communicate with one another. As shown in Section 3.7.6, "Data Exchange Between Procedures and Invoking Program Units," parameterless procedures can interface with one another only via nonlocal variables. Since the procedure describing a process is used as a parameter in NEWPROCESS (i.e., as a procedure variable; see Section 3.7.9), it cannot be declared locally in another procedure. The only nonlocal variables that can be considered for communication between processes are those that are declared at the outermost level of a program or implementation module. This is particularly true for process variables, which must be known to all affected processes.

In the following simple example, we demonstrate the communication of a pair of parallel processes in a simple producer/consumer problem. We will use two processes, p and c. p produces data (in our case characters) that are used (consumed) by c. Whenever c needs a new character to process, it allows the process p to step in. As soon as p has produced a character, it stores it in the variable char and steps back in favor of c, which can now consume the stored character. As soon as c has finished consuming, the cycle repeats. For the sake of simplicity, we allow p to produce a character by reading it with the procedure Read. The process c consumes the character by outputting it with the procedure Write:

```
MODULE ProcessDemo;
  FROM Terminal IMPORT
    Read, Write;
  FROM SYSTEM IMPORT
    PROCESS, NEWPROCESS, TRANSFER, ADR, SIZE;

  VAR
    p,c:  PROCESS;
    workspace:  ARRAY[1..100] OF CARDINAL;
    char:  CHAR;

  PROCEDURE Consumer;
  BEGIN
    LOOP
      IF char="$" THEN EXIT END;
      Write(char);
      TRANSFER(c,p)
    END
  END Consumer;
```

```
BEGIN
  NEWPROCESS(Consumer, ADR(workspace), SIZE(workspace), c);
  LOOP
    Read(char);
    TRANSFER(p,c)
  END
END ProcessDemo.
```

The module body forms the process p (producer) and the procedure Consumer represents the process c. The first statement in p creates the process c with the help of the procedure NEWPROCESS, which initializes the process variable c as though it had been suspended before execution of its first statement. The first invocation of TRANSFER (p, c) thus starts the procedure Consumer and stores the state of the module body in the process variable p. Note that the main process p is an infinite loop (a LOOP statement without an EXIT). Such constructs are common in the formulation of parallel processes. At least one process must be present that can cause the end of execution. In our case, this is the process c. Its corresponding procedure Consumer ends when the character stored by p proves to be "$".

Of course, our example has almost no practical value. We could have resolved the same problem in shorter and clearer form without parallel processes with a simple loop:

```
...
LOOP
  Read(char);
  IF  char = "$" THEN EXIT END;
  Write(char)
END
...
```

The importance of the process concept can be seen only when there are multiple points in various processes where control can be passed to another process. As an example, we will show a program fragment that executes at two levels:

- A dialog process reads and processes keyboard input from the user.

- A computing process simultaneously executes time-consuming calculations without the user's intervention.

From the user's point of view, the dialog process is in the *foreground*, while the computing process is in the *background*. This type of configuration is frequently used in personal computers, where the user can type in a program while a previously started program (a printing program or a compiler) runs "simultaneously" (actually alternately).

In order to allow two such processes to run to the satisfaction of the user, he/she has to have the feeling that the computer (i.e., the foreground process) reacts immediately to his/her keyboard input. There cannot be uncomfortable delays between the pressing of a key and the reaction of the computer. On the other hand, the background process needs to progress (preferably when the keyboard input has been processed, but the user has not pressed a new key).

This problem can be solved by first formulating the two processes independently of one another (e.g., the foreground process as module body and the background process as parameterless procedure). Then suitable locations need to be found for transfer between processes. In the dialog process, these would be locations where a user keyboard input is being awaited. As long as no key is pressed, the background process is to work on incrementally. In order to allow control to pass back to the dialog process, the background process must be divided into small sections whose execution can be handled so fast that the user does not notice it. After each such section is executed, the background process must check to see if a key has been pressed.

We will hide the actions required for process transfer in two procedures:

ReadKey waits until the user has pressed a key and returns the corresponding character. As long as there has been no keyboard input, control passes to the background process.

CheckKeyboard passes control from the background to the foreground process (i.e., to ReadKey). If a key was pressed in the interim, the foreground process has control until the next invocation of ReadKey; otherwise the background process receives control immediately.

To test whether a key has been pressed, we use a procedure called BusyRead from the module Terminal (see Section 4.2.1). In contrast to ReadKey, BusyRead does not wait until a key has been pressed, but returns the null character 0C if no key was pressed since the last invocation of Read or BusyRead.

```
MODULE BackgroundDemo;
  FROM Terminal IMPORT BusyRead, ...;
  FROM SYSTEM IMPORT
    PROCESS, NEWPROCESS, TRANSFER, ADR, SIZE;

  VAR
    foreground, background: PROCESS;
    workspace:  ARRAY[1..1000] OF CARDINAL;
    key:  CHAR;
    ...
  PROCEDURE ReadKey(VAR  key: CHAR);
  BEGIN
    LOOP
      BusyRead(key);
      IF key <> 0C  THEN EXIT END;
      TRANSFER(foreground,background)
    END
  END ReadKey;
  PROCEDURE CheckKeyboard;
  BEGIN
    TRANSFER(background,foreground)
  END CheckKeyboard;
```

```
PROCEDURE Background;
  VAR ready: BOOLEAN;
BEGIN
  REPEAT
    ...                    (* 1st section *)
    CheckKeyboard
    ...                    (* 2nd section *)
    CheckKeyboard
    ...                    (* 3rd section *)
    CheckKeyboard
  UNTIL ready;
  LOOP
    CheckKeyboard
  END
END Background;

BEGIN
  NEWPROCESS(Background,ADR(workspace),SIZE(workspace),background);
  LOOP
    ReadKey(key);
    ...                    (* process pressed key *)
  END
END BackgroundDemo.
```

When the background process has completed its work, it is not simply terminated since that would cause the termination of the dialog process as well. Instead, the infinite loop LOOP CheckKeyboard END provides that user input will continue to be accepted and processed. Since the dialog process also contains an infinite loop, the program never terminates, but reads and processes keyboard input.

Note that the two processes are completely independent of one another. The only thing they have in common is that they run "simultaneously." They do not work with shared data.

3.10.2   Interrupts and Priorities

The concepts discussed so far for process transfer and synchronization suffice for implementing processes as software aids where parallel execution is to be achieved. In reality, even higher expectations are placed on the process concept.

Most computers have mechanisms for interrupting a process from the outside. That is, in addition to voluntarily passing control on, a process can be forced to surrender control. A hardware signal (e.g., a printer connected to a special interrupt line showing that it has completed printing a line or that paper is about to run out) usually sets off the interrupt, and this is to be processed in a suitable fashion and without delay.

In conventional programming languages, such *interrupts* are usually handled by procedures. Some suitable mechanism ensures that the interrupt signal causes the procedure invocation. As soon as the procedure has been executed, control returns to the point where the interrupt occurred.

The concept of coroutines affords the possibility of considering external interrupts as a process transfer that comes from outside. This makes it possible to blend interrupts smoothly into the process concept of Modula-2. The programmer has to write processes for handling interrupts, called interrupt handlers. These processes are started at the beginning of program execution and move into a dormant state; i.e., they return control to the main process. As soon as an interrupt signal is received, the currently active process is interrupted and control is transferred to the corresponding process. Instead of the invocation of an interrupt procedure, this can be viewed as an invocation of TRANSFER(interrupted,handler). The state of the interrupted process is thus stored in the process variable interrupted and control passes to the process designated by handler. The latter then has the possibility of resuming execution of the interrupted process with the invocation of TRANSFER(handler,interrupted).

Beyond requiring processes as interrupt handlers, the computer needs to know which process corresponds to which interrupt. Exactly how this happens depends a great deal on the computer that is used, so we cannot present a general method here. Instead, we will show a procedure that is provided with Modula-2 on PDP-11 computers (compare Wirth 1985):

```
PROCEDURE IOTRANSFER(VAR from,to: PROCESS; intnr: CARDINAL);
```

The procedure IOTRANSFER (like TRANSFER) causes control to be passed from the process from to the process to. At the same time, it ensures that an invocation of TRANSFER(to,from) is inserted in the currently active process when interrupt number intnr is received. With the help of IOTRANSFER, a process can surrender control and at the same time announce that it wants control back at the next interrupt.

The following example shows how a local module for time management can be formulated with IOTRANSFER:

```
MODULE Clock[7];
  IMPORT
    PROCESS, NEWPROCESS, TRANSFER, IOTRANSFER, ADR, SIZE;
  EXPORT
    GetTime, SetTime;

  VAR
    hour:  [0..23];
    min, sec:  [0..59];
    timer, interrupted:  PROCESS;
    workspace:  ARRAY[1..100] OF CARDINAL;

  PROCEDURE GetTime(VAR h,m,s: CARDINAL);
  BEGIN
    h := hour;  m := min;  s := sec
  END GetTime;
```

```
    PROCEDURE SetTime(h,m,s:  CARDINAL);
    BEGIN
      hour := h;  min := m;  sec := s
    END SetTime;

    PROCEDURE EverySecond;
    BEGIN
      LOOP
        IOTRANSFER(timer,interrupted,24);
        IF sec<59
          THEN INC(sec)
          ELSE
            sec := 0;
            IF min<59
              THEN INC(min)
              ELSE  min := 0;  hour := (hour+1) MOD 24
            END
        END
      END   (* loop *)
    END EverySecond;

  BEGIN   (* Clock *)
    hour := 0;  min := 0;  sec := 0;
    NEWPROCESS(EverySecond,ADR(workspace),SIZE(workspace),timer);
    TRANSFER(interrupted,timer)
  END Clock;
```

The module body has the task of creating and initializing the timer process. Initialization occurs when the process is activated once by means of TRANSFER. The process timer does nothing more than return control to the module body, whose execution terminates thereupon, by means of IOTRANSFER. The invocation of IOTRANSFER, however, also causes the process timer to be invoked again as soon as interrupt number 24 occurs. We assume that a hardware clock generates interrupt number 24 at intervals of exactly one second. Thus, every second, whichever process is active at that time is interrupted and the execution of EverySecond is resumed immediately after the invocation of IOTRANSFER. The succeeding statements provide that the time represented by the variables hour, min and sec, which are encapsuled in the module Clock, are incremented by one second. Then the LOOP begins again, and the procedure IOTRANSFER returns control to the suspended process until the next interrupt.

Whenever control passes involuntarily from a process by means of an interrupt, there is the possibility of interference in the process' function on the part of the interrupt handler. Let's examine a process that reads the time with the help of GetTime. If the request for the time occurs at 9:59:59, there is the possiblity of an uncomfortable interrupt between the assignments h:=hour and m:=min because another second has elapsed in the procedure GetTime, whereupon the process timer updates the time (to 10:00:00 in our case). When the procedure GetTime resumes after the interrupt, the parameter h has already been assigned the value 9, and now m and s are each assigned the value 0. The time read differs from the actual time by a whole hour.

In order to be able to prevent such cases, Modula-2 has the possibility of precluding interrupts during the execution of certain parts of a program. This occurs only during the execution of a module body or of a procedure within the module by assigning a *priority* to a module. In Modula-2, every local, program and implementation module can be assigned a priority (see Sections 3.3, "Elemenary Program Structure," 3.8.1, "Local Modules," and 3.8.3.2, "Implementation Modules").

Priority$_{67}$

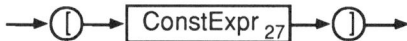

- A priority assignment immediately follows the module name in the module head. It consists of a constant expression in square brackets.

- The value of ConstExpr must be CARDINAL and is limited to a range determined by the implementation (e.g., 0 to 15).

Assigning priority is only practical if the computer being used has an *hierarchic interrupt concept*. This means that every interrupt has an assigned priority which expresses its urgency. For example, in an automated control unit, an interrupt that signals excessive steam pressure in a boiler would certainly have higher priority than an interrupt that reports that paper is running out on a printer.

In Modula-2, the assignment of priority p for a module means that all statements within it can be interrupted only by an interrupt with a higher priority. If a procedure from a module without a priority is invoked, this interrupt protection is maintained. If a procedure from a module with higher priority is invoked, the interrupt protection is increased accordingly during the execution of the procedure. Procedures from modules with lower priority cannot be invoked at all.

If an interrupt is temporarily blocked, it cannot be lost. It must be maintained until a program section with lower priority or without priority is executed. At that time, the *pending interrupt* causes a transfer to the corresponding process.

In our example, we assumed a priority of 7 for the interrupts arriving every second, so we assigned the module Clock the same priority level. This means that interrupts from the hardware clock are precluded during execution of GetTime and SetTime and the kind of interference that we portrayed above is avoided.

4 Writing Modula-2 Programs

Chapters 1 to 3 covered the rules that need to be taken into consideration when designing algorithms and formulating Modula-2 programs. This chapter seeks to round out the rough edges and go into certain particulars that tend to create difficulties for beginning programmers.

4.1 Some Simple Modula-2 Programs

Chapter 3 was written in handbook style to serve as a reference for Modula-2 users. Although individual elements of the language were illustrated with brief examples, complete Modula-2 programs were far less frequent. Using algorithms that are familiar to you from previous chapters, we now want to show how algorithms can be formulated in Modula-2.

(1)   Testing for Prime Numbers (Example 3 in Section 1.5)

Our solution used an input object n (the number which is to be tested to determine whether it is prime) and an output object prim. In order to formulate this algorithm as a Modula-2 program, we will need statements for reading the input object and for writing the result. Input and output have not been treated thus far. We refer the reader to Section 4.2. You will find, however, that the use of input and output statements is trivial and any reader who has been attentive so far will have no problem.

```
MODULE PrimeTest;
   (* reads a positive integer n and tests whether it is prime *)
   FROM InOut IMPORT ReadCard, WriteString, WriteCard, WriteLn;

   VAR
      n, q:  CARDINAL;
      prime: REAL;
```

```
BEGIN
  WriteString("Please enter the number to be tested:  ");
  ReadCard(n);      (* reads n from input medium *)
  WriteLn;
  IF  (n MOD 2 = 0) AND (n#2)
    THEN  prime := FALSE     (* n even and >2 *)
    ELSE
      prime := TRUE;         (* we assume that n is prime *)
      q := 3;
      WHILE  (q*q<=n) AND prime  DO
        IF n MOD q = 0
          THEN prime := FALSE    (* n divisible by q *)
          ELSE q := q + 2
        END (* IF *)
      END  (* WHILE *)
    END; (* IF (n MOD 2 = 0) AND (n#2) *)
  WriteCard(n,1);    (* write result *)
  IF prime
    THEN WriteString(" is a prime number")
    ELSE WriteString(" is not a prime number")
  END
END PrimeTest.
```

From the module InOut, we imported the following procedures for input and output of
given and resultant objects: ReadCard for reading a CARDINAL number,
WriteString to write a character string, WriteCard to write a CARDINAL number,
and WriteLn for advancing to the next line. The module InOut must be available on the
computer on which our PrimeTest program is to run. The rest of the program reflects
the algorithm that was presented in Section 1.5.

(2)   Eliminating Extraneous Blanks (Example 4 in Section 1.5)

The algorithm EliminateBlanks is to be written as a procedure exported from a
module called WordProcessing and thus made available to other modules. The
corresponding Modula-2 program looks like this:

```
DEFINITION MODULE WordProcessing;
  PROCEDURE  EliminateBlanks(n:CARDINAL; VAR text:ARRAY OF CHAR;
                             VAR len:CARDINAL);
  (* Given:  an array of characters text with length n>=1.
     The algorithm changes the array so that every sequence of blanks
     is replaced by a single blank and len represents the new size of
     the array. *)
  ...
  declarations of further procedures
  ...
END WordProcessing.
```

```
IMPLEMENTATION MODULE WordProcessing;
  ...
  PROCEDURE    EliminateBlanks(n:CARDINAL; VAR text:ARRAY OF CHAR;
                                VAR len:CARDINAL);
    CONST blank = " ";
    VAR i, j: CARDINAL;
  BEGIN
    len := 0;
    i := 1;
    WHILE i < n DO
      (* text[0..len] contains no sequence of multiple blanks *)
      IF (text[i] = blank) AND (text[len] = blank)
        THEN (* text[i] is extraneous blank *)
        ELSE (* text[i] is not extraneous blank, so transfer *)
          len := len + 1;
          text[len] := text[i]
      END;   (* IF *)
      i := i + 1
    END;   (* WHILE *)
    len := len + 1
  END EliminateBlanks;
  ...
BEGIN
  ...
END WordProcessing.
```

The Modula-2 version is only slightly different from the algorithm as it was written in pseudocode. We chose an open array type (with a variable index range) for the input/output object text (see Section 3.7.7, "ARRAY Parameters"). Within the procedure, the formal parameter text is thus handled as though its data type were ARRAY[0..maxindex] OF CHAR. This means that we have to initialize len with 0 (instead of 1, as in the design of the algorithm), and at the end of the program, we increment len by 1 to compensate, so that it then represents the actual length of the array.

(3)   Justification (from Section 2.2)

The following Modula-2 program system shows our solution based on the data capsule principle. Procedures and modules are used to accomplish the structuring. The program is divided into three compilation units: the program module Justify, the definition and implementation modules WordManagement, and the definition and implementation modules LineManagement. Procedures lend structure to each of the modules. The procedures reflect the subalgorithms arrived at by stepwise refinement.

```
MODULE Justify;
  FROM InOut IMPORT
    ReadCard, WriteString, WriteLn, WriteCard;
  FROM WordManagement IMPORT
    Word, ReadWord, ProcessWord;
  FROM LineManagement IMPORT
    ClearLine, PrintLine, linemax;
```

```
    VAR
      word:  Word;
      eot:   BOOLEAN;              (* end of text *)
      targetLen: CARDINAL;         (* target line length *)

  BEGIN
    WriteString("Please enter the target line length:  ");
    ReadCard(targetLen);
    IF targetLen>linemax THEN
      WriteString("The line length "); WriteCard(targetLen,1);
      WriteString(" is too large.  The default value ");
      WriteCard(linemax,1); WriteString(" was substituted.");
      WriteLn;
      targetLen := linemax
    END;
    ClearLine;
    REPEAT
      ReadWord(word, eot);
      ProcessWord(targetLen, word)
    UNTIL eot;
    PrintLine
  END Justify.
```

```
  DEFINITION MODULE WordManagement;
    TYPE Word =    RECORD
                      length: CARDINAL;
                      text:   ARRAY[1..132] OF CHAR
                   END;

    PROCEDURE ReadWord(VAR word:Word; VAR eot:BOOLEAN);
    (* Reads the next word of text.  IF "$" is read, then end
       of text (eot) is set to TRUE. *)

    PROCEDURE ProcessWord(targetLen:CARDINAL; word:Word);
    (* Appends a word to the current print line if that does
       not create a line longer than the value targetLen.
       Otherwise, the current line is justified and written,
       and the word becomes the first word in the next line.
       *)

  END WordManagement.
```

```
  IMPLEMENTATION MODULE WordManagement;
    FROM InOut IMPORT           Read, WriteLn;
    FROM LineManagement IMPORT  StretchLine, AppendWord, PrintLine,
                                ClearLine;
    PROCEDURE ReadWord(VAR word:Word; VAR eot:BOOLEAN);
      VAR ch: CHAR;
    BEGIN
      REPEAT  (* skip blanks *)
        Read(ch)
      UNTIL ch#" ";
```

```
    WITH word DO   (* RECORD type from definition module *)
      length := 0;
      WHILE  (ch#" ") AND (ch#"$")   DO   (* form word *)
        INC(length);
        text[length] := ch;
        Read(ch)
      END
    END;  (* WITH *)
    eot := ch="$"   (* end of text? *)
  END ReadWord;

  PROCEDURE ProcessWord(targetLen:CARDINAL; word:Word);
    VAR fits: BOOLEAN;
  BEGIN
    AppendWord(targetLen, word, fits);
    IF NOT fits THEN
      StretchLine;
      PrintLine;
      WriteLn;
      ClearLine;
      AppendWord(targetLen, word, fits)
    END
  END ProcessWord;
END WordManagement.
```

```
DEFINITION MODULE LineManagement;
  FROM WordManagement IMPORT Word;
  CONST linemax = 132;

  PROCEDURE ClearLine;
  (* initializes the length of the print line to zero *)

  PROCEDURE StretchLine(targetLen:CARDINAL);
  (* stretches the current line by increasing the spaces
     between words so that the first word begins at
     position 1 and the last word ends at position
     targetLen. *)

  PROCEDURE AppendWord(targetLen:CARDINAL; w:Word; VAR fits:BOOLEAN);
  (* appends the word w to the current line (with length x)
     if x+1+w.length <=  targetLen (i.e., fits=TRUE);
     otherwise, fits is set at FALSE and nothing is
     appended.  *)

  PROCEDURE PrintLine;
  (*  prints the current line *)

END LineManagement.
```

```
IMPLEMENTATION MODULE LineManagement;
  FROM WordManagement IMPORT Word;
  FROM InOut IMPORT Write;
```

```
VAR line:   RECORD
                  length: CARDINAL;
                  text:   ARRAY[1..linemax] OF CHAR
              END;

PROCEDURE ClearLine;
BEGIN
  line.length := 0
END ClearLine;

PROCEDURE StretchLine(targetLen:CARDINAL);
   VAR pos: CARDINAL;     (* position of white space in line. *)
BEGIN
  pos := 1;
  WHILE  line.length<targetLen  DO
    FindWhiteSpace(pos);   (* column pos contains a blank *)
    InsertBlank(pos)
  END
END StretchLine;

PROCEDURE AppendWord(targetLen:CARDINAL; w:Word; VAR fits:BOOLEAN);
   VAR i: CARDINAL;
BEGIN
  IF w.length=0
    THEN   fits := TRUE
    ELSE
       fits := line.length+1+w.length<=targetLen;
       IF fits THEN
         IF  line.length>0 THEN
           INC(line.length);
           line.text[line.length] := " " (* append blank *)
         END;
         FOR  i:=1  TO  w.length  DO
           INC(line.length);
           line.text[line.length] := w.text[i]
         END  (* FOR *)
       END  (* IF fits *)
  END   (* IF w.length=0 *)
END AppendWord;

PROCEDURE PrintLine;
   VAR i: CARDINAL;
BEGIN
  FOR i:=1 to  line.length  DO
    Write(line.text[i])
  END  (* FOR *)
END PrintLine;

PROCEDURE FindWhiteSpace(VAR pos:CARDINAL);
BEGIN
  WHILE  line.text[pos] = " "  DO
    INC(pos)
  END;    (* WHILE *)
```

```
    WHILE  line.text[pos] # " "  DO
      IF  pos=line.length
         THEN  pos:=1
         ELSE  INC(pos)
      END  (* IF *)
    END  (* WHILE *)
  END FindWhiteSpace;

  PROCEDURE InsertBlank(pos:CARDINAL);
    VAR i: CARDINAL;
  BEGIN  (* at this point, line.text[pos] = " "  *)
    FOR i:=line.length  TO  pos  BY  -1  DO
      line.text[i+1] := line.text[i]
    END;  (* FOR *)
    INC(line.length)
  END InsertBlank;

END LineManagement.
```

Unlike our original data-capsule solution, this Modula-2 version omits the procedure AppendChar (which occured only twice in the procedure AppendWord) and replaces its invocation with the actions contained in the procedure. In addition, we replaced WHILE loops with FOR loops wherever that seemed practical.

4.2 Input/Output

Although all language elements of Modula-2 were described in Chapter 3, readers with experience in other programming languages will have wondered what happened to commands for reading and writing data. How Modula-2 programs communicate with their environment still needs to be handled.

Communication between a person and a computer occurs via *peripheral devices* that are connected to the computer. The terms input and output encompass all transfers of data between the work space (in memory) used by a program and the peripheral devices. Most older programming languages attempted to address all possible peripheral devices by means of a scheme firmly established in the language definition. The advantage of this approach is the uniformity of all input/output (I/O) statements and greater machine independence. Among the disadvantages, however, is the fact that many of the functions of the computer or its operating system cannot be taken advantage of because the provided I/O mechanisms are not flexible enough.

In Modula-2 input/output is therefore treated in a different way. All I/O is handled exclusively by *procedure invocations*. Drivers for a particular device are packaged in a module that exports the "statements" for addressing the device in the form of procedures. This also makes it possible to handle different requirements on a particular device in a simple way. For example, if the user employs a graphic monitor simply for displaying text, a simple module for that purpose suffices, whereas a complicated module is necessary in order to take advantage of all of the monitor's graphic capabilities.

The configuration of a personal computer could include a keyboard, a screen, a disk drive and a printer. The direct interface with the user is then handled by the module Terminal, which contains routines for reading user input from the keyboard and for outputting text on the screen. Files can be stored on magnetic disks. This means that we do not want to access an entire disk, but only individual files, and the module FileSystem makes this possible. Still another module, Printer, handles output to the printer.

The high degree of flexibility of this concept has disadvantages as well. Different computers could provide different modules for driving the same device. This restricts the *portability* of programs; i.e., a program written on one computer cannot simply be installed on a different type of computer if the program uses such modules. In order to avoid such dificulties and pave the way for widespread commercial applications of Modula-2, efforts are underway to standardize the basic I/O modules.

Before detailing the interfaces of the I/O modules, we want to explain the term *file* more precisely:

A file is an ordered set of data which is on an external storage medium and which forms some manner of logical unit (e.g., a file on persons, a series of measurements, a text). We distinguish two kinds of files:

- *Temporary files* can be used for short-range storage of large amounts of data on a mass storage medium so that they can be used later by the same program. Their lifetime ends with the termination of the program.

- *Permanent files* are for long-term storage of data on external media for later use by some program. In contrast to temporary files, permanent files have names under which they are stored and by which they can be recalled.

Before a program can write to or read from a file, the file must be opened. For a temporary file, this means that an empty, nameless file must be created. There are two cases in the opening of a permanent file:

(a) If a file is to be written to for the first time, it must first be created (i.e., space must be reserved for it) and assigned a name. This name is also entered in a directory on the mass storage medium.

(b) If an existing file is to be accessed (e.g., read), then its name must first be found in the directory.

Only after a file has been successfully opened can it be accessed. In most cases, files are accessed *sequentially,* i.e., every writing operation appends new data to the file, and successive reading operations return the data in the same order in which they were stored. The reading or writing position always advances in one direction (from the beginning of the file to the end). Sequential operations can be compared to writing and reading a letter.

Sometimes, however, *direct access (random access)* to files is necessary. Analogous to referencing a telephone book, the reading or writing position has to be set to a certain position within the file. The subsequent read or write operation is carried out from that position. A write operation causes data previously at that position to be overwritten (replaced).

Every open file must be *closed* after its use. For a temporary file, this means deleting it, i.e., the space occupied by its data is released for other files to use. Closing a permanent file causes its current status to be recorded on the mass storage medium.

The following sections introduce several important basic I/O modules from Wirth (1985): `Terminal`, `InOut`, `RealInOut` and `FileSystem`. We will refrain from a detailed description of each of these modules and concentrate on their most important routines.

4.2.1 The Module Terminal

This module provides procedures for reading data from the keyboard and outputting data on the screen. The procedures serve the following functions:

- Reading from the keyboard

`Read`	reads a character
`BusyRead`	checks for keyboard input
`ReadAgain`	repeats a read operation

- Displaying on the screen

`Write`	displays a single character
`WriteString`	displays a character string
`WriteLn`	begins a new line on the screen

The definition module for `Terminal` looks like this:

```
DEFINITION MODULE  Terminal;

   PROCEDURE   Read(VAR ch:CHAR);
   (* The procedure Read waits until a key has been pressed,
      then assigns the corresponding character to the
      variable parameter ch.  The character read is not
      displayed on the screen. *)

   PROCEDURE   BusyRead(VAR ch:CHAR);
   (* The procedure BusyRead attempts to read a character
      from the keyboard.  If a key was pressed since the
      most recent invocation of either Read or BusyRead,
      then the variable parameter ch contains that
      character; otherwise, the null character 0C.  The
      character read is not displayed on the screen. *)

   PROCEDURE   ReadAgain;
   (* This procedure does not read a character; it only
      causes the next invocation of Read or BusyRead to
      again read the character that was read in the previous
      invocation of Read  or BusyRead. *)
```

```
PROCEDURE  Write(ch:CHAR);
(* Displays the character ch on the screen. *)

PROCEDURE  WriteLn;
(* This procedure ends a line.  The next write operation
   begins at the first column of the next line on the
   screen. *)

PROCEDURE  WriteString(s:ARRAY OF CHAR);
(* The entire character string s is displayed on the
   screen if it does not contain the null character 0C;
   otherwise, the first occurrence of 0C terminates the
   output *)
```

END Terminal.

This module provides us with procedures for input and output of characters and character strings. Only the definition module is relevant to us; the implementation module is hardware-dependent, as is the case with other I/O modules presented here. The implementation must be tailored to the properties of the computer on which Modula-2 is available, and it is provided with the compiler.

4.2.2 The Modules InOut and RealInOut

As an extension of the module Terminal, InOut contains routines for I/O of characters and numbers. This I/O can refer to keyboard and screen, but can also be channeled (redirected) to external files (e.g., disk files).

The module InOut exports procedures for opening and closing files as well as for reading and writing. Opening and closing is necessary only for external files since the reading and writing routines default to the keyboard and screen if no file is open. The procedures exported by InOut serve the following functions:

- Opening and closing

OpenInput	opens an input file (for reading)
OpenOutput	opens an output file (for writing)
CloseInput	closes the input file
CloseOutput	closes the output file

- Reading

Read	reads a single character
ReadString	reads a character string
ReadInt	reads an INTEGER number
ReadCard	reads a CARDINAL number

- Writing

Write	writes a single character
WriteString	writes a character string
WriteInt	writes an INTEGER number (decimal)

WriteCard	writes a CARDINAL number (decimal)
WriteOct	writes a CARDINAL number (octal)
WriteHex	writes a CARDINAL number (hexadecimal)
WriteLn	ends an output line

InOut does not contain routines for I/O of real numbers. For that purpose, the module RealInOut exports the following procedures:

ReadReal	reads a real number
WriteReal	writes a real number

The definition modules of InOut and RealInOut take the following form:

```
DEFINITION MODULE InOut;

  CONST  EOL = 36C;  (* ASCII code for end of line *)

  VAR
    done: BOOLEAN;     (* variable that reports the success or
                          failure of some procedures  *)
    termCH: CHAR;      (* character that terminated an input *)
    (* CAUTION:  The values of the exported variables done
       and termCH are not to be changed from outside this
       module. *)

  PROCEDURE OpenInput(defext:ARRAY OF CHAR);
  (* This procedure opens an input file, prompting the user
     to input the name of the file.  If the file name ends
     with a period, the character string  defext  is
     expanded.  The exported variable done is TRUE if the
     file could be opened correctly; otherwise it is FALSE.
     If a file was opened with OpenInput, all subsequent
     input procedures refer to this file. *)

  PROCEDURE  OpenOutput(defext:ARRAY OF CHAR);
  (* This procedure opens an output file, prompting the
     user to input the name of the file.  If the file name
     ends with a period, the character string defext is
     appended.  The exported variable done is TRUE if the
     file could be opened correctly; otherwise it is FALSE.
     If a file was opened with OpenOutput, all subsequent
     output procedures refer to this file. *)

  PROCEDURE  CloseInput;
  (* The file opened by means of OpenInput is closed.  All
     subsequent invocations of input procedures refer to
     the keyboard until another input file is explicitly
     opened. *)

  PROCEDURE  CloseOutput;
  (* The file opened by means of OpenOutput is closed.  All
     subsequent invocations of output procedures refer to
     the screen until another output file is explicitly
     opened. *)
```

```
PROCEDURE  Read(VAR ch:CHAR);
```
(* A single character is read from the input file or (by
   default) the keyboard and assigned to the variable
   parameter ch. The read character *is not displayed* on
   the screen. If the end of the input file is reached
   (i.e., no further character could be read from the
   input file), the variable done is FALSE; otherwise it
   is TRUE. Keyboard input precludes an (actual) end of
   file. *)

```
PROCEDURE  ReadString(VAR s:ARRAY OF CHAR);
```
(* ReadString reads a character string from the input
   file or (by default) the keyboard. Reading terminates
   with the first blank or control character (e.g., end
   of line). Leading blanks are skipped. The character
   that caused termination of the reading process is
   stored in the variable termCH. When reading from the
   keyboard, the character string being read *is displayed*
   on the screen *)

```
PROCEDURE  ReadInt(VAR x:INTEGER);
```
(* Like ReadString, this procedure reads a character
   string. The variable done is TRUE if the read string
   represents an INTEGER (with or without a leading
   sign); otherwise, it is FALSE. The variable parameter
   x contains the INTEGER which was read. If no INTEGER
   was read, the value of x is undefined. *)

```
PROCEDURE  ReadCard(VAR x:CARDINAL);
```
(* Like ReadString, this procedure reads a character
   string. The variable done is TRUE if the read string
   represents a CARDINAL number (without a leading sign);
   otherwise, it is FALSE. The variable parameter x
   contains the CARDINAL number which was read. If no
   CARDINAL number was read, the value of x is undefined.
   *)

```
PROCEDURE  Write(ch:CHAR);
```
(* The value parameter ch (a single character) is written
   to the output file or (by default) displayed on the
   screen. *)

```
PROCEDURE WriteLn;
```
(* This procedure outputs the end-of-line control
   character EOL to the output file or (by default) to
   the screen. Screen output begins a new line. *)

```
PROCEDURE  WriteString(s:ARRAY OF CHAR);
```
(* The entire character string s is written to the output
   file or (by default) displayed on the screen as long
   as it does not contain a null character 0C; otherwise,
   the first null character terminates output. *)

```
PROCEDURE  WriteInt(x:INTEGER;  n:CARDINAL);
(* The INTEGER x is written to the output file or (by
   default) displayed on the screen in decimal format
   with at least n digits.  If n is larger than the
   number of places required for x, then x is output with
   leading blanks.  If n is smaller that the number of
   places required for x, the output format of x is
   expanded. *)

PROCEDURE  WriteCard(x, n:CARDINAL);
(* The CARDINAL number x is written to the output file or
   (by default) displayed on the screen in decimal format
   with at least  n  digits.  If  n  is larger than the
   number of places required for  x,  then  x  is output
   with leading blanks.  If  n  is smaller that the
   number of places required for  x,  the output format
   of  x  is expanded. *)

PROCEDURE  WriteOct(x, n:CARDINAL);
(* The CARDINAL number x is written to the output file or
   (by default) displayed on the screen in octal format
   with at least n digits.  If n is larger than the
   number of places required for x, then x is output with
   leading blanks.  If n is smaller that the number of
   places required for x, the output format of x is
   expanded. *)

PROCEDURE  WriteHex(x, n:CARDINAL);
(* The CARDINAL number x is written to the output file or
   (by default) displayed on the screen in hexadecimal
   format with at least n digits.  If n is larger than
   the number of places required for x, then x is output
   with leading blanks.  If n is smaller that the number
   of places required for x, the output format of x is
   expanded. *)

END InOut.

DEFINITION MODULE RealInOut;

   VAR done:  BOOLEAN;  (* variable that reports the success or
                           failure of the procedure ReadReal  *)

   PROCEDURE  ReadReal(VAR x:REAL);
   (* Analogous to  ReadString in the module InOut, this
      procedure reads a character string.  The variable done
      is TRUE if the string read is a REAL number in Modula-2
      format; otherwise, it is FALSE.  The variable
      parameter x contains the REAL number which was read.
      If no REAL number was read, the value of x is
      undefined. *)

   PROCEDURE WriteReal(x:REAL; n:CARDINAL);
   (* The REAL number x is written to the output file or (by
      default) displayed on the screen with at least n
      digits in Modula-2 format (with mantissa and exponent).
```

```
If n is larger than the number of places required for
x, then x is output with leading blanks.  If n is
smaller that the number of places required for x, the
output format of x is expanded. *)
```

END RealInOut;

If I/O was channeled to a file by means of the procedures Open Input and/or
OpenOutput (procedures exported from InOut), this redirection applies to the routines
in RealInOut as well.

These simple I/O routines permit the programmer to implement sequential (stream) I/O,
which treats the entire external data set as a continuous stream of individual characters.
Sequential I/O suffices for many applications, particularly if only the keyboard and the
screen (or printer) are used as I/O media. The following example shows the input of names
with the help of routines imported from InOut .

```
MODULE ReadName;
  FROM InOut IMPORT
    EOL, Read, Write, WriteString;

  CONST  namelength = 30;

  VAR
    ch: CHAR;
    name: ARRAY[0..namelength-1] OF CHAR;

BEGIN
  . . .
  WriteString("Please enter name:  ");
  i := 0;
  Read(ch);         (* single character *)
  WHILE  (i<namelength) AND (ch#EOL)  DO
    Write(ch);      (* display on screen *)
    name[i] := ch;
    INC(i);
    Read(ch)        (* single character *)
  END;
  IF  i<namelength  THEN
    name[i] := 0C (* append null character to close *)
  END
  . . .
END  ReadName.
```

In this example, a name is input character-wise. ReadString cannot be used because it
does not accept blanks (refer to the description of the definition module InOut), but we
want to allow blanks in a name (e.g., "I. Newton"). Since the module InOut provides
the constant EOL (the ASCII end-of-line control character), we use it in our example to
terminate names that are shorter than namelength (=30) characters.

The modules InOut and RealInOut meet the needs of most simple programs. For
more sophisticated file operations (e.g., multiple files opened simultaneously), however,

they fall short. Thus we need additional procedures conceived especially for file processing.

4.2.3 The Module FileSystem

This module exports routines suitable for more than just sequential I/O. The procedures provided by this library module serve the following functions:

- Opening, closing and renaming files

Create	opens a temporary file
Lookup	opens a permanent file
Close	closes a (temporary or permanent) file
Rename	renames a file; can also be used to transform a permanent (named) file into a temporary (unnamed) file and vice versa.

- Reading and writing

ReadChar	reads a character
ReadWord	reads a word of storage
WriteChar	writes a character
WriteWord	writes a word of storage
Again	repeats a read operation

- Positioning

GetPos	determines the current position in a file
SetPos	changes the current position in a file
Reset	resets the current position to start of file
Length	determines the current file length

Beyond routines for processing files, FileSystem exports the data type File, which is implemented as a RECORD with variants. Among other things, it contains the components eof (which reports whether the end of file has been reached) and res (which discloses the success or failure of a file operation. A variable of type File must exist for every file used in order to provide information about that file. That is why the file variable is passed as a variable parameter in the invocation of all procedures in the module FileSystem.

The definition module for FileSystem on the Modula-2 computer *Lilith* (Wirth 1981) takes the following form (whereby only the most important elements that suffice for our purposes are described):

```
DEFINITION MODULE  FileSystem;
  FROM SYSTEM  IMPORT  WORD;
  TYPE
    ...
    Response =  (done, notDone,..., unknownFile, fileNameError,...);
            (* list of all possible error types for file operations *)
```

```
      File = RECORD
                eof:BOOLEAN;   (* end of file reached? *)
                res:Response;  (*result of most recent file operation*)
                ...
             END;
```
PROCEDURE Create(VAR f:File; mediumName:ARRAY OF CHAR);
(* This procedure opens a new temporary file f on a
    peripheral device designated by mediumName (e.g., "DK"
    for magnetic disk) *)

PROCEDURE Lookup(VAR f:File; fileName:ARRAY OF CHAR; new:BOOLEAN);
(* This procedure searches the directory of the mass
    storage medium for a file with the name fileName. If
    such a file is found, it is opened. If the file is
    not found, then the last parameter determines what is
    to happen in this case. If new is TRUE, a new file
    with the name fileName is created; otherwise, f.res
    reports why the file could not be found. *)

PROCEDURE Close(VAR f:File);
(* The file indicated by f is closed. If the file is
    temporary, it is deleted. After Close has been
    invoked, no operations are possible on the file f
    until the next invocation of Create or Lookup *)

PROCEDURE Rename(VAR f:File; fileName:ARRAY OF CHAR);
(* The name of file f is changed to the character string
    contained in the parameter fileName. If fileName is
    the null string, then file f is transformed into a
    temporary file. *)

PROCEDURE GetPos(VAR f:File; VAR highPos, lowPos:CARDINAL);
(* GetPos determines the current position within the file
    f, i.e., the variable parameters highPos and lowPos
    contain the addresses of the bytes within the file at
    which the next read/write operation will take place.
    *)

PROCEDURE SetPos(VAR f:File; highPos, lowPos:CARDINAL);
(* SetPos alters the current position within the file f,
    i.e., the position at which the next read/write
    operation will take place, to the position indicated
    by the addresses in the parameters highPos and lowPos.
    *)

PROCEDURE Length(VAR f:File; VAR highPos, lowPos:CARDINAL);
(* The current length of the file f (in bytes) is
    determined and assigned to the variable parameters
    highPos and lowPos. *)

PROCEDURE Reset(VAR f:File);
(* Resets the current position in file f to the beginning
    of the file. *)
```
```

```
PROCEDURE Again(VAR f:File);
(* This procedure causes the "rereading" of the most
   recent character or word of storage read by an
   invocation of ReadChar or ReadWord respectively. *)

PROCEDURE ReadChar(VAR f:File; VAR ch:CHAR);
(* This procedure reads the next character in the file f
   and assigns it to the variable parameter ch. If end of
   file has been reached (i.e., no further character
   could be read), then the value of ch is undefined and
   f.eof has the value TRUE. *)

PROCEDURE ReadWord(VAR f:File; VAR w:WORD);
(* This procedure reads the next word of storage in the
   file f and assigns it to the variable parameter w. If
   end of file has been reached (i.e., no further word
   could be read), then the value of w is undefined and
   f.eof has the value TRUE.   *)

PROCEDURE WriteChar(VAR f:File; ch:CHAR);
(* WriteChar writes the character ch to the file f. *)

PROCEDURE WriteWord(VAR f:File; w:WORD);
(* WriteWord writes the word w to the file f. *)
...

END FileSystem.
```

The success or failure of all these routines is stored in the component res of the file variable. Invocations of ReadChar or ReadWord can lead to the end of file, in which case the component eof is assigned the value TRUE.

The following example reads positive whole numbers (e.g., test readings) from the keyboard and writes the same numbers to the file with the name DK.NUM.OUT:

```
MODULE Numbers;
  FROM  FileSystem  IMPORT
    Close, Lookup, File, Response, WriteWord;
  FROM  InOut  IMPORT
    ReadCard, WriteString;

  VAR
    f:File;
    n:CARDINAL;

BEGIN
  Lookup(f, "DK.NUM.OUT", TRUE);  (* open file DK.NUM.OUT *)
  IF  f.res = done
    THEN
      ReadCard(n);          (* read a CARDINAL number *)
      WHILE n>0  DO
        WriteWord(f,n); (* write number  n  to file  DK.NUM.OUT *)
        ReadCard(n)        (* read CARDINAL number *)
      END;
```

```
        Close(f)
    ELSE
        WriteString("Could not open DK.NUM.OUT")
    END
END Numbers.
```

The procedure `Lookup` opens the file `DK.NUM.OUT`. The parameter `TRUE` tells `Lookup` that a new file is to be created if it does not already exist (see the explanation under the definition module `FileSystem`). The component `f.res` contains information about whether the file was correctly opened. In writing the CARDINAL numbers with the procedure `WriteWord`, we make use of the fact that a CARDINAL number occupies one word of storage.

If stored numbers are to be read and their average calculated (rounded to a whole number), the following module can help:

```
MODULE MeanValue;
    FROM  FileSystem  IMPORT
        Close, Lookup, File, Response, WriteWord;
    FROM  InOut  IMPORT
        WriteCard, WriteString;

    VAR
        f:File;
        count, n, sum:CARDINAL;

BEGIN
    Lookup(f, "DK.NUM.OUT", FALSE);   (* open file DK.NUM.OUT *)
    IF  f.res = done
        THEN
            sum := 0;  count := 0;
            ReadWord(f, n);      (* read value from  DK.NUM.OUT *)
            WHILE NOT  f.eof  DO
                sum := sum + n;
                INC(count);
                ReadWord(f, n)
            END;
            IF  count > 0
                THEN
                    WriteString("Mean value ");
                    WriteCard(sum DIV count, 5) (* write mean value *)
                ELSE
                    WriteString("No numbers stored")
            END;
            Close(f)
        ELSE
            WriteString("Could not open DK.NUM.OUT")
    END
END MeanValue.
```

The procedure `Lookup` opens the file `DK.NUM.OUT`. The parameter `FALSE` tells the procedure not to create a new file if `DK.NUM.OUT` is not found. The component `f.eof` is `TRUE` when the end of file is reached.

Recognize that the modules and procedures for I/O are in part system-dependent because they use the machine-dependent data type WORD and are tailored to the hardware interfaces.

The modules introduced so far give the impression that each data type in Modula-2 requires its own read/write routines. This is not the case. Other modules can be implemented that export routines for blockwise I/O (i.e., procedures that use a parameter of type ARRAY OF WORD to read/write a certain number of words of storage from/to a file). We have deliberately chosen to describe only the above basic modules for I/O. Suggestions for additional I/O modules can be found, for example, in Wirth 1985 and Odersky 1989.

4.3 Dynamic Data Structures

In introducing POINTER types in Section 3.4.1.3, we alluded to dynamic data structures. We now want to explain this concept in detail.

We have already mentioned that all the data types covered in Section 3.4 share the property that memory is assigned to them at compilation time. Such data types exist as long as the procedure or module in which they were declared (see Sections 3.7.5 and 3.8.2, "Scope and Lifetime of Objects in Procedures/Modules"). These *static objects* describe *static data structures*. They have the following disadvantages:

- The size and "structure" of the objects must already be know at compilation time.

- Memory must always be reserved for the *maximum* number of objects that might be needed. Memory is not used efficiently if only part of this storage space is then actually used.

- If the amount of data grows beyond the assumed maximum, a static data structure cannot grow to meet new needs.

Static objects alone therefore cannot meet the requirements of programming. Sometimes objects are required that alter not just their values but also their *structure*. We use structure here not to mean the data type, which is naturally established statically, but the size and form (e.g., the number of elements). An example of dynamic data structures is a list, whose size can change continuously.

Modula-2 makes programming with dynamic data structures possible with its data type POINTER (see Section 3.4.1.3) and its standard procedures NEW and DISPOSE (see Section 3.7.8). POINTER variables point to the region of memory that contains the values of other objects. Pointers can be components of structured objects (e.g., RECORDs). This makes it possible to link such objects at run time and to dissolve the links as well; i.e., data structures of any complexity can be created dynamically. We call these *dynamic data structures* and *dynamic objects*.

4.3.1 Working with Dynamic Data Structures

We will demonstrate the properties of dynamic data structures and how to work with them by means of a list processing example:

> An author catalog is to be produced as part of a library management package. The catalog is to contain a list of authors and a list of wroks (publications) for each author. Each publication needs to include a reference to its author.

Figure 4.1 shows how such an author catalog is to be constructed:

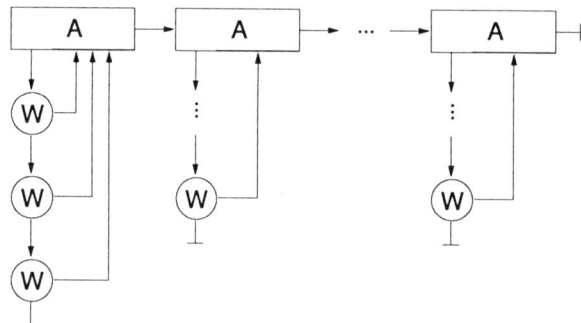

Fig. 4.1 Author list and publication list

Both the number of authors and the number of publications per author are unknown. We have to dynamically manage the objects in both the author list and the publication lists.

Creating Dynamic Objects

Two steps are required for creating dynamic objects:

*   the declarations of the data types that describe the authors and the publications and of pointers that point to each of them, and

*   the dynamic generation of the objects themselves at run time.

The following are our declarations:

```
TYPE
  AuthorPointer = POINTER TO Author;
  PublicationPointer = POINTER TO Publication;
  Author =        RECORD
                    name:ARRAY[0..29] OF CHAR;
                    publicationList:PublicationPointer;
                    nextAuthor:AuthorPointer
                  END;
  Publication = RECORD
                    title:ARRAY[0..29] OF CHAR;
                    author:AuthorPointer;
                    nextPublication:PublicationPointer
                  END;
```

With the help of these type declarations, we can now define the POINTER variables that point to objects in the author list or the publication list. We need three pointers: one variable to point to an object in the author list, one to point to an object in the publication list, and one to point to the beginning of the author list.

```
VAR
   authorPtr:  AuthorPointer;        (* pointer to an author *)
   authorList: AuthorPointer;        (* pointer to first author *)
   publicPtr:  PublicationPointer;   (* pointer to a publication *)
```

The standard procedure NEW (see Section 3.7.8) creates an object to which a pointer refers, e.g.:

```
NEW(authorPtr)
```

This invocation of NEW reserves memory for an object with data type Author. The parameter authorPtr points to the newly created object (after the invocation). The components of the newly created object Author (name, publicationList, nextAuthor) are undefined at this time (they have no value).

Accessing Dynamic Objects

In order to access an object created with NEW, we write the name of the respective POINTER variable followed by ^ (the pointer dereferencing operator), e.g., authorPtr^. Note that authorPtr is a POINTER, whereas authorPtr^ designates a RECORD. In order to access individual components of the RECORD, we have to reference them, e.g.:

```
NEW(authorPtr);        (* creates an object of type  Author *)
NEW(publicationPtr); (* creates an object of typle  Publication *)
authorPtr^.publicationList := publicationPtr;  (* links an author with
                                                a publication list *)
```

The following rules govern the use of pointer variables:

- A pointer variable x can only point to (dynamic) objects of a single data type.

- Pointer variables contain a value after they are used as parameters in an invocation of NEW or after an assignment (pointers of the same data type are assignment compatible).

- Aside from their use in assignments, pointer variables of the same data type can only be tested pairwise for equality or inequality; no other operations are permissible.

Deleting Dynamic Objects

When an object is no longer needed, the memory it occupies can be freed by invoking the standard procedure DISPOSE:

```
DISPOSE(authorPtr)
```

This invocation frees the memory occupied by the object to which `authorPtr` points. The value of `authorPtr` is undefined after the invocation of `DISPOSE`. Remember that in order to use `NEW` and `DISPOSE`, the procedures `ALLOCATE` and `DEALLOCATE` need to be imported from the module `Storage` (see Section 3.7.8).

Multiple pointer variables of the same type can all point to the same object. This also needs to be kept in mind when disposing of dynamically created objects. Consider the following program fragment:

```
TYPE
   AuthorPointer = POINTER TO Author;
   Author = RECORD
             ...
         END;
VAR
   wirth, jensen:  AuthorPointer;
...
   NEW(wirth);
   jensen := wirth;
   ...
   DISPOSE(wirth);
   ...
```

After the execution of the standard procedure `DISPOSE`, the object referenced by `wirth` has disappeared and the value of the pointer `wirth` is undefined. The value of the pointer variable `jensen`, which originally referenced the same object as `wirth`, was not changed by disposing of the RECORD stored at the address contained in `wirth`. This means that `jensen` points to an object that no longer exists. What happens if we use the pointer `jensen` after the above invocation of `DISPOSE` depends on the particular implementation of Modula-2. The programmer must always ensure that pointers used to reference objects do point to existing objects and that their value is not `NIL`.

Removing an element from a doubly linked list demands particular attention. Consider the list illustrated in Fig. 4.2:

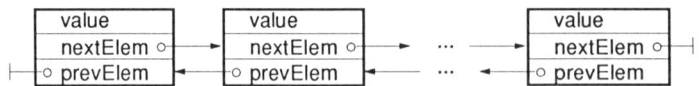

Fig. 4.2 Doubly linked list

This list can be described by the following data structure:

```
TYPE
   ListPtr =  POINTER TO ListElem;
   ListElem =  RECORD
               value: ...              (* information *)
               nextElem: ListPtr;      (* pointer to next element *)
               prevElem: ListPtr       (* pointer to previous element*)
             END;
```

In order to remove an element from this list, we need to update the pointer `nextElem` in the preceding element as well as the pointer `prevElem` in the subsequent element:

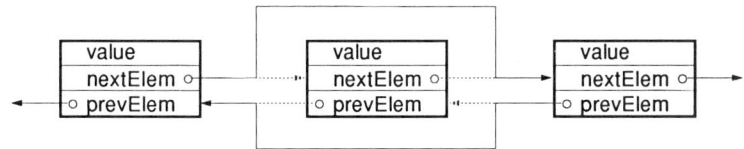

Fig. 4.3 Removing an element

Only after this update has been completed can we proceed with the deletion of the element with `DISPOSE`. Here is one solution in Modula-2:

```
VAR elem:  ListPtr;   (* pointer to ListElem *)
...
(* assert:  elem  points to erasable element *)
elem^.prevElem^.nextElem := elem^.nextElem;
elem^.nextElem^.prevElem := elem^.prevElem;
DISPOSE(elem);
...
```

This solution makes use of the knowledge that the pointers to the predecessor (`elem^.prevElem`) and to the successor (`elem^.nextElem`) are stored in the element to be deleted, and of the fact that Modula-2 permits multiple referencing.

In removing an element from a double-linked list, we must also be aware of the special cases: the element to be removed could be the first or the last element in the list (i.e., it has either no predecessor or no successor). We will leave it to the reader to think about how these last details can be handled.

Implementation of an Author Catalog

The following is a possible implementation of the author catalog. The example is limited to the procedures `NewDirectory` and `AppendPublication`, both of which are necessary for constructing a directory:

```
IMPLEMENTATION MODULE  AuthorCatalog;
  FROM  Storage  IMPORT
    ALLOCATE, DEALLOCATE;

  TYPE
    AuthorPointer = POINTER TO Author;
    PublicationPointer = POINTER TO Publication;
    Name   = ARRAY[0..29] OF CHAR;
    Author = RECORD
               name:  Name;
               publicationList:  PublicationPointer;
               nextAuthor:  AuthorPointer
             END;
```

```
    Publication = RECORD
                        title:  Name;
                        author:  AuthorPointer;
                        nextPublication:  PublicationPointer
                    END;

VAR authorList:  AuthorPointer;

PROCEDURE NewCatalog;
BEGIN
  authorList := NIL
END  NewCatalog;

PROCEDURE  AppendPublication(authorname, titleName:Name);
  VAR
    found:  BOOLEAN;
    auth, lastAuth:  AuthorPointer;
    publication, pubAuxil:  PublicationPointer;
BEGIN
  NEW(publication);              (* creates new publication object *)
  WITH publication^  DO
    title := titleName;        (* record title from parameter*)
    nextPublication := NIL  (* no successor yet *)
  END;    (* WITH *)
  auth := authorList;          (* search for author name in list *)
  found := FALSE;
  WHILE   (auth#NIL) AND NOT found  DO
    found := SameName(auth^.name, authorname);
    lastAuth := auth;
    auth := auth^.nextAuthor
  END;    (* WHILE *)
  IF NOT found
    THEN                            (* new author *)
      NEW(auth);              (* create new author object *)
      IF authorList = NIL
        THEN authorList := auth
        ELSE  lastAuth^.nextAuthor := auth
      END;    (* IF *)
      WITH auth^  DO
        nextAuthor := NIL;
        name := authorname;
        publicationList := publication   (* assign publication to
                                                           author*)
      END  (* WITH *)
    ELSE                   (* author found, find last publication *)
      pubAuxil := auth^.publicationList;
      WHILE  pubAuxil^.nextPublication # NIL  DO
        pubAuxil := pubAuxil^.nextPublication
      END;    (* WHILE *)
      pubAuxil^.nextPublication := publication (*append to list*)
  END;
  publication^.author := auth (* establish author reference *)
END AppendPublication;
```

```
PROCEDURE SameName(name1, name2:Name):BOOLEAN;
...
END  SameName;


  ...
END AuthorCatalog.
```

The procedure `AppendPublication` creates a new object `publication`. The next step is to test whether the publication's author is already in the list. If so, the new publication is appended to the end of the author's publication list. (For the sake of simplicity, we did not test whether the new publication already exists in the list.) If the author is not yet in the list, then a new object is created for this author and the publication is entered as his only one.

4.3.2 Dynamically Created RECORDs with Variants

The procedure `NEW` also permits constants as parameters if a RECORD with variants is to be created (see Section 3.7.8). These constants must serve to differentiate variants in the RECORD to be created. Consider the following extension of our library example:

```
TYPE
   AuthorPointer = POINTER TO Author;
   PublicationPointer = POINTER TO Publicaton;
   Name = ARRAY[0..29] OF CHAR;
   Author      =    RECORD
                      name:  Name;
                      nextAuthor:  AuthorPointer;
                      publicationList: PublicationPointer;
                      CASE hasPenName:  BOOLEAN OF
                        TRUE: penName: Name;
                      | FALSE: (* no further components *)
                      END;
                    END;
   Publication =    RECORD
                      ...
                    END;

   VAR authorPtr: AuthorPointer;
```

We can now dynamically create an object that is assigned storage for only the components `name`, `publicationList`, and `nextAuthor` by means of the invocation of NEW as follows:

```
NEW(authorPtr, FALSE)
```

Invoking the procedure with `TRUE` or without the boolean parameter, i.e., `NEW(authorPtr, TRUE)` or `NEW(authorPtr)`, would reserve memory for the additional component `penName`. The programmer must observe two points:

- Memory is only reserved for the dynamically created object; the component for differentiating the variants is not assigned a value.

- Freeing memory must proceed analogously to its allocation.

The second requirement means that the parameter lists in the invocation of the two procedures NEW and DISPOSE must be the same. The following invocation deletes the object created by NEW(authorPtr, FALSE):

```
DISPOSE(authorPtr, FALSE)
```

If the parameter lists do not match, then it is possible that more memory is freed than was originally reserved. The following invocations would include the component penName in the calculation of how much memory to deallocate (although no memory was reserved for penName in the creation of the object):

```
DISPOSE(authorPtr, TRUE)    or    DISPOSE(authorPtr)
```

This can lead to errors that are very difficult for the programmer to locate.

4.4 Recursion

Although vital to computer science, the principle of recursion is by no means the sole domain of this discipline. Recursion occurs each time that a definition is explained in terms of itself or parts of itself.

The following are examples of recursion:

- in mathematics:

  The factorial of n is defined recursively for $n \geq 0$:
  ```
  0! = 1,
  n! = n * (n-1)!      for n>0
  ```
- in optics:
  The multiple reflection of an object located between facing mirrors is a kind of recursion.

- in story telling:
  Once upon a time there was a man who had seven sons.
  The seven sons said, "Father, tell us a story."
  The father began:
      "Once upon a time there was a man who had seven sons.
      The seven sons said, "Father, tell us a story."
      ..."

The scope of a Modula-2 introductory book does not permit extensive handling of every imaginable application of the principle of recursion in programming. This section strives instead to explain recursion itself in fundamental terms and to demonstrate its application in programming by means of several examples.

4.4.1 Recursive Procedures

Recursive algorithms are implemented with the help of procedures. A procedure can be invoked at any point within a program at which its name is known. Since the procedure name is known in the statement part of the procedure itself, this means that any procedure can invoke *itself*.

The Euclidean algorithm for determining the greatest common divisor of two positive numbers m and n (introduced in Section 1.4) can be defined recursively as follows:

- GCD(m,n) := GCD(n,m)   for n > m
- GCD(m,n) := n   for m MOD n = 0
- GCD(m,n) := GCD(n, m MOD n)   for m MOD n <> 0

The definition of GCD uses the function GCD itself at two locations. This recursive definition can be transformed directly into the following procedure:

```
PROCEDURE GCD(m,n:CARDINAL):CARDINAL;
BEGIN
   IF  n>m  THEN  RETURN  GCD(n,m)  END;
   IF  m MOD n = 0
      THEN RETURN n
      ELSE RETURN  GCD(n, m MOD n)
   END
END GCD;
```

If we compare the above recursive solution to the original procedure at the end of Section 1.4, the following characteristics can be observed:

- The recursive procedure is considerably shorter than the nonrecursive solution. This outstanding compactness is a typical property of recursive procedures.

  Note : The recursive solution can be further shortened by simply omitting the first IF statement. Proving the correctness of this claim is left to the reader.

- The recursive approach requires neither local auxiliary variables nor assignment statements. (Assignments do, however, occur in covert form in the recursive invocations when the value of the actual parameter is passed to the respective formal parameter.)

- The recursive procedure does not call itself for all possible parameter combinations (specifically, not when n≤m and m is divisible by n without a remainder). All recursive procedures share this attribute since at some point the recursive invocation must end when no further invocation is necessary. Otherwise such a procedure would never return a result because yet another invocation would always be necessary and no invocation could bring about an end.

Note also that the loop in the nonrecursive procedure corresponds to the recursive invocation in our new solution. The nonrecursive branch is executed under the same conditions that lead to loop termination in the original procedure (when m is divisible by n).

Based on this observation, the transformability of any iterative algorithm (i.e., one containing loops) into a recursive algorithm can be shown. This is applied in what is known as *functional programming*. The following is a simple example of the transformation of an iterative into a recursive algorithm:

An array x is given whose first n elements are occupied and whose data type is

```
CardinalArray = ARRAY[1..100] OF CARDINAL;
```

Compute the sum of all its elements from x[1] to x[n].

An iterative solution:

```
PROCEDURE Sum(x:CardinalArray; n:CARDINAL):CARDINAL;
  VAR i, s: CARDINAL;
BEGIN
  s := 0;
  FOR  i:=1  TO  n  DO
    s := s+x[i]
  END;
  RETURN  s
END Sum;
```

A recursive solution:

```
PROCEDURE Sum(x:CardinalArray; n:CARDINAL):CARDINAL;
BEGIN
  IF  n=0
    THEN RETURN 0
    ELSE RETURN  Sum(x,n-1) + x[n]
  END
END Sum;
```

Here again, notice that the recursive solution is shorter than the iterative one and that the recursive procedure requires no local variables for loop control or for sum accumulation.

Our examples so far have used *direct recursion* , i.e., a procedures invokes itself. If a procedure P1 calls a second procedure P2 which in turn again invokes P1, we have an instance of *indirect recursion*. Such indirect recursion can extend through multiple levels of invocation. While direct recursion can clearly be read from the body of a procedure, indirect recursion is more elusive. Locating indirect recursion might require reading through an entire program. Figure 4.4 graphically depicts indirect recursion.

A procedure A invokes procedures B and C. Procedure C calls procedure D, which in turn invokes A. We have a case of indirect recursion: A ⇒ C ⇒ D ⇒ A ⇒...

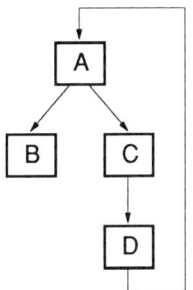

Fig. 4.4 Indirect recursion

4.4.2 Inner Structure of Recursive Procedures and How They Work

We have established that all recursive procedures must contain at least one nonrecursive branch that requires no further recursive invocations; otherwise the recursive algorithm would never end. Figure 4.5 shows the general structure of direct recursive procedures in flow chart form. The structure of indirect recursive procedures is analogous.

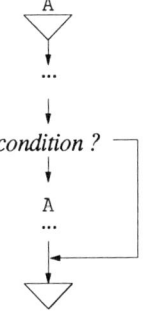

Fig. 4.5 Structure of a directly recursive procedure

We will use the example of factorial computation in order to follow the flow of a recursive procedure. Figure 4.6 shows a flow chart for factorial computation and execution with a concrete value of 3 for n :

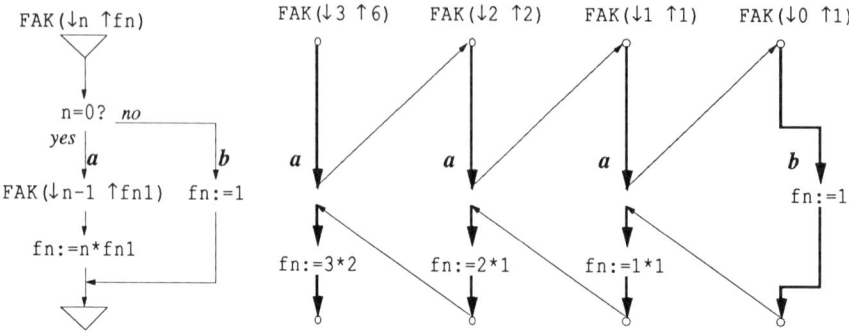

Fig. 4.6 Recursive computation of 3!

In this example, the recursive procedure invocation occurs in branch a. Branch b does not contain a recursive invocation. Execution of this branch leads to a normal end of the procedure for the first time. This causes a return to the previous recursion level, effecting a normal end for branch a of the invoking procedure.

A novice might get the wrong impression that the recursive invocation of a procedure amounts to nothing more than a branch to the beginning of the program (comparable to a GOTO in older programming languages). In actuality, a region of memory is reserved for the local variables and parameters in the procedure with each invocation. This means that changes occurring in the reserved memory of a recursively invoked procedure have no effect on the local variables and parameters of the invoking procedure. After a return from a recursively invoked procedure, the invoking procedure continues to work with values established before the recursive invocation (and with values returned by the invoked procedure).

4.4.3 Some Examples of Recursive Algorithms

This section shows examples of both direct and indirect recursive procedures in Modula-2.

(1)   Binary Search

A list of length len contains CARDINAL numbers sorted in ascending order. A procedure is required that determines whether the CARDINAL value x is contained in the list. If so, then the index i of the value is to be returned (so that list[i] = x); otherwise i is assigned the value −1.

We base our algorithm on the knowledge that the list is sorted, so that we need only search in sublists. If we take the middle element in the list and compare it to x, we can quickly determine whether the element x is contained in the first or second half of the list (if at all). By repeatedly applying this process, i.e., by halving the respective sublist each time, we either arrive at the element being sought or an empty sublist (in case the element is not in the list). A possible procedure in Modula-2 is:

```
PROCEDURE    BinSearch(list:ARRAY OF CARDINAL;x, first,last:CARDINAL;
                        VAR i:INTEGER);
VAR m:   CARDINAL;
BEGIN
   IF   first > last
      THEN  i := -1
      ELSE
         m := (first + last) DIV 2;
         IF  x = list[m]  THEN  i := m
            ELSIF  x < list[m]  THEN  BinSearch(list, x, first, m-1, i)
            ELSE  BinSearch(list, x, m+1, last, i)
         END
   END
END BinSearch;
```

In contrast to the problem description, the parameter list contains the first and last indices of
the list (instead of the length of the list) as value parameters. This readily permits an exact
description of the sublist which is currently being searched. For list[0..len-1] the
invocation would be BinSearch(list,x,0,len-1,i).

(2)   Test for Divisibility

A pipe has a length of totLen. Test whether the pipe can be cut into any number of
pieces with lengths len1, len2 or len3 in such a way that there is no waste. If such a
reduction is possible, then TRUE is to be returned by the function; otherwise, FALSE.

Our example is very simple. The total length of the pipe is reduced by len1, len2 or
len3. As long as the remaining total length is greater than zero, we continue the process.
If the total length is reduced to zero, the reduction is possible. If the total length drops
below zero, then at least that approach has failed. A possible Modula-2 solution is:

```
PROCEDURE Divisible(totLen,len1,len2,len3:INTEGER):BOOLEAN;
BEGIN
   IF  totLen = 0
      THEN RETURN TRUE
      ELSIF  totLen < 0   THEN RETURN FALSE
      ELSE RETURN Divisible(totLen-len1,len1,len2,len3)
                 OR Divisible(totLen-len2,len1,len2,len3)
                 OR Divisible(totLen-len3,len1,len2,len3)
   END
END Divisible;
```

This example shows how simple and compact recursive solutions can be. Although a large
number of combinations must be tested, we get by without nested loops and have only a
single IF construct. We must be aware, however, that every invocation of Divisible
can cause three further recursive invocations. The set of possible combinations is covered
by a multitude of recursive invocations.

(3)   Testing for Prime Numbers

For a given positive integer n greater than or equal to 2, a function procedure Prime is to return the boolean value TRUE if n is a prime number and FALSE otherwise. Our solution is based on the following algorithm:

Step 1 [initialization]
>   Set k:=2 (2 being the smallest prime number).

Step 2 [end?]
>   If k≥n then n is a prime number and the algorithm ends (n was not divisible by any prime number k); otherwise continue with step 3.

Step 3..[divisibility]
>   Determine the remainder of the division n/k. If it is zero, then n is not a prime number and the algorithm ends; otherwise continue with step 4.

Step 4 [next prime number]
>   Replace k with the next largest prime number and return to step 2.

Here is a possible solution using Modula-2 procedures:

```
PROCEDURE Prime(n:CARDINAL):BOOLEAN;
  VAR k:  CARDINAL;
BEGIN
  k := 2;       (* 2 is the smallest prime number *)
  LOOP
    IF  k*k > n   THEN
      RETURN TRUE END;   (* not divisible by any prime  k *)
    IF  n MOD k = 0   THEN
      RETURN FALSE END;
    k := NextPrime(k)
  END
END Prime;

PROCEDURE NextPrime(k:CARDINAL):CARDINAL;
BEGIN
  REPEAT
    INC(k)
  UNTIL Prime(k);
  RETURN k
END NextPrime;
```

The procedure Prime tests whether a given number n is prime by first testing its divisibility by the smallest prime number, 2. If n is not divisible by 2, then Prime continues to try successively larger prime numbers until either a divisor is found or the square of the assumed divisor is larger than the number n (see Example 3 in Section 1.5). The procedure NextPrime finds the next largest prime number, using the procedure Prime in the process. We have an example of indirect recursion.

4.4.4 Advantages and Disadvantages of Recursive Programming

In principle, every algorithm that can be formulated recursively can be implemented as a recursive procedure. The question arises of what advantages recursive programming has. Let us outline the most important ones:

- For many problem statements, a recursive solution is more natural than a nonrecursive one.

- The correctness of recursive solutions is usually more easily checked than is the case with their nonrecursive equivalents.

- Compared to nonrecursive alternatives, recursive solutions are usually shorter and more compact in terms of source code.

- Recursive solutions are more obliging when it comes to changes. Often a change needs to be made at only a single location, whereas a change in a nonrecursive equivalent often affects multiple locations in the code.

Recursive programs are, however, usually less efficient than equivalent iterative solutions. An example is the summation of the first n numbers in the array in Section 4.4.1. Every recursive invocation consumes memory. Each procedure call requires the reservation of memory for local variables and parameters. (In the procedure Sum, this means 101 words of memory for x and n.) For n=50, the procedure is invoked a total of 51 times, which means that 5151 words of memory are required for the summation of the first 50 elements of the array. Compare this to the 103 words of memory required in the iterative approach.

As a rule of thumb, recursive algorithms should be used when the problem is defined recursively. Wirth writes that recursion is to be avoided whenever there is an *obvious* nonrecursive solution (Wirth 1975).

4.5 Language Extension Modules

Most high-level programming languages provide a variety of standard procedures and functions that are built into the language and are intended to make the programmer's life easier. Modula-2 avoids such inflation of the language by providing only a small set of standard procedures (see Section 3.7.8). Instead, the module concept was employed to build up library modules of useful procedures for various areas of application. A programmer can write additional library modules to meet his specialized needs. Unfortunately, this leads to a large number of modules (as in the case of I/O) that can vary a great deal in terms of scope and capabilities from one computer to the next. (This simply echoes the need for binding standards.) We will thus introduce only a series of simple modules that should be available on most computers with little or no deviation.

4.5.1 The Module MathLib0

The library module `MathLib0` exports eight procedures for calculations with REAL numbers. Its definition module looks like this:

```
DEFINITION MODULE MathLib0;
(*  standard functions for REAL numbers *)

  PROCEDURE sqrt(x:REAL):REAL;
  (* sqrt(x) returns the square root of the number x *)

  PROCEDURE exp(x:REAL):REAL;
  (* exp(x) returns the value of the exponential function eˣ *)

  PROCEDURE ln(x:REAL):REAL;
  (* ln(x) returns the natural logarithm (base e) of x *)

  PROCEDURE sin(x:REAL):REAL;
  (* sin(x) returns the sine of the angle x, which is in radians *)

  PROCEDURE cos(x:REAL):REAL;
  (* cos(x) returns the cosine of the angle x, which is in radians *)

  PROCEDURE arctan(x:REAL):REAL;
  (* arctan(x) returns the angle (in radians) whose tangent is x *)

  PROCEDURE real(x:INTEGER):REAL;
  (* real(x) converts the INTEGER x into a REAL number *)

  PROCEDURE entier(x:REAL):INTEGER;
  (* entier(x) returns the largest INTEGER <= x *)

END MathLib0.
```

You will notice that `MathLib0` does not provide all possible mathematical functions. Instead, it avails some basic functions on which other related functions can be based. Thus, for example, a procedure `arcsin` could be implemented with the help of `arctan` and `sqrt` as follows:

```
PROCEDURE  arcsin(x:REAL):REAL;
BEGIN
  RETURN arctan(x/sqrt(1.0-x*x) )
END  arcsin;
```

In using the module `MathLib0`, care must be taken that function arguments (i.e., procedure parameters) fall within respective permissible ranges. For example, the parameter of `sqrt` cannot be negative and the parameter value of `entier` must be within the range of INTEGER values. If a procedure is called with an improper parameter value, the function value is undefined. Normally the program terminates with an error message.

4.5.2 The Module String

The library module String provides seven procedures for string manipulations. Since there is no data type to represent strings in Modula-2, these procedures work with ARRAY parameters. In this way, character strings of any length can be processed. The definition module takes the following form:

```
DEFINITION MODULE String;
(* procedures for string manipulations *)

  CONST
    first =     0;  (* position of the first character in a string*)
    last  = 65535;  (* position of the last character in a maximum-
                                              length string *)

  PROCEDURE Length(VAR s:ARRAY OF CHAR):CARDINAL;
    (* Length(s) determines the length of the string s. *)

  PROCEDURE Occurs(VAR s:ARRAY OF CHAR; start:CARDINAL;
                                    w:ARRAY OF CHAR):CARDINAL;
    (* Occurs(s,start,w) searches the character string s
       beginning at the character  s[start]  for the
       substring w.  If w is found,  Occurs  returns the
       index of w's first character in s.  If w is not found,
       the value last (=65535) is returned.
                  e.g.: s = "ABCDEFGHIJ"
                        Occurs(s,2,"EFG") = 4
                        Occurs(s,5,"EFG") = last *)

  PROCEDURE Insert(VAR s:ARRAY OF CHAR; at:CARDINAL;
                                    w:ARRAY OF INTEGER);
    (* Insert(s,at,w) inserts the string w in the string s
       immediately before the character s[at].  If the string
       variable s does not contain enough elements to absorb
       the resulting longer character string, this string is
       truncated.  If at=last, then w is appended to s.  If
       Length(s)<at<last, then blanks are added to the end of
       s to allow w to begin with s[at]. *)

  PROCEDURE InsertCh(VAR s:ARRAY OF CHAR; at:CARDINAL; ch:CHAR);
    (* InsertCh(s,at,ch) inserts the character ch at the
       position at so that s[at]=ch. *)

  PROCEDURE Delete(VAR s:ARRAY OF CHAR; start, length:CARDINAL);
    (* Delete(s,start,length) deletes the substring
       s[start..start+length-1] in the string s. *)

  PROCEDURE Copy(VAR s:ARRAY OF CHAR; w:ARRAY OF CHAR;
                                    start, length:CARDINAL);
    (* Copy(s,w,start,length) assigns the substring
       w[start..start+length-1] to the string s.  If the
       string variable s has less than length elements, the
       resultant character string is truncated.*)
```

```
PROCEDURE Same(VAR s:ARRAY OF CHAR; start, length:CARDINAL;
                                        w:ARRAY OF CHAR);
(* Same(s,start,length,w) tests whether the substring
   s[start..start+length-1] is characterwise identical to
   w. *)
```

```
END String.
```

Whenever a VAR parameter is required, the actual paramater at invocation time must be a character string *variable* . When ARRAY parameters are passed, the maximum length of the string is passed to the invoked procedure, where it can be accessed with the standard function HIGH (see Section 3.7.8). The current length of the string variable (i.e., the number of elements actually occupied) is marked by the null character 0C following the last character.

4.5.3 The Module Storage

In Sections 3.7.8, "Standard Procedures," and 4.3, "Dynamic Data Structures," we explained that every invocation of the standard procedures NEW and DISPOSE is translated by the compiler into invocations of ALLOCATE and DEALLOCATE, respectively. The latter procedures must be made available by the user, and the simplest way to do so is to import them from the module Storage, whose definition module follows:

```
DEFINITION MODULE Storage;
(* procedures for dynamic memory allocation *)

  FROM SYSTEM IMPORT ADDRESS;

  PROCEDURE ALLOCATE(VAR a:ADDRESS; size:CARDINAL);
  (* ALLOCATE(a, size) reserves a region of size words of
     available memory and returns its address a.  If less
     than size contiguous words of memory are available,
     the program is terminated. *)

  PROCEDURE DEALLOCATE(VAR a:ADDRESS; size:CARDINAL);
  (* DEALLOCATE(a, size)  frees the memory reserved in the
     corresponding  ALLOCATE  procuedure invocation. *)

  PROCEDURE Available(size:CARDINAL):BOOLEAN;
  (* Available(size)   returns TRUE if  size  contiguous
     words of memory are available, otherwise FALSE.
     Available  can be used to avoid an abnormal program
     termination caused by an unsuccessful invocation of
     ALLOCATE. *)

END Storage.
```

When using ALLOCATE and DEALLOCATE (or NEW and DISPOSE), it is important to free regions of memory with the same size as specified when they were reserved (refer to Section 4.3).

4.6 Parallel Processes

In Section 3.10, "Processes and Coroutines," we became acquainted with the elementary language elements that Modula-2 provides for programming parallel processes (more precisely, coroutines). This section shows how more abstract mechanisms can be implemented on the basis of this simple concept.

Modula-2 requires every change of processes with TRANSFER to identify which process is next in line. If a program system contains only two processes, this is superfluous because it is clear that the (only) other process is to assume control. When more than two processes are involved, care must be taken that no process is overlooked. The simple module below independently manages all the processes that exist in a given program. Such a module is often termed a *process scheduler*.

```
DEFINITION MODULE  SimpleScheduler;

    PROCEDURE  CreateProcess(P:PROC;  workspaceSize:CARDINAL);

    PROCEDURE  Pass;

END  SimpleScheduler.
```

The module SimpleScheduler exports only two procedures:

- CreateProcess generates a new process whose actions are established in the procedure P. The amount of memory in words required for execution of the process is given in workspaceSize.

- Pass can be invoked within a process to surrender control to some other process. The procedure Pass ensures that transferring from one process to another follows some orderly plan (schedule) that guarantees that each process has its turn.

Note that the definition module of SimpleScheduler does not contain any system-dependent language elements. Use of this module is therefore not restricted to any particular computer. (Remember: the elementary language elements for handling processes are exported by SYSTEM and as such are highly system-dependent.)

The following example shows how the module SimpleScheduler can be used. We again use the producer/consumer problem from Section 3.10.1:

```
MODULE ProcessDemo2;
   FROM Terminal IMPORT
      Read, Write;
   FROM SimpleScheduler IMPORT
      CreateProcess, Pass;

   VAR char: CHAR;
```

```
    PROCEDURE Consumer;
    BEGIN
      LOOP
        IF  char="$"  THEN EXIT END;
        Write(char);
        Pass
      END
    END Consumer;

  BEGIN
    CreateProcess(Consumer,100);
    LOOP
      Read(char);
      Pass
    END
  END ProcessDemo2.
```

The program module `ProcessDemo2` now contains nothing that has to do with scheduling the involved processes. The processes `p` and `c` as well as the `workspaceSize` for the procedure `Consumer` have disappeared; all are now hidden in the module `SimpleScheduler`.

We will now develop the implementation module for `SimpleScheduler`. First we need to consider a couple of points regarding process scheduling:

- In order to achieve *fair scheduling* (i.e., each process has a turn in some just distribution), all processes are to be arranged in a ring (a circular linked list). Each invocation of `Pass` causes the next process in this ring to assume control.

- When a process is created with `NEWPROCESS`, memory must be reserved for the process. We use the procedure `ALLOCATE` from the module `Storage` for this purpose (see Section 4.5.3).

```
    IMPLEMENTATION MODULE SimpleScheduler;
      FROM SYSTEM IMPORT
        PROCESS, NEWPROCESS, TRANSFER, ADDRESS;
      FROM Storage IMPORT ALLOCATE;

      TYPE
        ProcessPtr  =   POINTER TO Process;
        Process     =   RECORD
                          p: PROCESS;
                          next: ProcessPtr
                        END;

      VAR
        first: ProcessPtr;   (* first process in the ring *)
        last:  ProcessPtr;   (* last created process *)
        cp:    ProcessPtr;   (* current process *)
```

```
PROCEDURE CreateProcess(P:PROC; workspaceSize:CARDINAL);
  VAR workspaceAddr:  ADDRESS;
BEGIN
  ALLOCATE(workspaceAddr, workspaceSize);
  NEW(last^.next);
  last := last^.next;  (* append a new node to the ring *)
  WITH  last^  DO
    NEWPROCESS(P, wordspaceAddr, workspaceSize, p);
    next := first
  END
END CreateProcess;

PROCEDURE Pass;
  VAR old: ProcessPtr;
BEGIN
  old := cp;  cp := cp^.next;
  TRANSFER(old^.p, cp^.p)
END Pass;

BEGIN
  NEW(first);  first^.next := first;
  last := first;  cp := first
END  SimpleScheduler.
```

The reader might find it difficult to understand how the procedure Pass functions in process transfer. The following example is intended to clarify this mechanism:

```
MODULE M;
  . . .
  PROCEDURE P;
  BEGIN
    B;
    Pass;
    D;
    Pass
  END P;

BEGIN
  CreateProcess(P,100);
  A;
  Pass;
  C;
  Pass;
  E
END M.
```

In the execution of module M, the procedures A, B, C, D and E are to be executed (in that order). Figure 4.7 shows how the procedure Pass ensures that this order is maintained. We represent the two processes alongside one another and designate the program flow with a continuous line. The broken lines depict the duration of execution of the individual procedures.

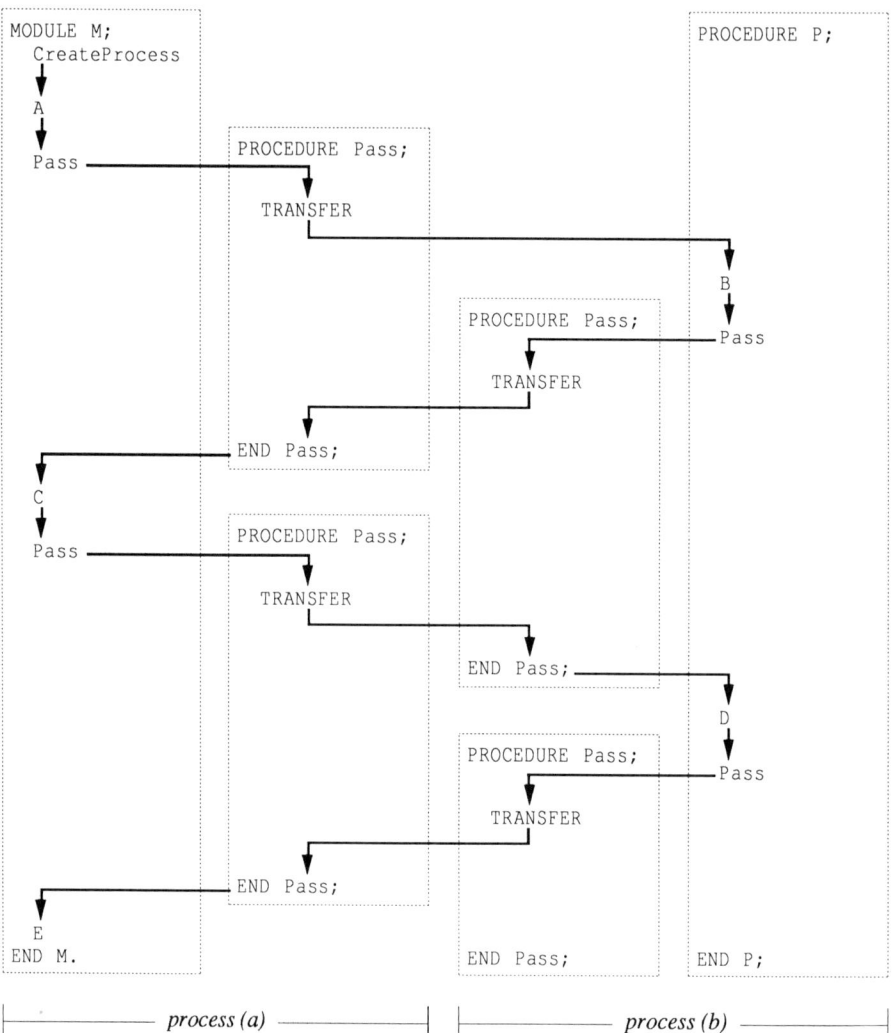

Fig. 4.7 Process switches by means of a procedure

As the illustration shows, each invocation of TRANSFER in the procedure Pass causes the current state of the process being executed (i.e., the state immediately before the end of the procedure Pass) to be saved and to be restored at the next invocation of TRANSFER. The continuation of the process occurs for a time within the procedure Pass; after the end of the procedure, execution resumes after its invocation.

The illustration furthermore shows that the procedure `Pass` can be active in both processes simultaneously. (*Caution!* This is not to be misinterpreted as recursion.) Note that the execution of the procedure `P` and the last invocation of `Pass` in process (b) never reach their ENDs.

The module `SimpleScheduler` shows how—based on the elementary process concept—the creation of processes and process transfer can be elevated to a higher level. This module does not contain mechanisms for process synchronization. Numerous concepts can be found in computer science literature that support language elements for synchronization (compare Wirth 1984). Even a general survey of these methods would be beyond the scope of this book, so we will limit ourselves to the introduction of one example.

In programming parallel processes, we often encounter the requirement that certain resources (e.g., a peripheral device) be used by not more than one process at a time (*mutual exclusion*). We presented one such example in Section 3.10 (the module `Clock`). By assigning priorities, we ensured that only one process at a time can adjust the time or read the clock. The situation becomes more challenging if process transfers occur while a process is using a given resource. Imagine a program with multiple processes, two of which want to print a long text. Since printing takes a rather long time, each of the two processes allows other processes to continue execution (for example, at intervals such as after the printing of a line):

```
...
FOR  i:=1  TO  n  DO     (* print n lines *)
   Print(line[i]);
   Pass
END;
...
```

With the above scheduling mechanism, if two processes wanted to print at the same time, `Pass` would ensure that they receive the resource alternately. You can imagine that the resulting printout would be scarcely decipherable.

A simple mechanism to guarantee mutual exclusion in such a case consists of the introduction of the state variable `printerReady` that indicates whether a text is currently being printed:

```
...
WHILE NOT  printerReady  DO  Pass  END;
printerReady := FALSE;
FOR  i:= 1  TO  n  DO
   Print(line[i]);
   Pass
END;
printerReady := TRUE;
...
```

Before a process can claim the printer, the printer must be available. As long as this is not the case, other processes are handled. As soon as the printer becomes available, it is reserved (`printerReady:=FALSE`) and released only after the last line has been printed. In the meantime, however, several processes might have requested the printer. The module `SimpleScheduler` transfers control in the same order in which they were created by `CreateProcess`. That does not agree with the order that we would prefer for fair scheduling. We would expect that the processes be allocated the printer in the same order in which they requested them.

The following module for scheduling parallel processes contains the synchronization mechanism known as a *semaphore*, first introduced by Dijkstra (1968).

Semaphores describe events . They permit the following operations:

> `Signal(s)`   announces the occurrence of event s.
>
> `Wait(s)`   waits until event s occurs.

Invocations of `Signal` and `Wait` always match pairwise. The nth invocation of `Signal(s)` reports that the the event s has occurred for the nth time. The nth invocation of `Wait(s)` waits for the nth occurrence of the event s. The effects of `Signal` and `Wait` depend on the chronological order in which they were invoked. Two cases need to be delineated:

(a) The nth invocation of `Signal(s)` takes place before the nth invocation of `Wait(s)`. At the time when `Wait(s)` is invoked, event s has already occurred n times. Neither `Signal(s)` nor `Wait(s)` has any effect on program execution. (In particular, the process which calls `Wait(s)` can continue to execute without interruption).

(b) The nth invocation of `Signal(s)` takes place after the nth invocation of `Wait(s)`. At the time when `Wait(s)` is invoked, event s has not yet occurred n times. In this case, the process which called `Wait(s)` for the nth time is placed in a wait state and is activated again only after the nth invocation of `Signal(s)`.

Semaphores can be implemented in Modula-2 with the help of an abstract data type. We still need a third operation, `InitSemaphore`, for the initialization of a semaphore. (The value of s after the invocation of `InitSemaphore` means that neither `Signal(s)` nor `Wait(s)` has been invoked so far.) Our definition module (named `Scheduler`) takes the following form:

```
DEFINITION MODULE Scheduler;

    PROCEDURE CreateProcess(P:PROC; workspaceSize:CARDINAL);
    PROCEDURE Pass;

    TYPE Semaphore;     (* abstract data type *)

    PROCEDURE InitSemaphore(VAR s:Semaphore);
    PROCEDURE Signal(s:Semaphore);
    PROCEDURE Wait(s:Semaphore);

END Scheduler.
```

Like SimpleScheduler, the module Scheduler exports the two procedures CreateProcess and Pass for generating processes and for transferring control to another process. In addition, Scheduler provides routines for process synchronization.

In order to achieve mutual exclusion during printing in our example, we can replace the boolean variable printerReady with a semaphore of the same name:

```
...
Wait (printerReady);
FOR  i:=1  TO  n  DO
   Print(line[i]);
   Pass
END;
Signal(printerReady);
...
```

But before we can work with this semaphore, we need to initialize it:

```
...
InitSemaphore(printerReady);
Signal(printerReady);
...
```

The invocation of Signal is required in our case to indicate that the printer is available at the beginning of program execution. The first process that wants to print a text thus has the go-ahead. If, however, a second process requests the printer by invoking Wait (for the second time) while the first is still printing, then the second process must wait until the first process invokes the procedure Signal (for the second time) and thereby releases the printer. If several processes request the printer in the interim, the second invocation of Signal assures that the first process in the queue gets its turn (i.e., the process that invoked the second Wait).

Before formulating the implementation module for Scheduler, we need to determine what kinds of data structures will be used. Since this module is an enhancement of SimpleScheduler, we will again use a linked circular list in order to connect all processes with one another. A semaphore can be implemented as a RECORD with two components:

events: CARDINAL

indicates how often the event described by the semaphore has occurred without a process waiting for it. Thus events>0 means that the procedure Wait can be called that number of times without a process having to wait.

firstWaiting: ProcessPtr

points to the process that has been waiting the longest for the event described by the semaphore. All succeeding processes are linked in the order in which they invoked Wait and thus form a queue.

A semaphore can thus assume the following values:

```
events=0, firstWaiting=NIL
```

Signal and Wait were invoked the same number of times.

```
events>0, firstWaiting=NIL
```

Signal was called events times more often than Wait.

```
events=0, firstWaiting≠NIL
```

Wait was invoked more often than Signal. The processes waiting on events are in a queue, and firstWaiting points to the first process in that queue.

Note that the case events>0, firstWaiting≠NIL cannot occur.

The semaphore concept places additional demands on the linked ring that schedules all the processes. Every element in the ring must have a flag indicating whether the process is ready or waiting for some event. A process in a waiting state must be skipped when Pass is invoked. If a process is waiting for an event, its corresponding element in the ring must be able to point to its successor in the queue. Two components need to be added to the data type Process of the module SimpleScheduler:

```
TYPE
  ProcessPtr = POINTER TO Process;
  Process =  RECORD
               p: PROCESS;
               next:  ProcessPtr;      (* next process in ring *)
               ready: BOOLEAN;         (* ready or waiting? *)
               successor:  ProcessPtr  (* next process in queue *)
             END;
```

With these considerations in mind, we can now formulate the implementation module for Scheduler:

```
IMPLEMENTATION MODULE Scheduler;
  FROM SYSTEM IMPORT
    PROCESS, NEWPROCESS, TRANSFER, ADDRESS;
  FROM Storage IMPORT ALLOCATE;
  FROM Terminal IMPORT WriteString;
  TYPE
    ProcessPtr = POINTER TO Process;
    Process =  RECORD
                 p: PROCESS;
                 next:  ProcessPtr;      (* next process in ring *)
                 ready: BOOLEAN;         (* ready or waiting? *)
                 successor:  ProcessPtr  (* next process in queue *)
               END;
    Semaphore =  POINTER TO RECORD
                   events:  CARDINAL;
                   firstWaiting:  ProcessPtr;
                 END;
```

```
VAR cp:  ProcessPtr;

PROCEDURE CreateProcess(P:PROC; workspaceSize:CARDINAL);
  VAR
    workspaceAddr: ADDRESS;
    newProc: ProcessPtr;
BEGIN
  ALLOCATE(workspaceAddr, workspaceSize);
  NEW(newProc);
  WITH  newProc^  DO
    NEWPROCESS(P, workspaceAddr, workspaceSize, p);
    next := cp^.next;
    ready := TRUE;
    successor := NIL
  END;
  cp^.next := newProc
END CreateProcess;

PROCEDURE Pass;
  VAR old: ProcessPtr;
BEGIN
  old := cp;
  REPEAT                   (* find a ready process *)
    cp := cp^.next
  UNTIL  cp^.ready  OR  (cp=old);
  IF  cp^.ready
    THEN TRANSFER(old^.p, cp^.p)
    ELSE WriteString("--deadlock--");  HALT
  END
END Pass;

PROCEDURE InitSemaphore(VAR s:Semaphore);
BEGIN
  NEW(s);
  WITH  s^  DO
    events := 0;
    firstWaiting := NIL
  END
END InitSemaphore;
```

```
PROCEDURE Signal(s:Semaphore);
  VAR old: ProcessPtr;
BEGIN
  WITH  s^  DO
    IF firstWaiting=NIL
      THEN INC(events)            (* no waiting processes *)
      ELSE                        (* activate waiting process *)
        old := cp;
        cp := firstWaiting;
        firstWaiting := cp^.successor;
        WITH  cp^  DO
          ready := TRUE;
          successor := NIL
        END;
        TRANSFER(old^.p, cp^.p)
    END  (* IF *)
  END  (* WITH *)
END Signal;

PROCEDURE Wait(s:Semaphore);
  VAR last: ProcessPtr;
BEGIN
  WITH  s^  DO
    IF  events>0
      THEN DEC(events)            (* event already occurred *)
      ELSE                        (* deactivate current process *)
        IF  firstWaiting=NIL      (* and append it to queue *)
          THEN  firstWaiting := cp
          ELSE
            last := firstWaiting;
            WHILE  last^.successor#NIL  DO
              last := last^.successor
            END;
            last^.successor := cp
        END;
        WITH  cp^  DO
          ready := FALSE;
          successor := NIL
        END;
        Pass                      (* transfer to next ready process *)
    END  (* IF *)
  END  (* WITH *)
END Wait;

BEGIN  (* Scheduler *)
  NEW(cp);
  WITH  cp^  DO
    next := cp;
    ready := TRUE;
    successor := NIL
  END
END Scheduler.
```

The procedure Wait first tests whether Signal has already been invoked more often than
Wait (events>0). If that is the case, then events (i.e., the difference between

invocations of Signal and Wait) is decremented by one and the process can proceed immediately. If the awaited event has not yet occurred, the currently active process is placed at the end of the queue for the semaphore and its ready flag is set to FALSE. Control is then passed to some other process by means of Pass.

The procedure Signal first tests whether there is a process waiting for its event (firstWaiting#NIL). If that is not the case, then the component events of the semaphore simply records an excess of invocations of Signal. If a process is waiting for the event, it is taken from the queue, marked as "ready" and activated.

The procedure Pass needs to skip over (in a loop) all processes that are in a waiting state (i.e., not ready). The case could arise that all processes are in a waiting state, a condition known as *deadlock*. Since there is no way out of a deadlock, program execution must be terminated.

Exercises

(1) The module Terminal exports procedures for characterwise I/O. Write a module that exports procedures for I/O of CARDINAL numbers. The module is to import only I/O procedures from Terminal.

(2) Write a module based on FileSystem that exports procedures for reading and writing entire RECORDs. Use parameters of type ARRAY OF WORD.

> procedure headings:

```
ReadRecord(VAR f:File; VAR rec:ARRAY OF WORD);
WriteRecord(VAR f:File; rec:ARRAY OF WORD);
```

(3) Someone wants to create a telephone directory. Each entry is to consist of a name and a telephone number. Write a data capsule that manages this directory as a dynamic list. Include procedures for making an entry and for searching by name or by number.

(4) Exercise 2 in Section 3.6.3 was the inversion of an array. Transform this iterative algorithm into a recursive one.

(5) Write a recursive function procedure Power(x:REAL;n:INTEGER):REAL to compute x^n. Note that n can be negative.

(6) Write a recursive procedure to answer the question:

> In how many different ways can $20 be changed?

You might want to use a table of coins and bills from 1¢ to $10.

(7) Consider the following recursive procedure:

```
PROCEDURE F(n, x, y:CARDINAL):CARDINAL;
BEGIN
  IF  n=0  THEN RETURN  x+y  END;
  IF  y=1  THEN RETURN  x   END;
  RETURN  F(n-1, F(n, x, y-1), x)
END F;
```

Determine what values the procedure returns with respect to n. Note: Consider only parameter combinations with n<=3.

(8) When the module SimpleScheduler is used, the processes are arranged in the ring in the same order in which they are created by CreateProcess. For Scheduler, this is not the case.

•   Determine how the order of processes in the ring is established in the module Scheduler.

•   How do the processes have to be created with CreateProcess so that their order is the same in SimpleScheduler and Scheduler?

(9) Think about how deadlock occurs. Give a simple example of deadlock.

In a broader sense, we could designate a situation wherein only part of the processes can never be reactivated as the result of a deadlock. Give such an example and consider why the module Scheduler cannot recognize such cases.

5 Programming Style and Program Testing

In Chapter 2 we showed how to reduce a task by stepwise refinement until the resulting subtasks are so simple that they can be formulated with elementary actions. In Chapter 3 we introduced the programming language Modula-2, and in Chapter 4 we handled specialized problems that can arise in the course of programming in Modula-2. This chapter shares with the reader some rules for programming that have proved themselves in the field. In the first section, we discuss what we consider good programming style; in the second section, we treat the problem of program testing and debugging.

5.1 Programming Style

The most important elements of good programming style are:

structure, expressive power, outward form, and *efficiency* .

This is true for both the *design* and the *formulation* of algorithms in a programming language. We applied these principles in the design of the algorithms that were included in this book, but we did not draw the reader's attention to them because we had not yet built up the required foundation. We want to make that up in the following pages.

Although the efficiency of an algorithm is an important criterion of quality, we will not handle that aspect. The question of efficiency only makes sense after a problem and its solution are really understood. Furthermore, methods for run-time measurements of programs and for locating critical parts of programs are required. Since this book is intended as an introductory-level text, we will refrain from treatment of efficiency.

5.1.1 Structure

On the one hand, structuring refers to the stepwise reduction of a problem into constituent subproblems with the goal of mastering complexity with abstraction and striving for simplicity and clarity. We call this *structuring in the large*.

On the other hand, structuring also refers to the choice of appropriate programming elements in the formulation of the subalgorithms. This is called *structuring in the small*.

Structuring in the Large

The principle of structuring in the large was discussed in detail in Chapter 2. The result of this process is modules and their associated functions. Programming is the implementation of the modules and functions defined in the design process so that they are executable on a computer. The medium for this implementation is the programming language. The implementation of a program system requires that the modular reduction defined in the design process can be expressed in the programming language; that the objects with which the various actions work can be expressed in the chosen language; and that the language provides control structures that permit the description of the desired or required functions (see Pomberger 1986).

Modula-2 fulfills these requirements in every respect. For structuring in the large, we use *modules* and *procedures* (see Sections 3.7 and 3.8). The data type concept in Modula-2 permits us to express the abstractions of data objects and the operations permitted on them in programs as they were established in the design of the algorithm.

For an example of structuring in the large, refer to Section 4.1, "Some Simple Modula-2 Programs."

Structuring in the Small

For the sake of understanding and testing algorithms, it is necessary for the algorithms to be easy to read. Complexity-related problems are rooted in the free use of transfers of control (GOTOs), i.e., in the construction of unlimited flow structures. The underlying idea behind *structured programming* is the exclusive use of structures that have a *single entry* point and a *single exit* point. This results in a correspondence between the static description of an algorithm and its dynamic execution. In other words, actions that occur sequentially in the progam text will generally be executed sequentially. This lends clarity to algorithms and makes their verification, modification or extension easier.

Böhm and Jacopini (1966) demonstrated that every algorithm can be represented in terms of the basic elements *sequence*, *branch* and *while loop* (all of which have a single entry point and a single exit point).

Figure 5.1 shows these basic elements in the form of flow diagrams. Algorithms that consist of only these elements are called D-diagrams (named after the computer scientist Dijkstra). We include the additional two elements *multiway decision* and *repeat loop* in Figure 5.2 because they have no negative effect on the clarity of algorithms.

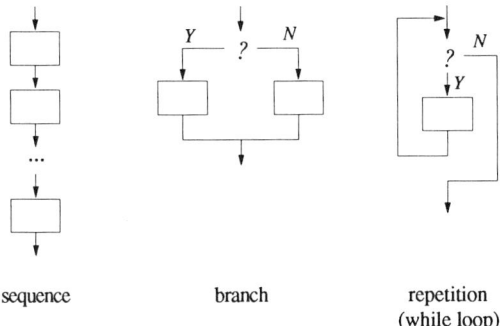

sequence   branch   repetition
                                                      (while loop)

Fig. 5.1 D-diagram elements

When algorithms are formulated with combinations of these elements, there is no need for other transfers of control (e.g., GOTOs). Modula-2 permits the implementation of all the elements shown in Figs. 5.1 and 5.2 and prevents unlimited flow structures simply by the absence of a GOTO statement. Programming without GOTOs does not, however, guarantee structured programs. By choosing unsuitable program elements, poorly structured programs can be created, albeit they do not contain a single GOTO.

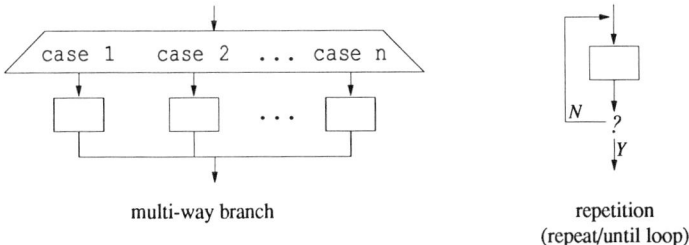

multi-way branch   repetition
                                              (repeat/until loop)

Fig. 5.2 Additional elements

The LOOP statement (see Section 3.6.3.4) in Modula-2 does not meet the above requirements. It can contain multiple EXIT statements, and the EXITs can occur at any point in the body of the loop. Considered as a whole, however, a LOOP statement has only one exit point. The RETURN statement, which can occur at any point in a PROCEDURE, behaves similarly (see Section 3.7.3). All other Modula-2 statements reflect elements of structured programming as explained above.

    The following three examples show how unlimited flow structures, which are found often in the field, can be transformed into structured solutions.

Example 1

The following (poor) program structure is given:

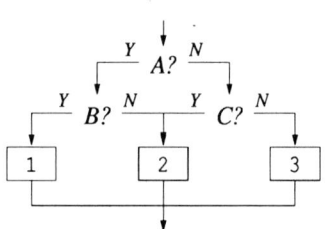

Transform it into a structured form.

Solution 1: transformation of the test conditions

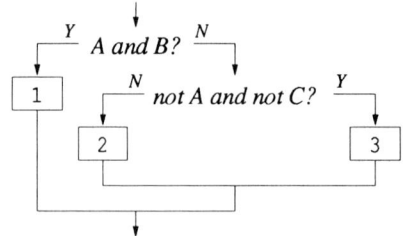

Solution 2: code duplication

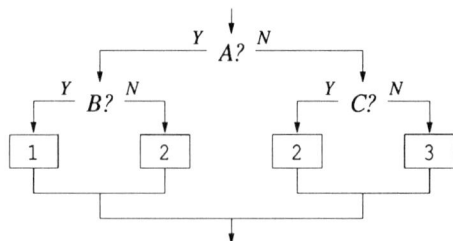

Example 2

The following *n+1/2 loop*, as it often occurs in LOOP statements, is given.

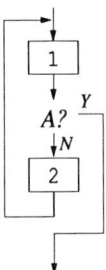

Devise a loop construction that conforms to the rules of structured programming.

Solution 1: introduction of a boolean auxiliary variable (looping)

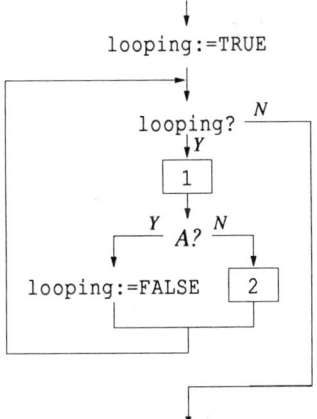

Solution 2: code duplication

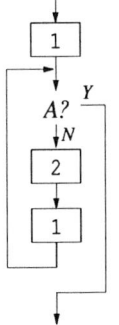

Example 3

The following program structure (a cross structure) is given. It is often found in dialog programs.

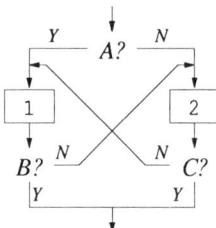

Find a form that does not violate the rules of structured programming.

Solution:

Upon closer examination, we find that 1 and 2 are executed alternately until B or C is true. This flow is reminiscent of a game with two players. First they draw to see which player is to begin (test A); after each turn, they must decide whether the game is to be continued with the other player or terminated. We can formulate a structured solution to this algorithm by introducing an auxiliary variable next, whose value can be 1, 2 or 0, depending on whether player 1 or player 2 is to take his/her turn or whether the game is to be terminated.

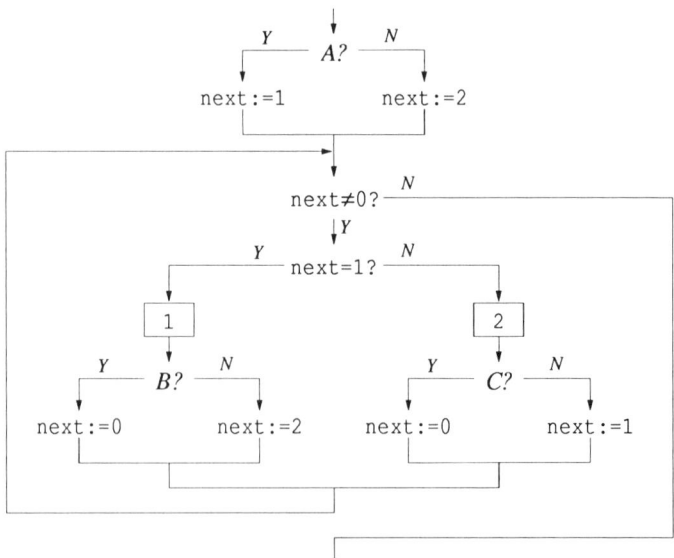

This structure corresponds to the while loop, a basic element of structured programming.

5.1.2 Naming Conventions

Formulating algorithms includes naming the objects and describing the actions that manipulate these objects. The choice of names plays an important role in writing algorithms.

In some programming groups, a practice was adopted that begins each identifier with an abbreviation of the project name or even the initials of the programmer. Thus names like HPRJSL (a *limit* value for a *heat pump regulation* project programmed by *John Smith*) are no rarity. It can scarcely be contested that such names prove detrimental to the understanding of an algorithm.

We therefore recommend vesting an expressive power in identifiers and adhering to the following rules for naming objects:

- Choose pregnant names, even if that makes the names longer. The additional written work pays off when the program needs to be modified, corrected or expanded.

- Use only common abbreviations that can be understood without additional explanation. Remain consistent in the use of abbreviations (i.e., don't use temp for "temperature" at one point and for "temporary" at another).

- Use upper case and lower case to differentiate classes of identifiers (e.g., first letter upper case for data types, procedures and modules; lower case for variables) and to make long names more readable (e.g., CheckInputValue).

- Use nouns for values, verbs for actions and adjectives for conditions in order to make the meaning of identifiers transparent (e.g., width, ReadKey, valid).

- Set up your own rules and apply them consistently.

5.1.3 Commentary

Good programming style is also expressed in the use of comments. They influence the readability of a program and are thus important parts thereof. Correct commentary in programs is not simple and requires experience, imagination and the ability to concisely and precisely express what is important (compare Pomberger 1986). Here are some rules to help you generate good commentary:

- Every program (indeed, every module) should begin with a detailed comment that answers some general questions about the program:
    - What does the program do?
    - What is the program used for (contextually)?
    - How does the program work (special methods, etc.)?
    - Who is the author of the program?
    - When was the program written?
    - What modifications have been made in the program?

- Each procedure should be provided with commentary that describes its task and possibly how it works. This is especially important for procedure headings in definition modules.

- The meaning of variables should be explained in a comment.

- Parts of a program that are responsible for isolated subtasks should be marked with comments.

- At important points in the program (e.g., at the start of procedures or loops), the state of the program should be described in comment form (so-called *assertions*).

- Statements that are difficult to understand (e.g., tricky methods or program parts that exploit a trait of a particular computer) need to be explained in commentary so that they can be understood without unnecessary trouble.

- Comments in a progam should be as few and as brief as possible, but as many and as detailed as necessary.

- Particularly note that program modifications affect not only declarations and statements, and so the commentary needs to be updated as well. Incorrect commentary is worse than none at all!

These rules are deliberately general because there are no rules that can be applied in the same way to every program and every area of application. Writing commentary is just as much an art as designing and writing programs.

5.1.4 Outward Form of Programs

Beyond commentary and the choice of names, the readability of a program is dependent upon its outward form. We therefore recommend the following rules for structuring the outward form of programs:

- In every program, module or procedure, the declaration part (data types, constants, variables, procedures) should be clearly separated from the statement part.

- The declaration parts of various modules and procedures in a program should apply a uniform order of declarations, e.g., constants, data types, variables, modules, and procedures.

- The parameter lists of procedures should separate input, output and input/output objects, e.g.:

```
PROCEDURE AppendWord(b:CARDINAL; w:Word;
                     VAR line:LineOfText;
                     VAR fits:BOOLEAN);
```

First come the input objects (b, w), then the input/output object (line), and finally the output object (fits). Unfortunately, Modula-2 does not permit the distinction of output and input/output objects.

- Indention should be used to make the program structure visible, e.g.:

```
...
REPEAT
Read(char,eof);
   IF NOT eof THEN
      IF char = " "
         THEN AddSeparator(text,t1)
         ELSE INC(t2); text[t2]:=char
      END
   END
UNTIL eof;
...
```

- Commentary and program text should be distinctly separated.

We have made an effort to consistently abide by these rules in this book. Detailed examples can be found in Section 4.1.

5.2 Program Testing

Experience has shown that the production of error-free program systems is nearly impossible. Thus it is usually an illusion to assume that a new program is perfect. Every program has to be diligently tested to determine whether it does what it is expected to do. Program testing and debugging is thus an important part of a programmer's work.

5.2.1 Types of Error

Two types of error need to be distinguished: *formal* errors and *content* errors.

Formal errors are those that occur as violations of the rules of the programming language used. These errors are identified by the compiler during program translation; i.e., the compiler marks the position of each error and (as a rule) gives the programmer an indication of what type of error occurred by means of error messages, which make correction possible.

Example

A Modula-2 programmer writes the following (syntactically incorrect) program fragment:

```
WHILE   a<b   REPEAT
```

During compilation, the error location is marked and an error message is output for the programmer, for example:

```
WHILE   a<b   REPEAT
                 ↑ Syntax Error:  DO expected
```

Formal errors result from mistakes made during the formulation of the algorithm description and from infamiliarity with the syntax rules. These errors are easy to find and easy to correct because the compiler provides support.

Content errors are errors in logic on the part of the programmer that lead to incorrect results in the algorithm. They cannot be recognized by the compiler. Detecting such errors is the real task of testing.

5.2.2 The Testing Procedure

Testing is a matter of showing evidence of errors. Understandably, an author of a program attempts to get it running as quickly as possible and therefore hopes not to find any errors during testing. The attitude and motivation of the tester should be tuned to finding *as many errors as possible*. Every program should be approached with the utmost mistrust.

There is a difference between testing simple programs and extensive program systems. The larger the program system is, the harder it is to test, for not only do its individual modules need to be tested in isolation, but also their interplay in the system needs to be meticulously tested. Although an intensive handling of testing goes beyond the limits of an introductory book, we do want to list the most important basic rules that govern the process.

Rules for Program Testing

(1)   Test preparation

- Testing begins with the attempt to verify an algorithm even before it ever runs on a computer. The simplest approach to verification is the manual simulation of the finished algorithm. This forces us to reconsider design decisions and helps to identify errors.

- We need to assume that there could be errors in any section of the program. The test data (both for the manual simulation and for the test run on the computer) must be chosen so that every branch of the program is executed at least once.

- Test data must be chosen in such a way that restrictions and special cases are especially tested. For example, a variable with a restricted range should assume the limit of this range during testing; loops should be tested with a minimum and maximum number of runs; iterative loops (WHILE and REPEAT) need to be tested for a condition that might cause infinite execution; and so on.

- Testing a program only with input data that produce correct results is by no means enough. How the program performs when incorrect data are input is just as important.

- It is bad practice to run a program and then check its results afterwards. This approach tends to bias the programmer toward accepting the results as correct.

Instead, the expected results should be computed in advance and then compared with the results from the program.

- In preparation for localizing errors, auxiliary print statements that output information on the current state of the program at critical points (e.g., before the start of a loop, at the beginning and end of a procedure) should be inserted. For *loops*, that would mean the output of all variables used for loop control. For *procedures*, the input parameters ought to be printed out at the beginning and the output parameters at the end (see also Section 5.2.3).

(2)   Debugging measures

- If an error is detected during testing, the error must first be localized. This process is known as *debugging* and requires knowing the order in which the various parts of the program are executed and determining to what point the execution had been correct. For this purpose, we activate the auxiliary print statements that were inserted at critical points (see Section 5.2.3) and follow the execution until the error occurs.

- Once the error has been localized, the respective section is to be examined by manual simulation.

- If an error is found, that by no means precludes other errors in the program, and the results of a new run must again be compared with the expected results (calculated by hand) to determine whether other errors are present.

- After an error has been corrected, consider the possibility that new errors have been introduced. All previous tests must be repeated. Therefore, store all test data and document each test run that is made with the data.

- If the source of the error cannot be found, try presenting the program to another programmer. Alone the need to explain a program to a colleague often leads the programmer to insights and a new point of view that helps him/her track down the error.

- There are certain typical perpetual errors (e.g., index overflow in working with arrays, exceeding a range restriction, division by zero) that deserve special attention in debugging. It is good practice to record all sorts of errors one has made and to use this record as a check list during inspection of programs.

5.2.3 Built-In Testing and Debugging Aids

As we mentioned above, preparing a program for error localization is an important part of testing and debugging. The simplest and most natural way of localizing errors is following the flow of a program and monitoring the state (i.e., value) of important variables at critical points in the program.

In order to follow the *flow of a program*, auxiliary print statements are useful for providing information about procedure invocations, loop executions, and execution of particular statements.

In order to monitor the *state of program variables*, we need to be able to observe the values of important variables at critical points in the algorithm.

A programmer can build auxiliary output statements into a Modula-2 program in order to easily monitor both program flow and variable states:

```
MODULE TestObject;
  ...
  VAR testswitch:  ARRAY [1..n] OF BOOLEAN;
  ...
  PROCEDURE Proc1(in:Type; VAR out:Type);
    local declarations
  BEGIN
    IF testswitch[1] THEN
      WriteString("Procedure Proc1 started");
      Write(in)    (* write input parameter(s) *)
    END;
    ...
    statement part
    ...
    IF testSwitch[1] THEN
      WriteString("Procedure Proc1 ended");
      Write(out)  (* write output parameter(s) *)
    END;
  END Proc1;
  ...
BEGIN  (* body of MODULE TestObject *)
  FOR i:=1 TO n DO
    ReadBoolean(testSwitch[i])
  END
  ...
END TestObject.
```

In the main module of a program system, we declare an array (testSwitch) that contains an element for every procedure in the system. At the start and end of every procedure, we insert statements to output information about program flow and the state of variables (e.g., information that a procedure was begun or terminated, values of parameters). These types of auxiliary print statement can be inserted anywhere else as well. They should only be executed if the tester wants them to be (i.e., when the flag for that variable is set to TRUE). For this purpose, the program reads the values for these flags at the start of the program (the invocation of ReadBoolean at the start of the body of the main program).

This technique makes it possible to incorporate auxiliary output statements for monitoring program flow and states of variables. These statements are included during the design of the program and activated or suppressed by setting the values of the corresponding flags. Should the resulting information not suffice, the same technique can be employed to insert statements and flags at other points in the program.

The *advantage* of this flagging technique is that the degree of monitoring can be regulated (i.e., all procedures or only procedure X could be tabulated) without changing the program itself. The auxiliary output statements could even be left in the program after debugging; instead of reading in the values of the flags, they would simply be initialized to

FALSE. If another error is found at a later date, minimal changes in the program restore its monitoring capability.

The *disadvantage* of the technique is that testing whether the auxiliary output statements are to be executed is time consuming. This reduces program efficiency. As a rule, however, a majority of run time is consumed by a small percentage of the code. If care is taken that these sections of the program receive few or no auxiliary output statements, then the negative effect on efficiency is negligible.

5.2.4 Debuggers

Modern programming environments—collections of tools that provide support for the programmer—also contain tools with the capability of providing information about program flow and states of variables without amendments to the program text. Such tools are called *debuggers*. They support successive testing of programs by means of analysis of states at any given time and at any given location in the program code. Modern debuggers present the analysis results in an understandable form that is tuned to the programmer's way of thinking. Sometimes a programmer has access to additional tools (e.g., test-case generators). Tools on the market today are so different in quality and capabilities that we will not describe them here.

6 Software Engineering with Modula-2

Stated simply, software engineering is a collective term for all methods of economical production of reliable and efficient software products, including methods for their specification, design, implementation, testing, documentation and maintenance.

Various programming languages support the methods of software engineering in very different ways. Modern programming languages (such as Modula-2 and Ada) were designed especially in view of these methods, while older languages often only minimally support (or even impede) the application of these methods. Thus the choice of a programming language decidedly influences the quality and production costs of a software package.

This is an introductory programming book rather than a text on software engineering. Nevertheless, we want to round out the introduction with a short discussion of how Modula-2 supports the principles of software engineering.

6.1 Modula-2 as a Tool for Specification

The development of a software product can be divided into several project phases (see Fig. 6.1). The first phase, *problem analysis*, has the goal of establishing a *definition of the expectations* placed on the program. A programming language cannot provide assistance in this project phase since this is a matter of task definition.

The *design phase* establishes which program components (algorithms) are to be used to meet the expectations defined during problem analysis. The result of the design phase is a collection of program specifications that are to serve as a basis for the formulation and implementation of the individual program components.

One of the most important tasks in the design of a software product is the definition of the modules that will make up the program system and their interfaces. The concept of export interfaces (definition modules) in Modula-2 can already be employed in the design phase for interface descriptions of the program components. This manner of module specification is quite suitable for design documentation and helps to avoid inconsistent interfaces (assuming that Modula-2 is also used as the implementation language). The concept of interface description can even be used in the design phase if individual program components are later implemented in another language.

Although Modula-2 is not a specification language, it does support the specification of program components.

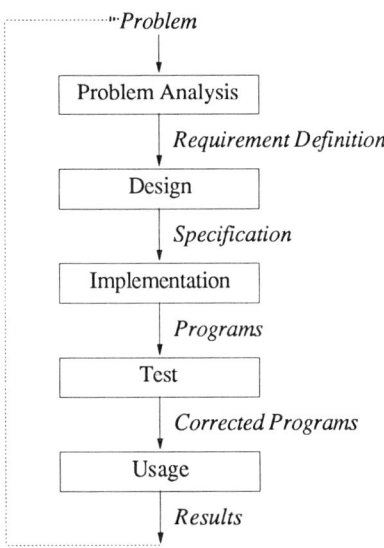

Fig. 6.1 Project phases

6.2 Modularizing and Structuring

In Chapter 2, we showed how to successively reduce a problem by stepwise refinement until the resulting subproblems can be formulated algorithmically. We also identified criteria for combining the ensuing algorithms into modules.

Clearly we want the writing of programs in a programming language to reflect our design decisions as closely as possible. We expect that the structures (modules, procedures) and the interface descriptions derived from stepwise refinement can be formulated in the programming language. For many older programming languages, this is possible only to some limited extent because the language elements for the description of modules are usually completely lacking, the separation of specification (definition) and

Modula-2 elegantly supports the transformation of the design results into programs and permits the formulation of modules and procedures as well as the separation of interface definition and implementation (which is useful for data capsules and abstract data types).

Beyond modularization, another important aspect of programming is the structuring of the individual algorithms. In Section 5.1.1 ("Structuring"), we introduced the term *structured programming* and explained the measures required to achieve a well-structured algorithm. A program that is well-structured contains exclusively the following elements: sequences, conditional branches, multiway selections, and repetitions (see Figures 5.1 and 5.2).

Modula-2 provides statements for formulating exactly these elements. The lack of a GOTO statement in the language definition removes the temptation of creating unlimited flow structures. Thus Modula-2 supports structured programming far better than older programming languages such as COBOL, Fortran, and BASIC.

6.3 Data Capsules and Data Abstraction

The principle of data capsules has a great deal of practical value. Particularly in the implementation of larger program systems, the use of data capsules attains a significantly higher degree of program reliability than in conventional implementation methods.

In Section 2.2 ("Data Capsules") we gave a detailed explanation of data capsules and an example thereof. However, our handling of the subject was very general and independent of any programming language.

The principle of data capsules says that algorithms that want to use encapsulated data objects can only do so by means of *access algorithms*, and that the implementation of the encapsulated objects is not visible to the user (*principle of information hiding*). Therefore a change in the organization of the encapsulated objects and the access routines must not have any effect on the programs that use the data capsule.

The module concept with its separation of definition and implementation modules (see Section 3.8.3, "Global Modules and Separate Compilation") is exactly what we need in order to describe data capsules in a programming language. The capsule is divided into two parts: the one visible to the user describes the access routines (i.e., the export of the operations permitted on the encapsulated objects), while the one invisible to the user contains the implementation details for the encapsulated objects and the algorithmic structure of the access routines.

The concept of separate compilation with interface checking allows the internal structure of a data capsule to be changed without chain reactions for the user of the data capsule. The module `LineManagement` (section 4.1, point (3)) shows an example of the implementation of a data capsule in Modula-2.

Not only procedures but also variables can be exported in accordance with Modula-2's import and export rules for modules (listed in Section 3.8.1, "Local Modules"). The importing module can access the variables it imports from another module as though they had been declared in the importing module itself; i.e., the implemented structure of the variable is known and its value can be changed. Use of this possibility, however, violates the principle of information hiding, for we are in effect working with global variables (see Section 2.2 under "Advantages of data capsules") and all their associated drawbacks (poor modification capability, no protection from unauthorized access).

The terms *abstract data structure* and *abstract data type* are closely related to data capsules.

As we explained in Section 2.1, in the design process using the principle of stepwise refinement, it is important not to focus on a concrete representation of data too early. This guideline is intended to prevent the designer from concentrating on details too soon and thereby neglecting the solution of the basic problem or matching his design to the data structures. Thus we also applied the principle of stepwise refinement to the design of data structures and worked in this sense with abstract data types.

> "An *abstract data structure* defines a set of objects (its components) and a set of operations which can manipulate these components or the data structure as a whole." (Pomberger 1986, p. 111)

This definition immediately leads us to the connection with the data capsule: every data capsule represents an abstract data structure. The data managed by the data capsule are the objects and the access routines are the defined operations.

The term abstract data type is closely related but not identical to the abstract data structure.

> "An *abstract data type* defines a set of objects, all of which have the same abstract data structure, by means of the operations permissible on them." (Pomberger 1986, p. 111)

An abstract data type is necessary whenever we want to define multiple copies of an abstract data structure. The following example, the implementation of multiple queues, will clarify this point.

Let us define the abstract data type Queue, the valid operations EnQueue (append an element to a particular queue) and DeQueue (remove the first element of a particular queue), and the three queues q1, q2 and q3 of data type Queue. The three variables (q1, q2 and q3) thereby have the same properties, hence the same operations can manipulate them.

The implementation of abstract data types is possible in Modula-2 with a combination of the module concept and the concept of opaque data types (see Section 3.8.3.1, "Definition Modules"). Only the name of the abstract data type is written in the definition module; the complete declaration is provided in the implementation module. Thus we can write the specification of an abstract data type for queues as follows:

```
DEFINITION MODULE Queues;

  TYPE Queue;        (* abstract data type *)

  PROCEDURE EnQueue(VAR q:Queue; elem:INTEGER; VAR full:BOOLEAN);
  (* Appends the element elem to the queue q.  If the queue
     was already full before the invocation of EnQueue,
     full=TRUE is set and the element is not appended.
     Otherwise full has the value FALSE. *)

  PROCEDURE DeQueue(VAR q:Queue; elem:INTEGER; VAR empty:BOOLEAN);
  (* Returns the first element (elem) in the queue q and
     removes that element from q.  If the queue was empty
     before the invocation of DeQueue, then empty=TRUE is
     set and the value of elem is undefined.  Otherwise
     empty has the value FALSE. *)
END Queues.
```

The Module Queues can be used in the following way by other modules:

```
FROM Queues IMPORT
  Queue, EnQueue, DeQueue;
...
VAR
  q1, q2, q3: Queue;
  elem: INTEGER;
  empty, full: BOOLEAN;
...
EnQueue(q1,10,full);
...
DeQueue(q2,elem,empty);
...
```

This makes it possible to work with an abstract data type (Queue). The concrete implementation of the type Queue and the construction of the operations defined by the procedures EnQueue and DeQueue is hidden from the user in the implementation module.

Unfortunately, the use of opaque data types in Modula-2 has one snag since the concrete data type assigned to an abstract data type in the implementation module can only be a POINTER type according to the language definition. All other data types, ARRAYs and RECORDs in particular, are not permissible.

This restriction of abstract data types seems uncomfortable at first glance. In our example, we need an array or a dynamically linked list in order to implement our queue. Since objects of any type can be generated dynamically (see Section 4.3), the pointer to any type can be viewed as its abstract data type.

This requires that we incorporate an additional procedure NewQueue(VAR q:Queue) in our module Queues in order to enable us to generate any number of queues dynamically. Before we can work with a variable of data type Queue, it has to be initialized with an invocation of NewQueue.

```
DEFINITION MODULE Queues;

   TYPE Queue;      (* opaque data type *)

   PROCEDURE EnQueue(VAR q:Queue; elem:INTEGER; VAR full:BOOLEAN);

   (* Appends the element elem to the queue q.  If the queue
      was already full before the invocation of EnQueue,
      full=TRUE is set and the element is not appended.
      Otherwise full has the value FALSE. *)

   PROCEDURE DeQueue(VAR q:Queue; elem:INTEGER; VAR empty:BOOLEAN);

   (* Returns the first element (elem) in the queue q and
      removes that element from q.  If the queue was empty
      before the invocation of DeQueue, then empty=TRUE is
      set and the value of elem is undefined.  Otherwise
      empty has the value FALSE. *)

   PROCEDURE NewQueue(VAR q:Queue);

   (* Generates a new (empty) queue of type Queue. *)

END Queues.


IMPLEMENTATION MODULE Queues;

   FROM Storage IMPORT ALLOCATE, DEALLOCATE;

   CONST queuesize = 100;

   TYPE
      QueueIndex = [0..queuesize]
      QueueRec = RECORD
                       queue: ARRAY QueueIndex OF INTEGER;
                       front, rear: QueueIndex;
                    END;
      Queue = POINTER TO QueueRec;

   PROCEDURE NewQueue(VAR q:Queue);
   BEGIN
      NEW(q);
      q^.front := 0;
      q^.rear := 0;
   END NewQueue;

   PROCEDURE EnQueue(VAR q:Queue; elem:INTEGER; VAR full:BOOLEAN);
      VAR h: QueueIndex;
   BEGIN
      WITH q^ DO
         h := (rear+1) MOD queuesize;
         full := h=front;
         IF NOT full THEN
            rear := h;
            queue[rear] := elem
         END
      END   (* WITH *)
   END EnQueue;
```

```
PROCEDURE DeQueue(VAR q:Queue; elem:INTEGER; VAR empty:BOOLEAN);
BEGIN
  WITH q^ DO
    empty := front=rear;
    IF NOT empty THEN
      front := (front+1) MOD queuesize;
      elem := queue[front]
    END
  END   (* WITH *)
END DeQueue;
END Queues.
```

The RECORD component `rear` always points to the last element entered in the queue; `front` points to the last element removed. If `front=rear` applies, then the queue contains no elements.

Clearly the definition module is completely independent of the chosen implementation of a queue, so that `Queue` really is an abstract data type. We could have implemented the queue as a list of dynamically created RECORDs (which would remove the length restriction) without changing anything for the user of the module.

6.4 Separate Compilation and Type Binding

In small-scale programming, the entire program is written by an individual who is often the sole user. In such program design, the programmer has all the details, such as interfaces for modules and procedures, in his/her head and does not need to adhere to any guidelines or standards. Complex programming systems, on the other hand, are generally written by project teams. Programming languages intended for the implementation of large program systems need to meet certain requirements that enable and facilitate this division of labor. These include:

- separate compilation of the individual program components;

- interface definitions that are independent of the implementation of the program components; and

- automatic consistency checking of interfaces in the compilation of the individual program components.

Separate compilation was realized in earlier programming languages such as Fortran and PL/I. Individual program components, however, were compiled *independently* of all other components. The disadvantage of this approach is that incompatible interfaces (e.g., the number or types of the actual parameters do not agree with the formal parameters) are detected only at run time. Yet the advantage is that any order of compilation of the components is possible. The programmer is responsible for checking the consistency of the interfaces in the program sections he/she implements.

Modula-2 enables separate compilation of modules with simultaneous interface consistency checks. When translating a given module, this requires all definition modules (the interface descriptions) of modules imported by that module to have been compiled beforehand. This requires a certain sequence in the compilation of the components of a program system. The following import graph (Fig. 6.2) clarifies this point.

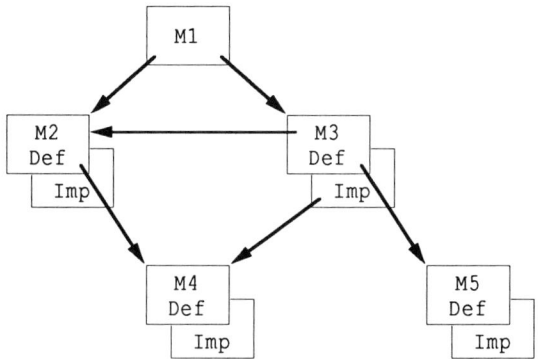

Fig. 6.2 Import graph of the relation "x imports objects from y"

As the import graph shows, the module M2 imports objects from M4, and module M3 imports objects from M2, M4 and M5. The following points apply to the compilation of these modules:

- Only the compilation of their respective definition modules is prerequisite for the translation of each of the implementation modules M4 and M5.

- In order to translate the implementation module M2, its definition module and that of M4 must have been compiled.

- The translation of the implementation module M3 and the program module M1 require the previous compilation of all definition modules.

This leads to the following possible compilation sequences for the definition modules:

```
M4 – M2 – M5 – M3
M5 – M4 – M2 – M3
M4 – M5 – M2 – M3
```

The prerequisite for the compilation of an implementation module is the successful compilation of its definition module and all definition modules from which it imports. Apart from that, the implementation modules and the program module can be compiled in any order. There are multiple possibilities for the compilation sequence in the above example. Another example might lead to a single possiblity. Let us examine the interdependence of the modules by means of a graphic representation in Fig. 6.3. Every arrow A → B means that module A must be compiled before module B.

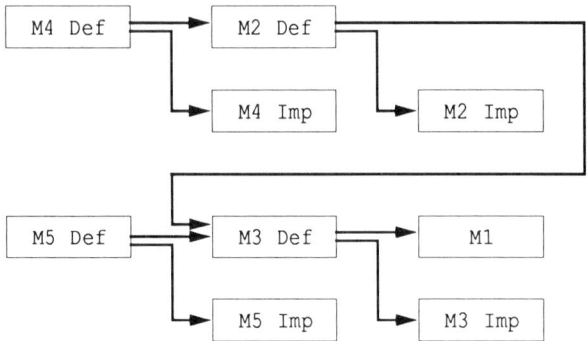

Fig. 6.3 Module dependencies with the relation "x must be compiled before y"

Modification of a definition module (i.e., changing the interface of a program component) means that no program using this module can run because the consistency of the interfaces is no longer guaranteed. Therefore all modules using this modified definition module have to be compiled anew in order to check whether the interfaces still match after the modification. This applies even if the definition module is simply recompiled without changes in its text, because this violates the required compilation sequence.

As Fig. 6.3 shows, modification of definition module M4 would affect all other modules except M5, and all affected modules would have to be recompiled. If the definition module M3 were modified, only its implementation module and the program module M1 would be affected. Modifying an implementation module requires nothing more than its own recompilation since no interface descriptions are affected.

The concept of separate compilation of modules supports the division of labor in software design. The measure of security required for separate compilation is offered by interface consistency checking at compile time.

Another step in the direction of security is Modula-2's strict type binding. Most older programming languages (e.g., PL/I and Fortran) permit the combination of objects of different data types. For example, if an INTEGER object a and a CHAR object b can be combined in an expression (e.g., a+b), then there must be rules that govern what "+" means in such a case, or how one of the two objects is to be projected onto the other's range of values. Such rules are often compiler-dependent rather than being established in the language definition, and they are often used by programmers for elegant tricks with interesting results that cannot be understood by the uninitiated. Things get worse when objects of different data types are unintentionally combined. If the compiler carries out automatic type conversions according to rules that are unknown to the programmer, this leads to a misinterpretation of the program. This can produce an apparently correct program that returns incorrect results, and it is often very troublesome to locate such errors.

These disadvantages are avoided in Modula-2 because the type concept permits the combination of different types only under certain conditions. These conditions were treated in Chapter 3 and are summarized in Appendix C under type equality, expression compatibility and assignment compatibility.

This type concept imposes more discipline on us and often limits our flexibility, but it reduces our programs' susceptibility to errors. It also improves the readability of programs because hidden transformation rules do not need to be filtered out when studying expressions, assignments and interface descriptions. If we really want to combine a pair of incompatible objects, this can be done by applying the standard procedures (e.g., FLOAT or CHR) or type transfer functions (see Section 3.9.2). This means, however, that a transformation is explicitly stated in the program text and the reader thus receives the information directly. This strict type binding also helps in the early detection of errors and in efficient program testing.

Appendix A: Syntax Diagrams

Chapter 3 provides a syntax diagram for every language element of Modula-2. These diagrams have been collected in this appendix for easy reference when questions arise concerning the formulation of particular program constructs. The syntax diagrams are listed and numbered in the same order as in Chapter 3. The following alphabetical list is intended to assist in locating individual syntax diagrams.

Ident$_1$

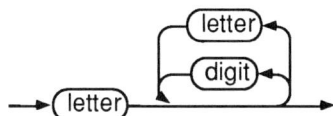

QualIdent$_2$

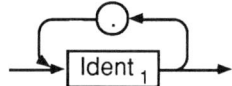

Number$_3$

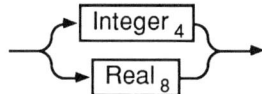

Integer$_4$

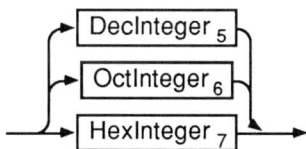

DecInteger$_5$

OctInteger$_6$

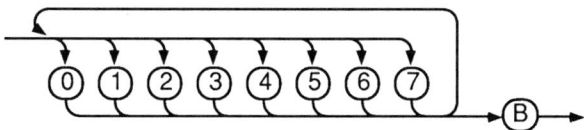

HexInteger₇

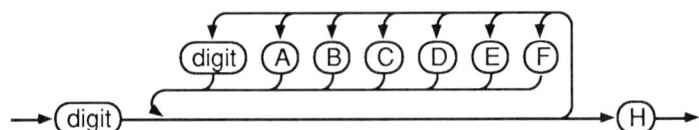

Real₈

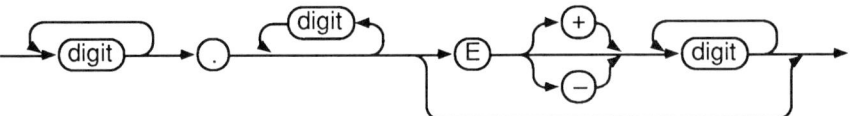

String₉

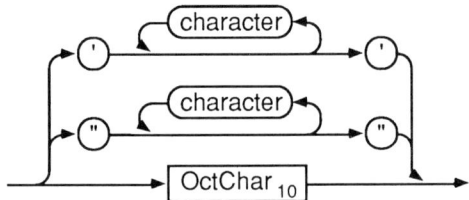

OctChar₁₀

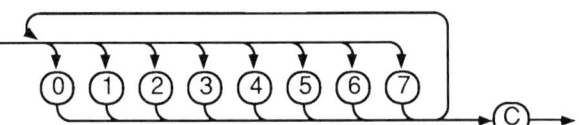

ProgramModule₁₁

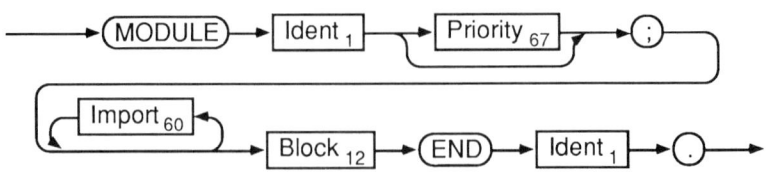

Block₁₂

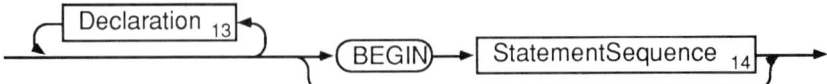

Declaration$_{13}$

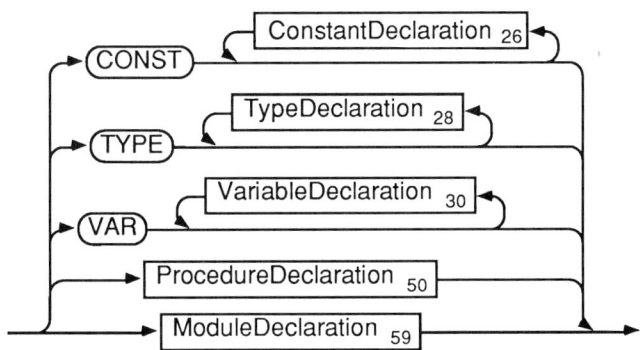

StatementSequence$_{14}$

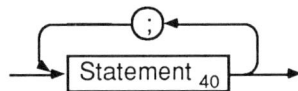

Enumeration$_{15}$

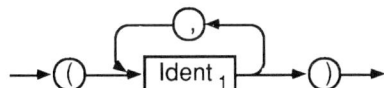

Subrange$_{16}$

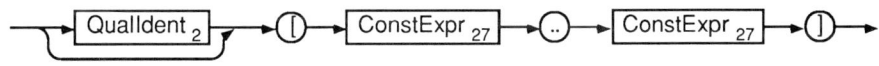

SetType$_{17}$

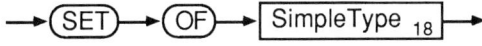

SimpleType$_{18}$

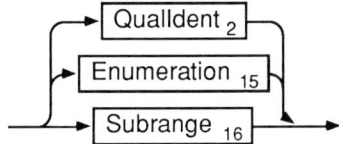

ArrayType$_{19}$

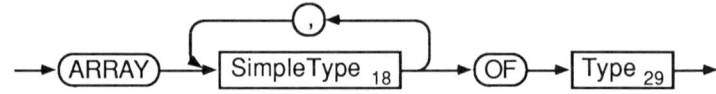

RecordType$_{20}$

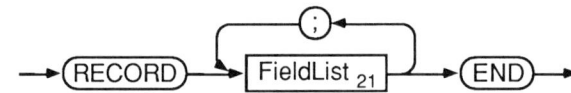

FieldList$_{21}$

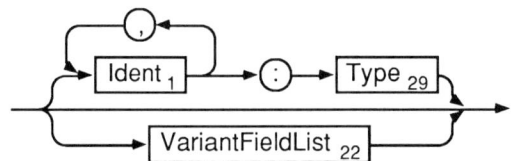

VariantFieldList$_{22}$

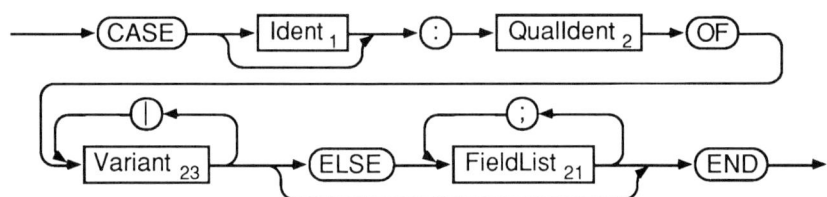

Variant$_{23}$

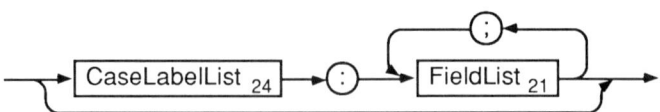

CaseLabelList$_{24}$

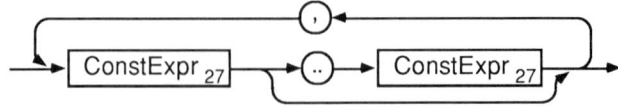

PointerType$_{25}$

ConstantDeclaration$_{26}$

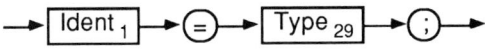

ConstExpr$_{27}$

TypeDeclaration$_{28}$

Type$_{29}$

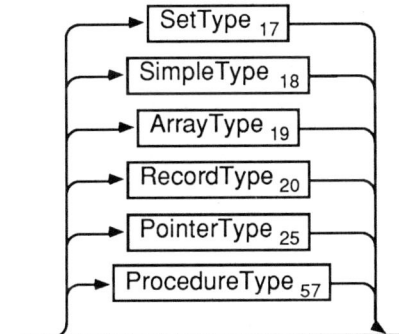

VariableDeclaration$_{30}$

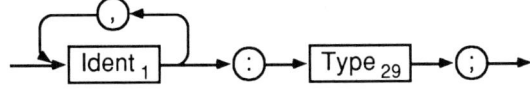

Designator$_{31}$

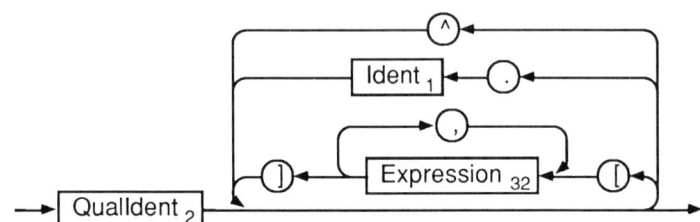

Expression$_{32}$

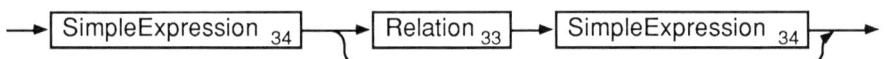

Relation$_{33}$

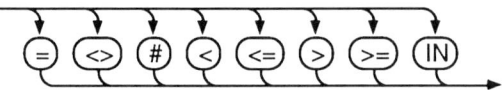

SimpleExpression$_{34}$

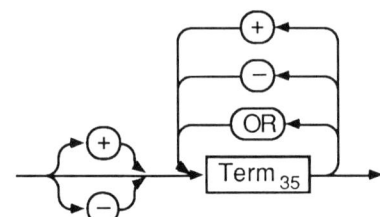

Term$_{35}$

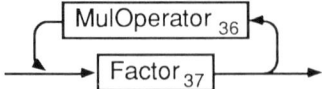

MulOperator$_{36}$

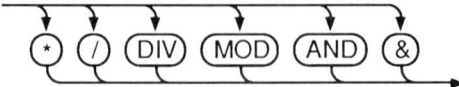

Factor$_{37}$

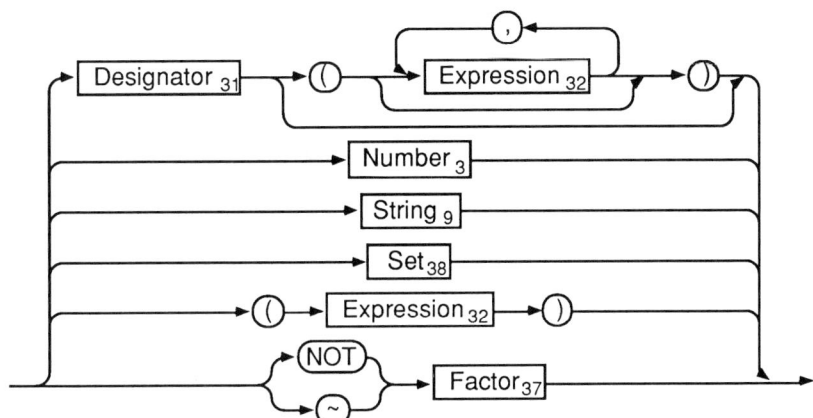

Set$_{38}$

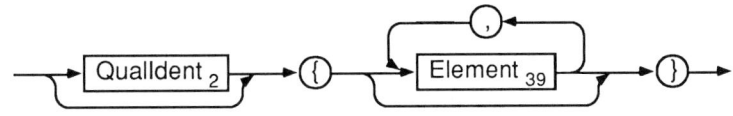

Element$_{39}$

Statement$_{40}$

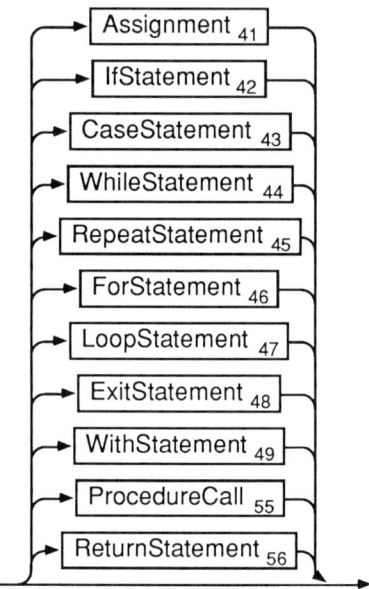

Assignment$_{41}$

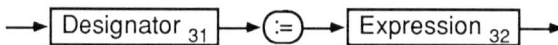

IfStatement$_{42}$

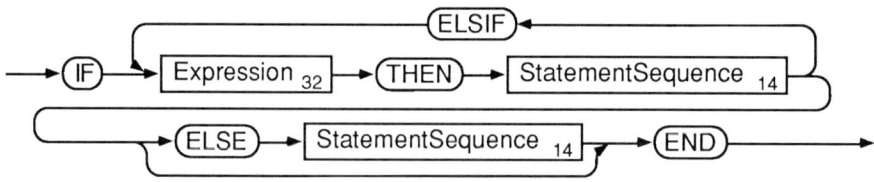

CaseStatement₄₃

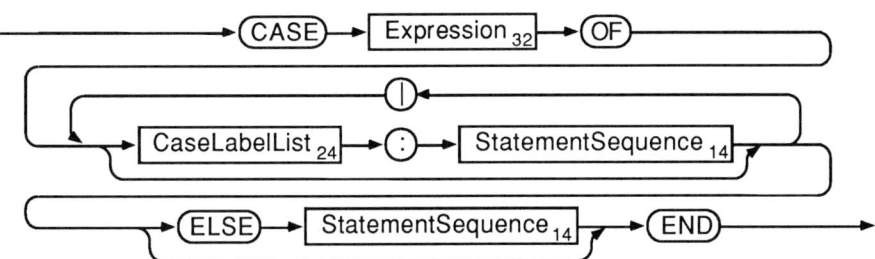

WhileStatement₄₄

→(WHILE)→ Expression ₃₂ →(DO)→ StatementSequence ₁₄ →(END)→

RepeatStatement₄₅

→(REPEAT)→ StatementSequence ₁₄ →(UNTIL)→ Expression ₃₂ →

ForStatement₄₆

→(FOR)→ Ident ₁ →(:=)→ Expression ₃₂ →(TO)→ Expression ₃₂
→(BY)→ ConstExpr ₂₇ →(DO)→ StatementSequence ₁₄ →(END)→

LoopStatement₄₇

→(LOOP)→ StatementSequence ₁₄ →(END)→

ExitStatement₄₈

→(EXIT)→

WithStatement₄₉

→(WITH)→ Designator ₃₁ →(DO)→ StatementSequence ₁₄ →(END)→

ProcedureDeclaration₅₀

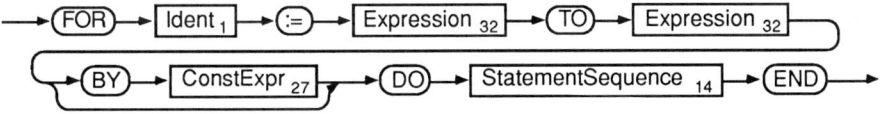

ProcedureHeading$_{51}$

FormalParameters$_{52}$

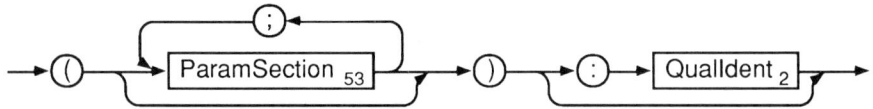

ParamSection$_{53}$

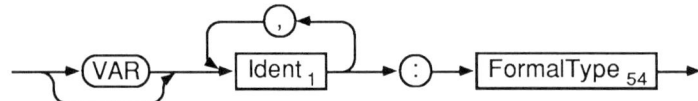

FormalType$_{54}$

ProcedureCall$_{55}$

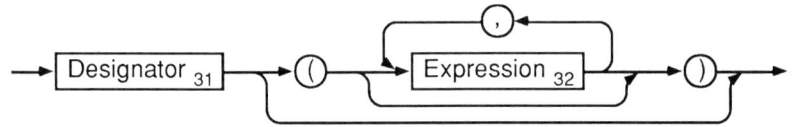

ReturnStatement$_{56}$

ProcedureType$_{57}$

FormalTypeList₅₈

ModuleDeclaration₅₉

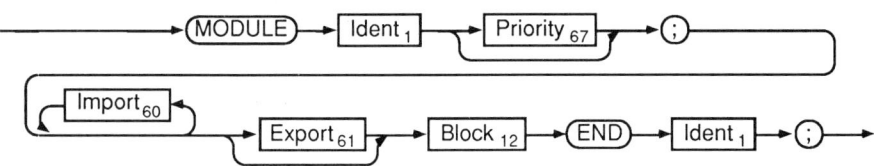

Import₆₀

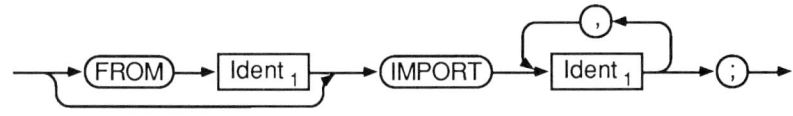

Export₆₁

DefinitionModule₆₂

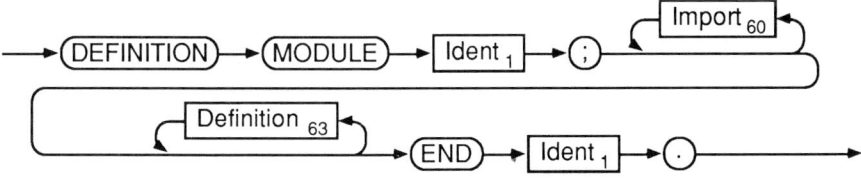

Definition$_{63}$

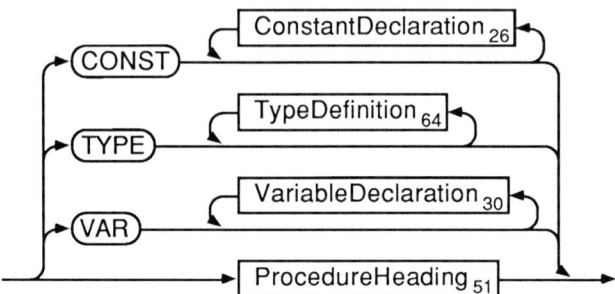

TypeDefinition$_{64}$

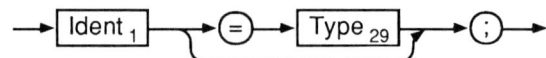

ImplementationModule$_{65}$

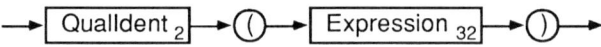

TypeTransfer$_{66}$

Priority$_{67}$

Appendix B: Predefined Identifiers

Modula-2 contains a number of predefined identifiers for constants, elementary data types and standard procedures. The following summary provides an overview of what they mean. A more detailed explanation can be found in Sections 3.4.1.1 ("Predefined Data Types") and 3.7.8 ("Standard Procedures").

Predefined Constants

FALSE	boolean value "false"
NIL	POINTER value that points to no object
TRUE	boolean value "true"

Predefined Data Types

BITSET	set
BOOLEAN	logical values "true" or "false"
CARDINAL	natural numbers (≥ 0)
CHAR	characters
INTEGER	whole numbers (positive or negative)
PROC	parameterless procedures
REAL	real numbers

Standard Procedures

DEC(x)	reduces (decrements) the value of x by 1
DEC(x,n)	reduces (decrements) the value of x by n
DISPOSE(p)	frees the storage to which p points
EXCL(s,e)	removes (excludes) the element e from the set s
HALT	terminates program execution
INC(x)	increases (increments) the value of x by 1
INC(x,n)	increases (increments) the value of x by n
INCL(s,e)	includes the element e in the set s
NEW(p)	allocates dynamic storage

Standard Functions

ABS(x)	returns the absolute value of x
CAP(ch)	changes the character ch to a capital letter
CHR(c)	returns the character whose ordinal number is c
FLOAT(c)	transforms the CARDINAL number c into a REAL number
HIGH(a)	returns the highest index of the array a
MAX(T)	returns the greatest value that can be represented by the data type T
MIN(T)	returns the smallest value that can be represented by the data type T
ODD(x)	returns the boolean value of the expression"x is odd"
TRUNC(r)	transforms the REAL number r to a CARDINAL number
VAL(T,c)	returns the value of data type T having the ordinal number c

Appendix C: Compatibility Rules

The strict type concept in Modula-2 forces the programmer to keep in mind which data types are compatible under which conditions. All the respective rules were covered in Chapter 3, but they are spread throughout the entire chapter. Thus we have summarized all the rules governing compatibility in this appendix.

Type Identity (see Section 3.4.5)

The two objects x1 and x2 with the data types t1 and t2 are of the *same data type* if one of the following conditions is met:

- t1 and t2 are identified by the same name, e.g.:

  ```
  VAR                          VAR
      n:      INTEGER;             material:   Material;
      val:    INTEGER;            substance:  Material;
  ```

- x1 and x2 are declared within the *same variable list* , e.g.:

  ```
  VAR
      n,val:  INTEGER;        PROCEDURE P(x,y:CHAR);
      die,dot: [1..6];
  ```

- t1 and t2 are identified by names that are designated as *synonyms* in the type declaration, e.g.:

  ```
  TYPE                         TYPE
      Minute = [0..59];            t  = (a,b,c);
      Second = Minute;             t1 = t;
  VAR                              t2 = t;
      sec: Second;             VAR
      min: Minute;                 x1:  t1;
                                   x2:  t2;
  ```

- x1 and x2 are *constants of the same enumeration type*, as low and high or red and yellow in these examples:

  ```
  VAR                          VAR
      voltage: (low,high);     color: (red,blue,yellow);
  ```

Type equality is required

- *with VAR parameters*

  The data types of formal and actual parameters must be the same.

  Exceptions:

  - If the formal parameter is an *ARRAY parameter*, only the *element types* must be identical in the formal and actual parameters.

  - *ADDRESS* is compatible with *CARDINAL* and with all *POINTER types*.

- *WORD* is compatible with every data type that occupies exactly *one word of memory*.

- *ARRAY OF WORD* is compatible with *any and all data types*.

• *with procedure variables*

If a procedure P is to be assigned to a procedure variable pv, the parameters of all data types in P and pv must be identical. If P and pv are function procedures, the data types of their function values must also be identical.

Expression Compatibility (see Section 3.5.5)

Two operands x1 and x2 with data types t1 and t2 are *expression compatible* if any one of the following conditions is met:

• t1 and t2 are the *same data type*.

• t1 is a subrange type with base type t2 (or vice versa).

• t1 and t2 are subrange types with the *same base types*.

• t1 is INTEGER or CARDINAL and t2 is a subrange type (or x2 is a constant) in the range [0..MAX(INTEGER)] (or vice versa). The value of MAX(INTEGER) depends on the particular computer used, but in any case it is the largest INTEGER that can be represented (which is simultaneously a CARDINAL number).

• x1 is the predefined constant NIL (see POINTER types in Section 3.4.1) and t2 is any POINTER type (or vice versa).

• t1 and t2 are *procedure compatible*.

• t1 is an ADDRESS and t2 is CARDINAL or any POINTER type (or vice versa).

Expression compatibilty is required

• *in expressions*

Whenever two operands are combined with an operator, they must be expression compatible.

Exception:

For the expression "e IN s" (where s is of data type SET OF T), e must be expression compatible with T.

• *in FOR statements*

In the expression "FOR x:=first TO last DO..." both first and last must be expression compatible with x.

• *in CASE statements*

In the expression "CASE x OF c_1:...|c_2:...END" all the constants c_i must be expression compatible with x.

Assignment Compatibility (see Section 3.6.1)

For the assignment d:=e, we will denote the designator d of the data type td and the expression e of the data type te as *assignment compatible* if one of the following statements applies:

- The designator d and the expression e are *expression compatible*.

- td is INTEGER (or a subrange thereof) and te is CARDINAL (or a subrange thereof), or vice versa. In the execution of the assignment under these conditions, we must guarantee that the value of the expression e is in the range determined by td, otherwise the value of the assignment is undefined.

- td is an ARRAY [0..N-1] OF CHAR (i.e., an array of n characters) and e is a character string constant with length len and len<=n. (If len<n, the string e is stored in d[0] to d[len-1] and d[len] is assigned the value 0C (null character).

- td is WORD and te is any data type that occupies exactly one word of memory (or vice versa).

Assignment compatibility is required

- *with assignments*

  In "d:=e" d and e must be assignment compatible.

- *with index referencing*

  If x is of data type ARRAY T OF E, then for every index reference x[i], the expression i must be assignment compatible with T.

- *with VAL parameters* (those without VAR)

  The actual parameter (expression) e must be assignment compatible with the corresponding formal parameter.

  Exceptions:

  - If the formal parameter is an *ARRAY parameter*, then the *element types* of the formal and actual parameters must *the same*.

  - *ARRAY OF WORD* is compatible with *any data type*.

- *with function procedures*

  In a function procedure that returns a value with function data type T, every expression occurring in a RETURN statement must be assignment compatible with T.

Procedure Compatibility (see Section 3.7.9)

Procedure compatibility between a procedure variable pv and a procedure P means that:

- pv and P have the same number of formal parameters.

- The formal parameters of pv and P match one to one, that is, the ith parameter in pv and the ith parameter in P must

  - be of the *same data type* (FormalType), and

  - both be value parameters or both be variable parameters.

- pv and P must either not be function procedures, or their function values must be of the *same type*.

Procedure compatibility is required

- in every occurrence of procedures or procedure variables (not procedure invocations!) in expressions, assignments or parameter lists (see also "Expression Compatibility").

Appendix D: ASCII Table

The following table lists the ASCII characters along with their corresponding ordinal numbers, which are given in decimal, octal and hexadecimal form respectively. For example

$$CHR(42) = CHR(52B) = 52C = CHR(2AH) = "*"$$

The characters with ordinal numbers 0 to 31 and 127 are control characters that can be interpreted by certain peripheral devices. For example, the character FF (CHR(12) or 14C) causes a form feed when output to a printer.

0	0B	00H	NUL	32	40B	20H	" "	64	100B	40H	"@"	96	140B	60H	"`"
1	1B	01H	SOH	33	41B	21H	"!"	65	101B	41H	"A"	97	141B	61H	"a"
2	2B	02H	STX	34	42B	22H	'"'	66	102B	42H	"B"	98	142B	62H	"b"
3	3B	03H	ETX	35	43B	23H	"#"	67	103B	43H	"C"	99	143B	63H	"c"
4	4B	04H	EOT	36	44B	24H	"$"	68	104B	44H	"D"	100	144B	64H	"d"
5	5B	05H	ENQ	37	45B	25H	"%"	69	105B	45H	"E"	101	145B	65H	"e"
6	6B	06H	ACK	38	46B	26H	"&"	70	106B	46H	"F"	102	146B	66H	"f"
7	7B	07H	BEL	39	47B	27H	"'"	71	107B	47H	"G"	103	147B	67H	"g"
8	10B	08H	BS	40	50B	28H	"("	72	110B	48H	"H"	104	150B	68H	"h"
9	11B	09H	HT	41	51B	29H	")"	73	111B	49H	"I"	105	151B	69H	"i"
10	12B	0AH	LF	42	52B	2AH	"*"	74	112B	4AH	"J"	106	152B	6AH	"j"
11	13B	0BH	VT	43	53B	2BH	"+"	75	113B	4BH	"K"	107	153B	6BH	"k"
12	14B	0CH	FF	44	54B	2CH	","	76	114B	4CH	"L"	108	154B	6CH	"l"
13	15B	0DH	CR	45	55B	2DH	"-"	77	115B	4DH	"M"	109	155B	6DH	"m"
14	16B	0EH	SO	46	56B	2EH	"."	78	116B	4EH	"N"	110	156B	6EH	"n"
15	17B	0FH	SI	47	57B	2FH	"/"	79	117B	4FH	"O"	111	157B	6FH	"o"
16	20B	10H	DLE	48	60B	30H	"0"	80	120B	50H	"P"	112	160B	70H	"p"
17	21B	11H	DC1	49	61B	31H	"1"	81	121B	51H	"Q"	113	161B	71H	"q"
18	22B	12H	DC2	50	62B	32H	"2"	82	122B	52H	"R"	114	162B	72H	"r"
19	23B	13H	DC3	51	63B	33H	"3"	83	123B	53H	"S"	115	163B	73H	"s"
20	24B	14H	DC4	52	64B	34H	"4"	84	124B	54H	"T"	116	164B	74H	"t"
21	25B	15H	NAK	53	65B	35H	"5"	85	125B	55H	"U"	117	165B	75H	"u"
22	26B	16H	SYN	54	66B	36H	"6"	86	126B	56H	"V"	118	166B	76H	"v"
23	27B	17H	ETB	55	67B	37H	"7"	87	127B	57H	"W"	119	167B	77H	"w"
24	30B	18H	CAN	56	70B	38H	"8"	88	130B	58H	"X"	120	170B	78H	"x"
25	31B	19H	EM	57	71B	39H	"9"	89	131B	59H	"Y"	121	171B	79H	"y"
26	32B	1AH	SUB	58	72B	3AH	":"	90	132B	5AH	"Z"	122	172B	7AH	"z"
27	33B	1BH	ESC	59	73B	3BH	";"	91	133B	5BH	"["	123	173B	7BH	"{"
28	34B	1CH	FS	60	74B	3CH	"<"	92	134B	5CH	"\"	124	174B	7CH	"	"
29	35B	1DH	GS	61	75B	3DH	"="	93	135B	5DH	"]"	125	175B	7DH	"}"
30	36B	1EH	RS	62	76B	3EH	">"	94	136B	5EH	"^"	126	176B	7EH	"~"
31	37B	1FH	US	63	77B	3FH	"?"	95	137B	5FH	"_"	127	177B	7FH	DEL

References

Aho, A. V., J. E. Hopcroft and J. D. Ullman. *The Design and Analysis of Computer Algorithms.* Addison-Wesley, 1975

Bauer, F. L., and G. Goos. *Informatik - eine einführende Übersicht.* Berlin, Heidelberg, New York: Springer, 1982

Böhm, D., and G. Jacopini. "Flow Diagrams, Turing Machines and Languages With Only Two Formation Rules." *Communications of the ACM*, 9/5, 1966, pp. 366-371

Dijkstra, E. W. "Cooperating Sequential Processes." In *Programming Languages.* Ed. E. Gunuys. Academic Press, 1968, pp. 43-112

Goos, G. "Systemprogrammiersprachen und strukturiertes Programmieren." In *Programming Methodology.* Berlin, Heidelberg, New York: Springer, Lecture Notes on Computer Science series, Vol. 23, 1973, pp. 203-224

Jensen, K., and N. Wirth. *Pascal User Manual and Report.* 3rd ed. Berlin, Heidelberg, New York: Springer, 1985 (1978)

Knuth, D. E. *The Art of Computer Programming.* 3 vols. Addison Wesley, 1973

Kronsjö, L. I. *Algorithms: Their Complexity and Efficiency.* Wiley, 1979

Nassi, I., and B. Shneiderman. "Flowchart Techniques for Structured Programming." *Sigplan Notices*, 8/8, 1973, pp. 12-26

Odersky, M. "MINOS: A New Approach to the Design of an Input/Output Library for Modula-2." *Structured Programming*, Springer-Verlag, April 1989

Parnas, D. L. "On the Criteria to be Used in Decomposing Systems into Modules." *Communications of the ACM*, 14/4, 1972, pp. 1053-58

Pomberger, G. *Software Engineering and Modula-2.* Englewood Cliffs, NJ: Prentice Hall, 1986

Rechenberg, P. *Programmieren für Informatiker, Band 1 und 2.* Oldenbourg, 1974

Wirth, N. "Program Development by Stepwise Refinement." *Communications of the ACM*, 14/4, 1971, pp. 221-227

Wirth, N. Algorithms and Data Structures. Prentice Hall International, 1986

Wirth, N. *Systematisches Programmieren.* Stuttgart: Teubner, 1978

Wirth, N. "Lilith - a Modula-2 Machine." In *Proceedings: NBS/IEEE/ACM Software Tool Fair.* San Diego, 1981

Wirth, N. *Schemes for Multiprogramming and Their Implementation in Modula-2.* Zurich: ETH, Report No. 59, 1984

Wirth, N. *Programming in Modula-2.* New York: Springer, 1985

Index